The Best Caribbean Travel Tips

Other titles in this series:

The Best European Travel Tips
The Best Mexican and Central American Travel Tips

The Best Caribbean Travel Tips

John Whitman

HarperPerennial

A Division of HarperCollinsPublishers

HarperCollins books may be purchased for educational, business, or sales promotional use. For information, please write to: Special Markets Department, HarperCollins Publishers, Inc., 10 East 53rd Street, New York, New York 10022.

Maps: Donna Whitman of Creative Designs

FIRST EDITION

Library of Congress Cataloging-in-Publication Data

Whitman, John, 1944–
    The best Caribbean travel tips / by John Whitman. — 1st ed.
      p. cm.
    Includes index.
    ISBN 0–06–273393–1
    1. West Indies—Guidebooks. 2. Caribbean Area—Guidebooks. I. Title.
I. Title.
F1609.W49 1996
917.2904852—dc20   96–19999

96 97 98 99 00 ❖/RRD 10 9 8 7 6 5 4 3 2 1

To Chad

Contents

Foreword   xi

PART I: TRIP PLANNING

Travel Documents   3
Money   7
Medical Preparations   13
Getting Information   18
Where to Go   32
When to Travel   72
Using Time Wisely   77
Whom to Go With   79
Tours and Cruises   90
Getting to the Islands   107
Transportation Between the Islands   124
Transportation on the Islands   134
Where to Stay   141
Packing   180
Final Steps   187

PART II: THE TRIP

Clearing Customs   199
Getting to Your Hotel   202
Hotel Strategies   205
Money Matters   215
Protecting Property   221
Personal Safety   225
Travel Between Islands   232

Travel on the Islands   239
Staying Healthy Once Abroad   246
Eating and Drinking   255
Communicating   265
Doing Things   271

Index   309

Foreword

The Caribbean covers a million square miles with coral cays and volcanic islands sweeping in a 2,800-mile arc from Florida to Venezuela. These islands are diverse and accessible to North Americans seeking sun and a chance to enjoy many of their favorite outdoor activities. The Bahamas, the Turks and Caicos (an extension of the Bahamas), and Bermuda are technically in the Atlantic. They are included in the guide because they offer many of the same attractions as their Caribbean counterparts. In this guide you'll find critical information on how to get the very best from each of these unique islands. Not included in the guide are Cuba and Haiti (the latter is half of the island of Hispaniola), because they are still in political turmoil. I hope that the tips in this book will make your trip enjoyable and safe. They should also save you lots of time and money. If you would like to add a tip or correct any misinformation, please write.

John Whitman
P.O. Box 202
Long Lake, MN 55356

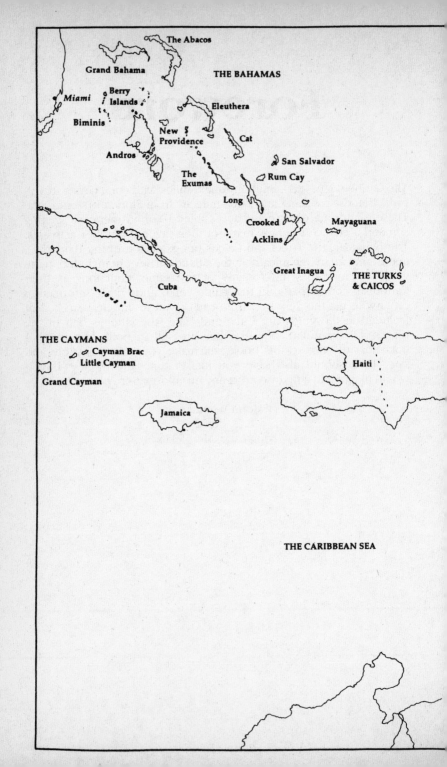

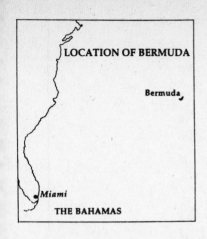

LOCATION OF BERMUDA

Bermuda

Miami

THE BAHAMAS

BERMUDA,
THE BAHAMAS, &
CARIBBEAN ISLANDS

THE ATLANTIC OCEAN

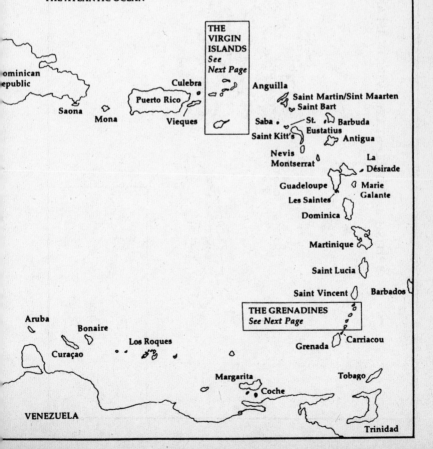

Dominican Republic

Saona

Mona

Puerto Rico

Culebra

Vieques

THE VIRGIN ISLANDS
See Next Page

Anguilla

Saint Martin/Sint Maarten
Saint Bart

Saba

St. Eustatius

Saint Kitt's

Barbuda

Antigua

Nevis
Montserrat

La Désirade

Guadeloupe

Marie Galante

Les Saintes

Dominica

Martinique

Saint Lucia

Saint Vincent

Barbados

THE GRENADINES
See Next Page

Aruba

Bonaire

Los Roques

Curaçao

Grenada

Carriacou

Margarita

Coche

Tobago

VENEZUELA

Trinidad

BRITISH & UNITED STATES VIRGIN ISLANDS

ANEGADA

Necker
Mosquito
Prickly Pear
VIRGIN GORDA
The Dogs

Ginger
Cooper
Salt
Beef
Camanoe
Great
Guana
TORTOLA
Dead
Chest
Peter
Norman
Frenchman's Cay

Little Jost
Van Dyke
JOST VAN DYKE
Great Thatch
SAINT JOHN

Great Tobago

SAINT THOMAS

SAINT CROIX

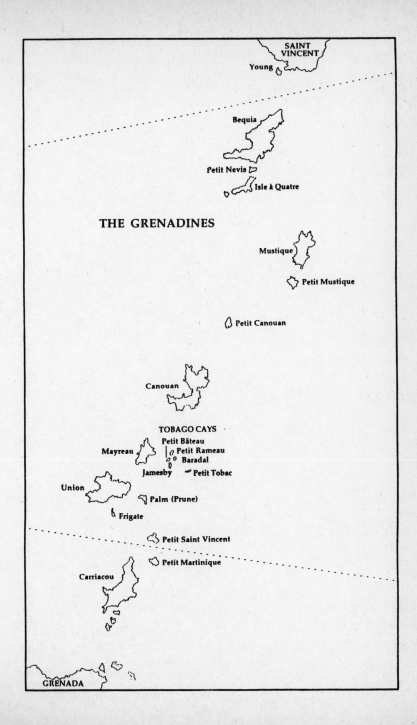

SAINT
VINCENT

Young

Bequia

Petit Nevis

Isle à Quatre

THE GRENADINES

Mustique

Petit Mustique

Petit Canouan

Canouan

TOBAGO CAYS

Petit Bâteau

Mayreau
Petit Rameau
Baradal
Jamesby   Petit Tobac

Union

Palm (Prune)

Frigate

Petit Saint Vincent

Petit Martinique

Carriacou

GRENADA

Part I
Trip Planning

Travel Documents

You'll need certain documents to travel freely through the Caribbean.

Passports

Although passports are not required on all islands in the area, get one because it's the best form of identification and most useful in cashing traveler's checks. If you already have one, check the expiration date to verify that it will be valid for the entire length of your trip. Technically, some islands can insist that it be valid for 6 additional months from the date of entry. Get yours renewed if it is about to expire.

Visas

Visas are special notations and stamps, added to your passport by officials of foreign countries, which allow you to enter and leave those countries. The islands in this guide do not require citizens of the United States to have visas except for study, long-term stays, and business travel. Canadians may have to get visas for some countries. Regulations change frequently, so to be sure, ask.

Special Tips on Getting Visas

- Use registered mail and keep the receipt.
- Include a check for the visa as well as enough money to cover *return postage* by registered mail.
- Always apply for visas at the foreign consulate or embassy in your city or the city nearest you. Most embassies and consulates are located in Chicago, New York, San Francisco, and Washington, DC. You'll find the addresses in individual city directories or in the Congressional Directory, found in most major libraries.
- Allow an extra 3 to 6 weeks for *each* necessary visa.

Insurance

If you carry any insurance at all, it will probably cover part of your trip. Exceptions to this general rule, and additional information on the subject, are detailed below.

Accident Insurance

- Check to see whether your policy, if you have one, is valid abroad.
- Many auto and travel clubs offer free accident insurance.
- So do some travel agents if you buy your tickets through them.

Baggage Insurance

- Avoid the need for this insurance by traveling with carry-on luggage and by leaving valuables at home. This includes engagement rings and wedding bands.
- If you can't, ask about a *personal articles floater.* It is most useful for expensive camera equipment, which some people insist on having.

Car Rental Insurance

- This is extremely complicated. See p. 138 for full details on getting foreign auto insurance.

Default Insurance

- Tour operators sometimes go belly up. This leaves you with no trip and little chance of recouping money spent for it unless you have default insurance.
- Travel agencies may pull the same stunt by taking your money and going out of business. Get a policy that covers both possibilities—tours or agencies going under.

Evacuation Insurance

- If you're seriously injured while in the islands, you may require surgery or blood transfusions. If possible, get back to Canada or the United States. To cover this contingency, consider evacuation insurance (see p. 16).
- If you have a serious illness, take out this insurance. Study the fine print to make sure it covers *pre-existing* conditions. Get a statement in writing that your condition is covered if the fine print seems vague. Otherwise, you're paying for fairy dust.

Health Insurance

- Younger travelers without their own medical insurance should check with the student and youth agencies at the nearest university. They often offer coverage for limited times at favorable rates.
- Older travelers should note that Medicare and Medicaid is not valid for travel in the islands. Check to see whether the law has changed recently, however. Buy temporary health insurance as necessary. Check with the AARP (see p. 88).
- Most health policies cover you worldwide, but ask. You'll pay for expenses on any given island to be reimbursed on your return. Many Caribbean hospitals require immediate cash payment for services.
- Carry your insurance card, your agent's telephone number, and your insurance company's telephone number when you travel. This way you can always get in touch with them for advice in an emergency.
- Having a *credit card* will help you get care quickly in a foreign clinic or hospital. Such a card could save your life.

Home Insurance

- Your home may not be covered if you are away for more than 30 days. Check with your agent for advice.

Trip Cancellation Insurance

- Some airline tickets, especially charter and special fares, have a rigid and steep penalty for cancellation. For these, consider trip cancellation insurance.
- Many different types of trip cancellation insurance exist, but most are related to illness or death—either yours or someone close to you in your family.
- If you take out insurance, it should cover *pre-existing* conditions, illnesses already known about or treated for.
- It should pay for your return from a foreign country in case of serious illness. If it doesn't, refer to evacuation insurance outlined earlier.
- It should cover all activities in which you might be engaged, such as biking, hiking, parasailing, rafting, riding horses, riding motorbikes, scuba diving, snorkeling, yachting, and so on. Many policies exclude any kind of strenuous outdoor activity. Policies with exclusions are essentially worthless for the adventuresome traveler.
- And, finally, the insurance should cover potential dangers, such as hurricanes and volcanic eruptions. The broader the coverage, the more valuable the insurance.

- You can get trip cancellation insurance from travel agencies or directly from the following companies (*read the fine print*):

Access America Service
  Organization
6600 West Broad Street
Richmond, VA 23230
Tel: (800) 284–8300

American Express
P.O. Box 919010
San Diego, CA 92191
Tel: (800) 234–0375

Health Care Abroad (Global)
Wallach & Company, Inc.
107 West Federal Street
P.O. Box 480
Middleburg, VA 22117
Tel: (800) 237–6615

Tele-Trip Company, Inc.
(Mutual of Omaha)
3201 Farnam Street
P.O. Box 31685
Omaha, NE 68131
Tel: (800) 228–9792

Travel Guard International
1145 Clark Street
Stevens Point, WI 54481
Tel: (800) 826–1300

Travel Insured International, Inc.
52-S Oakland Avenue
P.O. Box 280568
East Hartford, CT 06128
Tel: (800) 243–3174

Money

The reputation of the Caribbean is that it is expensive. It can be. However, if you want to reduce costs, there are hundreds of tips throughout this guide to help you do it. And, if you want to travel inexpensively, it is possible. Following are basic tips for trip preparation.

How Much Will a Trip Cost?

You probably have a certain amount of money to spend. Following are a few things to keep in mind.

Normal Trip Expenses

How much you spend will depend on how willing you are to trade time and energy to save money. If you're wily and willing, you can save a lot. However, a bare-bones budget will include the following:

- Medicines and medical preparation.
- Basic travel gear that you don't already have.
- The expense of getting to and from your destination.
- Departure taxes from each country.
- Travel within the region (between and on islands).
- Places to stay.
- Food.
- Entry fees to places of interest.
- Purchases of any kind.
- Costs for any special interest activity.
- Reserve money for emergencies.

Basic Cost-Cutting Tips

The following tips, all of which are outlined in greater detail throughout the guide, are especially important:

- Some islands tend to be much more expensive than others. If money is a major consideration, then travel to less expensive islands.
- From most major cities there are certain travel agencies specializing in cut-rate air fares to specific destinations. These are generally 1-week to 2-week charters. Even if your primary destination is not the island you fly into, you can often save money by taking a charter to one island and then flying to another.

- Buy all of your tickets before traveling to the islands. If you buy them once there, you'll often pay more and have additional taxes.
- Most of the major travel guides written for the general public and books specifically written for the travel industry do not contain information on extremely inexpensive rooms. These include small guest houses (boarding houses), modest hotels with just a few rooms, apartment complexes, and private homes. It can be difficult getting lists of these from the tourist offices listed on pp. 18–26, but try by writing or calling these offices directly for such information. Request equivalent information from local hotel associations (see p. 144).
- Traveling in the off-season will reduce your costs by as much as 50 percent. Depending upon why you're traveling, this can be a wise decision. However, most people want to travel during the peak season to avoid long, cold winters, so the off-season option is really out—though constantly promoted.
- Whenever possible, travel with someone so that you can split room expenses. Doubles are often just a few dollars more than singles.
- If you plan to stay in just one area, consider a package tour that includes airfare, accommodations, and meals. Some of these are reasonably priced and offer good value.
- Food can be expensive on many Caribbean islands because it must be imported. If you'll eat in local restaurants serving regional dishes and drinks, you'll cut costs dramatically. When this is not possible, you can make your own meals as the locals do by shopping in markets and small stores.
- Exchange your money wisely as outlined in appropriate sections of the guide. The longer you're traveling and the more you spend, the more important this tip is.
- Be flexible and learn to bargain. You can bargain on just about everything. It simply takes the courage to do it.
- For entertainment, follow the locals' lead. Go to public beaches, use public transportation (buses and shared taxis), listen to music and dance with the local people, and so on. Yes, in some instances safety can be an issue, but local people will let you know when and where not to go.
- If you're into sports, bring your own gear as suggested in the separate sections of the chapter on Doing Things (pp. 271–308). The costs of sporting equipment, from lures to tennis and golf balls, is exorbitant throughout the region.
- Make international calls from public phones that allow you to use a calling card.

Carrying Money

Once you've decided where you want to go and how much you plan to spend, how you carry your money becomes the next decision.

Bank Cards for ATMs (Automated Teller Machines)

The number of cash machines is growing throughout the Caribbean, but it is often quite difficult to pinpoint their locations in advance. Ask, but don't expect to get an answer.

- Ask about fees associated with each transaction.
- Make sure that your personal identification number (PIN) is not too long to work in the islands. Call the bank to abbreviate and *activate* it for foreign use.
- Many credit cards are now valid in ATMs. Verify this possibility by calling the 800 number on your credit card invoice.
- I have read, but have been unable to confirm, that ATM cards can become demagnetized and, therefore, useless if allowed to go through x-ray machines and metal detectors during baggage and body checks at airports. As with film, pass your card to a guard to avoid damage to the magnetized strip on the back of the card.

Traveler's Checks

Each year, more than a million travelers lose cash due to theft and negligence. For this reason, rely on traveler's checks as your main way of carrying money throughout this region.

- Traveler's checks are available from American Express, Bank of America, Barclay's Bank, Citibank, Thomas Cook, and many other institutions.
- There is suspicion, however, about lesser-known traveler's checks in many areas. This is as true in a bank as in a small shop or hotel. Traveler's checks from American Express remain the easiest checks to cash—and even they can occasionally be hard to cash in rural or remote areas.
- Some places simply refuse to take traveler's checks. They'll tell you to go the local bank, even in places where there are no banks.

Fee-Free Traveler's Checks

Many banks charge a 1 percent service fee for traveler's checks. This is a rip-off. Shop around. Find a bank offering checks for free.

- Free checks are offered with specific types of accounts. These often require a modest minimum initial deposit. If your bank doesn't offer such an account, call around. You will find one.
- Many travel clubs offer traveler's checks free to members. Of course, you're paying a fee to be a member of most clubs, so these checks are not quite free.

Credit Cards

Carrying at least two credit cards makes sense for travel in this region. Following are tips in regards to cards.

Credit Card Basics

Credit cards are accepted by many hotels, restaurants, and shops throughout the Caribbean. However, never assume that a place will accept a credit card. Even some of the fanciest places do not. Most do, although a few will only take a specific company's card. Credit cards are extremely helpful for renting cars and paying for plane flights. Many smaller establishments only accept cash.

- The best credit cards are American Express, Carte Blanche, Diners Club, MasterCard, and Visa. American Express and Visa are the most universally recognized.

Advantages of Credit Cards

- A number of credit cards are available with special programs that offer frequent flyer miles or discounts at hotels. Some also offer rebates on total purchases during the year.
- Many credit cards offer free flight insurance if you use them to purchase airline tickets.
- Credit cards are safer to carry than cash, because if they're lost or stolen, you have limited liability and no liability at all if you report the loss before they're used.
- You don't need to carry large amounts of cash at any time to pay for big expense items.
- You can use many of them to get cash from ATMs, although locations can be hard to find. And, I would avoid the use of ATM machines as much as possible for safety reasons. Thieves know where they are, too.
- Thieves are less interested in credit cards than cash. Still, they will steal them, so protect them like cash.
- If you plan to rent a car, you need a credit card or a large amount of cash for the deposit.

- Your signed receipt is all that's needed for a rental agreement—even if you choose to pay with cash later. You then ask for and destroy the original receipt.
- Some credit cards cover the deductible on car rentals abroad. This is very important if you plan to rent a car, but also full of loopholes (see p. 138).
- When you use credit cards, you have excellent records of your expenses. This is good for trip planning and for the IRS at tax time, if your trip can be used as a tax deduction.
- Credit card companies allow you to use their money on a float—you may not have to pay the bill for a month or two. This ends up being an interest-free loan.
- Companies automatically convert all charges to dollars at the rate of exchange prevailing at the time the charges are submitted. This means you can avoid much of the currency exchange hassle by using the card frequently.
- Credit cards are easy to carry and honored in many shops, restaurants, car rental agencies, and hotels.
- Request a pamphlet from your credit card company outlining the establishments honoring its card.
- *Disadvantages:* Some hotels, restaurants, and shops insist on adding a surcharge to the bill for their use. If you intend to use a credit card, always ask in advance if any surcharge will be added. You may decide to pay the bill in cash instead.
- Also, some hotels put a "hold" on a card, which amounts to a maximum potential charge you might make against it. Sometimes, they forget to clear this hold after you've paid the bill. So get the highest limit on any card you can and carry more than one card in case a card gets maxed out by these holds, which are mostly a problem on longer trips.

How to Bring Money into the Region

The following tips will help you avoid common pitfalls in carrying money into the region, giving you peace of mind and an edge on the market.

- Carry fifty to one hundred $1 bills depending upon your length of stay. Small bills can be used in a number of ways, for everything from paying a departure tax to a cab ride.
- The bulk of the bills is a nuisance outweighed by their usefulness.
- Carry as much U.S. currency as you can afford to lose. Carry notes in varying denominations, mostly smaller—five, ten, and twenty.

- *Note that $100 bills are impossible to cash because counterfeit notes in this denomination have flooded the area. Even $50 bills are suspect. The government created a new bill, but suspicion may continue for quite some time.*
- Canadians should convert their money into U.S. currency.
- You'll find that U.S. currency, referred to as hard currency by travelers, is often worth more in a bank than traveler's checks. Ironically, the reverse can also be true.
- Hard currency is also more valuable wherever there is a black market (see p. 218).
- Carry this money in different places on your body as outlined in the section on Protecting Property (see pp. 221–222).

Medical Preparations

A recent survey indicated that over 60 percent of travelers get sick during a trip abroad. The tips in this chapter can help you prevent major health problems.

Preparing for the Trip

Before traveling to the Caribbean, see a doctor and get prescriptions for appropriate medications, update or get vaccinations as recommended, have a dental checkup, and take out any appropriate insurance. If you are pregnant or have a chronic health problem, follow the tips outlined later. After reading this chapter, also read the section on Staying Healthy Once Abroad (see p. 246). Reading this additional chapter before traveling is important, because it will help you decide what medications to buy in advance. Read it before you see a doctor so that you can get up-to-date advice on specific questions you may have.

Seeing a Doctor

Go to a public travel clinic. You'll find these in most major cities. Or, see a doctor specializing in tropical medicine. The advantages of following this tip are simple. Travel clinics are in constant contact with the Centers for Disease Control in Atlanta, and they offer many shots at reduced cost. Any doctor specializing in tropical medicine will be equally well informed. If you have any problems after your trip, this is the person you're going to want to go to. If you have trouble locating such a doctor, send an 8 1/2" x 11" stamped (presently 98 cents), self-addressed envelope to the following address:

Traveler's Health and Immunization Services
148 Highland Avenue
Newton, MA 02165
Tel: (617) 527–4003

Medical Insurance

Having good medical insurance is important for all people, but especially for those traveling to the islands where you may be turned away from a hospital without it. Here are a few tips.

General Tips for Different Age Groups

- If you're older, you may not be covered in the islands under Medicare unless regulations have changed by the time this guide is published. Find out. If you are not, then check into short-term policies (see p. 15).
- If you're young, you can often get special policies through schools or organizations that represent young people and students.
- If you're neither young nor old, you may have a health insurance policy through your work or on your own. Call their toll-free number to verify that your insurance is valid outside of the United States. If not, take out short-term health insurance.

Inoculations

Get vaccinations in Canada or the United States before traveling to the islands. Doctors sometimes disagree on what vaccinations and medications are appropriate. However, you can prevent the following diseases almost entirely through inoculations: Diphtheria, hepatitis A and B, polio, rabies, tetanus, typhoid, and yellow fever. Prevention of hepatitis B is important for anyone with sexual contact, which includes kissing. Polio is said to be eradicated in the Western Hemisphere, but cases are reported. Avoid the oral vaccine since complications are rare but possible. You need yellow fever protection only if you'll be traveling to South America en route to some of the islands off its coast. Malaria is only a concern on Hispaniola (the countries of Haiti and the Dominican Republic). Prevent it with appropriate pills (Chloroquine phosphate, commonly sold as Aralen). Travel clinics or doctors specializing in tropical medicine will tell you exactly what to do.

- Many vaccinations are given free of charge or for a token charge at public clinics. By calling around, you may save as much as $50 to $100 on shots. If you have children, watch for discounted or free inoculations given at different times of year.
- Start immunizations well ahead of your trip. Some must be given in a series over weeks or even months.

- Some have side effects, which could affect your trip if you wait until the last minute.
- Keep a complete history of your inoculations. The easiest way to do this is to have a "yellow card," technically known as an International Certificate of Vaccination card. Keep updating this card for as long as you live.

Useful Medical Organizations

If you have a chronic illness or medical problem, you may be interested in contacting the following organizations for information on their services, which include everything from lists of English-speaking doctors to insurance. Medic Alert is noted for its engraved bracelets giving information on medical conditions and allergies to drugs. Such identification can save your life in a critical situation. TravMed includes a free copy of *International Travel Health Guide* with its insurance. Compare the offerings of all companies before deciding which one best matches your needs.

Access America
P.O. Box 90315
Richmond, VA 23286
Tel: (800) 284–8300

Assist-Card International
1001 South Bayshore Drive
Suite 2302
Miami, FL 33131
Tel: (305) 381–9959

Carefree
P.O. Box 310
120 Mineola Boulevard
Mineola, NY 11501
Tel: (800) 645–2424
    (516) 294–0220

Global Assistance
P.O. Box 18100
Philadelphia, PA 19116
Tel: (800) 523–8930

Healthcare Abroad
107 West Federal Street
P.O. Box 480
Middleburg, VA 22117
Tel: (800) 237–6615
    (703) 281–9500

Intercontinental Medical
2720 Enterprise Parkway
Suite 106
Richmond, VA 23294
Tel: (804) 527–1094

International Association
    of Medical Assistance to
    Travelers (IAMAT)
417 Center Street
Lewiston, NY 14092
Tel: (716) 754–4883

International Health Care Service
440 East 59th Street
New York, NY 10021
Tel: (212) 746–1601

International SOS Assistance, Inc.
(mailing address)
P.O. Box 11568
Philadelphia, PA 19116
(office location)
8 Neshaminy Interplex
Suite 207Trevose, PA 19053
Tel: (800) 523–8930
   (215) 244–1500

Medic Alert Foundation
P.O. Box 1009
Turlock, CA 95381
Tel: (800) 344–3226
   (209) 668–3333

TravMed
P.O. Box 10623
Baltimore, MD 21285
Tel: (800) 732–5309
   (410) 296–5225

WorldCare Travel
   Assistance
1995 West Commercial
   Boulevard
Suite H
Fort Lauderdale, FL 33309
Tel: (800) 521–4822
   (305) 776–4201

Worldwide Assistance
   Services
1133 15th Street N.W.
Suite 400
Washington, DC 20005
Tel: (800) 821–2828
   (202) 331–1609

Medical Evacuation Insurance

Medical evacuation is rarely necessary. If you'll be doing high-risk
activities or have a serious health condition, take out medical evacuation insurance. If you have a serious illness or accident requiring
surgery or blood transfusions and have the time to get back to
Canada or the United States, do it.

Questions to Ask

- Does the insurance cover all pre-existing medical problems?
- What is the daily charge for coverage?
- How quickly do they guarantee that they'll be on the scene?
- What medical emergencies are covered? Or, more importantly,
  what emergencies are not covered? What constitutes a medical
  emergency?
- Will the company fly you to the nearest hospital or to the one
  most suited to taking care of your problem?

Air Evacuation Companies

Aeromedical Group, Inc.
21893 Skywest Drive
Hayward, CA 94541
Tel: (800) 982–5806
 (510) 786–1592

Air Ambulance Network
905 Martin Luther King
 Junior Drive
Suite 330
Tarpon Springs, FL 34689
Tel: (800) 327–1966
 (813) 934–3999

Critical Air Medicine, Inc.
4141 Kearney Villa Road
San Diego, CA 92123
Tel: (800) 247–8326
 (619) 571–0482

International SOS Assistance
P.O. Box 11568
Philadelphia, PA 19116
Tel: (800) 523–8930
 (215) 244–1500

Life Flight
6411 Fannin Drive
Herman Hospital
Texas Medical Center
Houston, TX 77030
Tel: (800) 231–4357
 (800) 392–4357 (TX)
 (713) 704–3590

National Jets
P.O. Box 22460
Ft. Lauderdale, FL 33335
Tel: (800) 327–3710
 (954) 359–9900

NEAR (Nationwide
 Emergency
 Ambulance Return)
P.O. Box 1339
450 Prairie Avenue
Calumet City, IL 60409
Tel: (800) 654–6700
 (708) 868–6700

Schaefer's Ambulance,
 Inc.
4627 Beverly Boulevard
Los Angeles, CA 90004
Tel: (800) 229–4727
 (213) 469–1473

Getting Information

This book outlines the very best of what to see and do in the Caribbean. Still, it's missing detailed maps, which you can get for free; specific listings of hotels and restaurants; and detailed information on sights or destinations, also free if you know where to ask. By using the resources mentioned in this chapter, you'll get exactly what you want for your upcoming trip for free.

National Tourist Offices

Tourist offices usually offer free maps. Every person in your party should have a map appropriate to the kind of travel you're doing. It makes travel more exciting, makes kids feel special, divides the responsibility, and costs nothing. Free maps vary in quality but are generally good enough for trip planning. The National Tourist Offices can give you general information. Some have excellent pamphlets. Others are poorly organized. The more specific your question, the more unlikely it will get answered. These offices shy away from any kind of comparison: Is one beach better than another? Is a certain hotel the best in town? The tourist offices of the Dominican Republic and Venezuela are next to useless; I visited them in person and still couldn't get information, so I've included information on travel companies under these islands as alternative sources of information:

- Write the office nearest you well ahead of your planned departure, preferably several months in advance, to allow as much time as possible for a reply.
- A number of these offices produce pamphlets with more information than you could possibly believe. A few have extremely limited funds and may give you next to nothing. When writing these offices, be specific about what you want. For instance, you might want a list of hotels and prices or just a general map or everything they've got.

Anguilla
The Anguilla Tourist Information Office
c/o Medhurst & Associates, Inc.
The Huntington Atrium
775 Park Avenue
Huntington, NY 11743
Tel: (800) 553–4939
   (516) 271–2600

Antigua
Antigua & Barbuda
   Department of
   Tourism
610 Fifth Avenue
Suite 311
New York, NY 10020
Tel: (212) 541–4117

Antigua & Barbuda
  Department of Tourism
60 Saint Claire Avenue East
Suite 205
Toronto, ON M4T 1N5
Tel: (416) 961-3085

Aruba
Aruba Tourism Authority
1000 Harbor Boulevard
Weehawken, NJ 07087
Tel: (800) 862-7822
  (201) 330-0800

Aruba Tourism Authority
2344 Salzebo Street
Coral Gables, FL 33134
Tel: (305) 567-2720

Aruba Tourism Authority
86 Bloor Street West
Suite 204
Toronto, ON M5S 1M5
Tel: (800) 268-3042
  (416) 975-1950

Bahamas
Bahamas Tourist Office
10 East 52nd Street
28th Floor North
New York, NY 10022
Tel: (800) 422-4262
  (212) 758-2777

Bahamas Tourist Office
One Turnberry Place
19495 Biscayne Boulevard
Suite 809
Aventura, FL 33180
Tel: (800) 422-4262
  (305) 932-0051

Bahamas Tourist Office
8600 West Bryn Mawr Avenue
Suite 820
Chicago, IL 60631
Tel: (800) 422-4262
  (312) 693-1500

Bahamas Tourist Office
World Trade Center
Suite 186
2050 Stemmons Freeway
Dallas, TX 75258
Tel: (800) 422-4262
  (214) 742-1886

Bahamas Tourist Office
2957 Clairmont Road
Suite 150
Atlanta, GA 30345
Tel: (800) 422-4262
  (404) 633-1793

Bahamas Tourist Office
3450 Wilshire Boulevard
Suite 208
Los Angeles, CA 90010
Tel: (800) 422-4262
  (213) 385-0033

Bahamas Tourist Office
121 Bloor Street East
Suite 1101
Toronto, ON M4W 3M5
Tel: (416) 968-2999

Barbados
Barbados Tourism Authority
800 Second Avenue
17th Floor
New York, NY 10017
Tel: (800) 221-9831
  (212) 986-6516

Barbados Tourism Authority
3440 Wilshire Boulevard
Suite 1215
Los Angeles, CA 90010
Tel: (800) 221–9831
    (213) 380–2198

Barbados Tourism Authority
615 Boulevard Dorchester West
Suite 960
Montreal, PQ H3B 1P5
Tel: (514) 861–0085

Barbados Tourism Authority
5160 Yonge Street
Suite 1800
North York, ON M2N 6L9
Tel: (800) 268–9122
    (416) 512–6569

Barbuda
(see **Antigua**)

Bermuda
Bermuda Department
    of Tourism
310 Madison Avenue
Suite 201
New York, NY 10017
Tel: (800) 223–6106
    (212) 818–9800

Bermuda Department of Tourism
245 Peachtree Center Avenue
    Northeast
Suite 803
Atlanta, GA 30303
Tel: (404) 524–1541

Bermuda Department of Tourism
44 School Street
Suite 1010
Boston, MA 02108
Tel: (617) 742–0405

Bermuda Department of
    Tourism
150 North Wacker Drive
Suite 1070
Chicago, IL 60606
Tel: (312) 782–5486

Bermuda Department of
    Tourism
c/o Tetler, Moyer, & Associates
3151 Cahuenga Boulevard West
Suite 111
Los Angeles, CA 90068
Tel: (800) 421–0000
    (800) 252–0211 (in CA)
    (213) 436–0744

Bermuda Department of
    Tourism
1200 Bay Street
Suite 1004
Toronto, ON M5R 2A5
Tel: (800) 387–1304
    (416) 923–9600

Bonaire
Tourism Corporation of Bonaire
444 Madison Avenue
Suite 2403
New York, NY 10016
Tel: (800) 826–6247
    (212) 832–0779

Tourism Corporation of Bonaire
512 Duplex Avenue
Toronto, ON M4R 2E3
Tel: (416) 485–8724

British Virgin Islands
B.V.I. Tourist Board
370 Lexington Avenue
Suite 1605
New York, NY 10017
Tel: (800) 835–8530
    (212) 696–0400

B.V.I. Tourist Board
6245 Mosley Avenue
Los Angeles, CA 90056
Tel: (800) 835–8530
   (213) 293–2331

B.V.I. Tourist Board
1804 Union Street
San Francisco, CA 94123
Tel: (800) 835–8530
   (415) 775–0344

Carriacou
(see **Grenada**)

Cayman Islands
Cayman Islands Department
  of Tourism
420 Lexington Avenue
Suite 2733
New York, NY 10170
Tel: (212) 682–5582

Cayman Islands Department
  of Tourism
18484 Preston Road
Dallas, TX 75252
Tel: (214) 335–3540

Cayman Islands Department
  of Tourism
Two Memorial City Plaza
820 Gessner
Suite 170
Houston, TX 77024
Tel: (713) 461–1317

Cayman Islands Department
  of Tourism
3440 Wilshire Boulevard
Suite 1202
Los Angeles, CA 90010
Tel: (213) 738–1968

Cayman Islands Department
  of Tourism
6100 Blue Lagoon Drive
Suite 150
Miami, FL 33126
Tel: (305) 266–2300

Cayman Islands Department
  of Tourism
9525 West Bryn Mawr
  Avenue
Suite 160
Rosemont, IL 60018
Tel: (708) 678–6446

Cayman Islands Department
  of Tourism
234 Eglinton Avenue East
Suite 306
Toronto, ON M4P 1K5
Tel: (416) 485–1550

Culebra
Culebra Tourism Office
P.O. Box 56
Culebra, Puerto Rico 00645
Tel: (809) 742–3521

Curaçao
Curaçao Tourist Board
475 Park Avenue South
Suite 2000
New York, NY 10016
Tel: (800) 270–3350
  (212) 683–7660

Curaçao Tourist Board
330 Biscayne Boulevard
Suite 808
Miami, FL 33132
Tel: (800) 445–8266
  (305) 374–5811

Dominica
Consulate of Dominica
820 Second Avenue
9th Floor
New York, NY 10017
Tel: (212) 599–8478

Dominica National
    Development Corporation
P.O. Box 293
Valley Road
Roseau, Commonwealth
    of Dominica
West Indies
Tel: (809) 448–2045

Dominican Republic
Dominican Tourism
    Promotion Council
1501 Broadway
Suite 410
New York, NY 10036
Tel: (800) 752–1151
    (212) 768–2480

Inter-Island Tours
419 Park Avenue South
4th Floor
New York, NY 10016
Tel: (800) 245–3434
    (212) 686–4868

French West Indies
French West Indies
    Tourist Board
444 Madison Avenue
16th Floor
New York, NY 10022
Tel: (900) 990–0040
    (per minute charge)

Grenada
Grenada Board of Tourism
820 Second Avenue
Suite 900D
New York, NY 10017
Tel: (800) 927–9554
    (212) 687–9554

Grenada Board of Tourism
439 University Avenue
Suite 820
Toronto, ON M5G 1Y8
Tel: (416) 595–1339

Grenadines
(see **Saint Vincent**)

Guadeloupe
(see **French West Indies**)

Iles des Saintes or Les Saintes
(see **French West Indies**)

Isla Margarita
(see **Venezuela**)

Jamaica
Jamaica Tourist Board
801 Second Avenue
20th Floor
New York, NY 10017
Tel: (800) 233–4582
    (212) 856–9727

Jamaica Alternative
    Tourism, Camping, and
    Hiking Association
P.O. Box 304
Atlanta, Georgia 30319
Tel: (404) 452–7799

Jamaica Tourist Board
500 North Michigan Avenue
Suite 1030
Chicago, IL 60611
Tel: (312) 527–1296

Jamaica Tourist Board
1320 South Dixie Drive
Suite 1100
Coral Gables, FL 33146
Tel: (305) 665–0557

Jamaica Tourist Board
3440 Wilshire Boulevard
Suite 1207
Los Angeles, CA 90010
Tel: (213) 384–1123

Jamaica Tourist Board
1 Eglinton Avenue East
Suite 616
Toronto, ON M4P 3A1
Tel: (416) 482–7850

Les Saintes
(see **French West Indies**)

Margarita
(see **Venezuela**)

Martinique
Martinique Promotion Bureau
444 Madison Avenue
16th Floor
New York, NY 10022
Tel: (800) 391–4909

Montserrat
Montserrat Tourist Information
  Office
c/o Medhurst & Associates, Inc.
775 Park Avenue
Suite 105
Huntington, NY 11743
Tel: (800) 646–2002
  (516) 351–4922

Nevis
(see **Saint Kitt's**)

Puerto Rico
Puerto Rico Tourism Company
575 Fifth Avenue
23rd Floor
New York, NY 10017
Tel: (800) 223–6530
  (212) 599–6262

Puerto Rico Tourism Company
901 Ponce de Leon Boulevard
Suite 604
Coral Gables, FL 33134
Tel: (305) 445–9112

Puerto Rico Tourism Company
3575 West Cahuenga Boulevard
Suite 560
Los Angeles, CA 90068
Tel: (213) 874–5991
  (800) 223–6530

Puerto Rico Tourism Company
2 Bloor Street West
Suite 700
Toronto, ON M4W 3R1
Tel: (416) 969–9025

Saba
Saba Tourist Office
P.O. Box 6322
Boca Raton, FL 33427
Tel: (407) 394–8580
  (800) 722–2394

Saint Barthélémy, Saint Barth,
or **Saint Bart**
(see **French West Indies**)

Saint Christopher
(see **Saint Kitt's**)

Saint Croix
(see **United States Virgin Islands**)

Saint John
(see **United States
Virgin Islands**)

Saint Kitt's
St. Kitt's and Nevis
    Department of Tourism
414 East 75th Street, 5th Floor
New York, NY 10021
Tel: (800) 582–6208
    (212) 535–1234

St. Kitt's and Nevis
    Department of Tourism
1464 Whippoorwill Way
Mountainside, NJ 07092
Tel: (908) 232–6701

St. Kitt's and Nevis
    Department of Tourism
11 Yorkville Avenue
Suite 508
Toronto, ON M4W 1L3
Tel: (416) 921–7717

Saint Lucia
Saint Lucia Tourist Board
820 Second Avenue, 9th Floor
New York, NY 10017
Tel: (800) 456–3984
    (212) 867–2950

Saint Lucia Tourist Board
3 Robert Speck Parkway
Suite 900
Mississauga, ON L4Z 2G5
Tel: (905) 270–9892

Saint Martin
(see also **Sint Maarten**)
(see **French West Indies**)

Saint Thomas
(see **United States
Virgin Islands**)

Saint Vincent
Saint Vincent and the Grenadines
    Tourist Information Office
801 Second Avenue
21st Floor
New York, NY 10017
Tel: (800) 729–1726
    (212) 687–4981

Saint Vincent and the Grenadines
    Tourist Information Office
6505 Cove Creek Place
Dallas, TX 75240
Tel: (800) 235–3029
    (214) 239–6451

Saint Vincent and the Grenadines
    Tourist Information Office
32 Park Road
Toronto, ON N4W 2N4
Tel: (416) 924–5796

Sint Eustatius
Sint Eustatius Tourist Information
c/o Caribbean Connection Plus Ltd.
USA
P.O. Box 261
Trumbull, CT 06611
Tel: (203) 261-8603

Sint Eustatius Tourist Bureau
Fort Oranjestraat 3
Oranjestraat
Sint Eustatius
Netherlands Antilles
Tel: (011) 599 38 2433

Sint Maarten
(see also **Saint Martin**)
Sint Maarten Tourist Office
675 Third Avenue
Suite 1806
New York, NY 10017
Tel: (800) 786–2278
    (212) 953–2084

Sint Maarten Tourist Office
243 Ellerslie Avenue
Willowdale, ON M2N 1Y5
Tel: (416) 223–3501

Statia
(see **Sint Eustatius**)

Tobago
(see **Trinidad**)

Trinidad
Trinidad and Tobago
   Tourism Information
7000 Boulevard East
Guttenberg, NJ 07093
Tel: (800) 748–4224
   (201) 662–3403

Trinidad Development Company
c/o Cheryl Andrews Marketing,
   Inc.
1500 San Remo
Suite 145
Coral Gables, FL 33146
Tel: (305) 663–1660

Turks and Caicos
Turks and Caicos Islands
   Tourist Board
c/o Trombone Associates, Inc.
420 Madison Avenue
New York, NY 10017
Tel: (800) 241–0824
   (212) 223–2323

**United States Virgin Islands
(USVI)**
United States Virgin Islands
   Division of Tourism
1270 Avenue of the Americas
Suite 2108
New York, NY 10020
Tel: (800) 372–8784
   (212) 332–2222

United States Virgin Islands
   Division of Tourism
225 Peachtree Street Northeast
Suite 760
Atlanta, GA 30303
Tel: (404) 688–0906

United States Virgin Islands
   Division of Tourism
500 North Michigan Avenue
Suite 2030
Chicago, IL 60611
Tel: (312) 670–8784

United States Virgin Islands
   Division of Tourism
2655 Le Jeune Road
Suite 907
Coral Gables, FL 33134
Tel: (305) 442–7200

United States Virgin Islands
   Division of Tourism
3460 Wilshire Boulevard
Suite 412
Los Angeles, CA 90010
Tel: (213) 739–0138

United States Virgin Islands
   Division of Tourism
3300 Bloor Street West
The Mutual Group Centre
Suite 3120-Centre Tower
Toronto, ON M8X 2X3
Tel: (800) 465–8784
   (416) 233–1414

United States Virgin Islands
   Division of Tourism
The Farragut Building
900 17th Street Northwest
Suite 500
Washington, DC 20006
Tel: (202) 293–3707

Venezuela
Venezuelan Information Center
(Venezuelan Permanent
   Mission to the United Nations)
7 East 51st Street
Suite 1515
New York, NY 10022
Tel: (212) 826–1660

Inter-Island Tours
419 Park Avenue South
4th Floor
New York, NY 10016
Tel: (800) 245–3434
   (212) 686–4868

KAM Tours International
135 West 18th Street
New York, NY 10011
Tel: (800) 326–0339
   (212) 886–6685

Vieques
(see **Puerto Rico**)

Caribbean Coalition for Tourism

The Caribbean Coalition for Tourism will send you a free 300-page magazine, covering descriptions and attractions of many of the islands in the region. Since it's free, it contains lots of advertisements and leaves out hotels, restaurants, and information that would be helpful to any potential traveler. But it's a good beginning. Since it costs nothing, what do you have to lose? Call (800) 356–9999 and ask for the current *Caribbean Vacation Planner*.

Agents and Agencies

Travel agents can be excellent resources, especially those specializing in travel to the Caribbean. Always ask for an agent who has traveled to the area you plan to visit. Specific agencies or tour operators have been mentioned for special-interest activities in the chapter on Doing Things (see pp. 271–308). General agencies specializing in the Caribbean are clearly covered in the Yellow Pages of any major city directory.

Good Agents Should Give You Good Information

Travel agents are excellent sources of travel information. Unfortunately, many of them are now beginning to charge for their services, since the airlines have changed their commissions. However, many good agents don't have upfront charges. The first tip is to find an agent not charging a service fee. Then, the following tips apply:

- A good agent will save you lots of time and aggravation by telling you the options for travel to and within the Caribbean.
- A good agent really works the computer to come up with the best plane fares from A to B. These often are lower than ones quoted directly to you by the airline.
- A good agent will use the computer to compare car rental rates and make reservations.
- Few agents deal with ground transportation other than car rental and tours. It's best to get this kind of information locally, since it changes without notice.
- Good agents will give you access to specialized books: *Official Airline Guide, Official Hotel and Resort Guide, STAR (Sloane Travel Agency Reports),* and *World Travel Directory.* These all contain helpful, if dry, information. Once you learn to read between the lines in these books, you'll be surprised how helpful they can be.
- A good agent has traveled in an area or has the resources to find out exactly which hotel will match your personality and pocketbook.
- In many instances agents will be able to make hotel reservations for you free of charge. In some instances, you will be charged for faxes or telephone calls. Always ask about any potential charges upfront. Charges are most common for reservations in small hotels, which do not pay commissions to agents.
- If you want to take a cruise or a tour, definitely go to a travel agent. This is the very heart of their business.
- If you're going on a special-interest tour, compare what a local agent has to offer with one of the companies listed in the chapter on Doing Things (pp. 271–308).
- A good agent will put you on a cruise or tour that matches your personality. You pay nothing extra for this service.
- Many agencies also have a library of offbeat or unusual travel books, which you can look through to help you make decisions. These books are often not available in local libraries, are out of print, or would take you weeks to order from the publisher.

Picking an Agency

- Larger agencies tend to have more clout than smaller ones. It may be more personal and more convenient to go to a neighborhood agent, but what happens if something goes wrong? Find out whether the agency has representatives abroad, just in case something does go awry.
- Ask the agency what kind of travel it specializes in. If it doesn't match your travel plans, ask the agency to refer you to another one specializing in your brand of travel.

- In special cases, you may want to work with agents in other cities. If the best agency for a specific-interest tour happens to be in Los Angeles, carry on your business through the mail. Always ask for a toll-free number to avoid long-distance phone bills.

Recognizing a Good Agent

A good travel agent is one who has your best interest in mind. A good agent will find you the best possible price for any type of travel, even though commissions are based on cost. A good agent gets back to you as quickly as possible and carries through with all promises. An excellent agent is someone who does the above but also knows the area in which you'll be traveling and has personal experience with the places he or she recommends. Reward such an agent with all of your business. A letter of praise to a supervisor is highly recommended.

- Most travel agents are members of the American Society of Travel Agents (ASTA), so be wary of those who are not. ASTA maintains a file of complaints. You can write or call them:

  ASTA
  1100 King Street
  Alexandria, VA 22314
  Tel: (703) 739–2782

- Look for the initials CTC—for Certified Travel Consultant—after an agent's name. This designation signifies that the person has a good reputation and has been through a specialized course.

Other Sources of Information

Following are commonly used and not so commonly known sources of information on the Caribbean.

Travel Magazines

Read the following magazines for good travel information: *Caribbean Travel and Life, Condé Nast Traveler, Gourmet, Islands, National Geographic Traveler, Travel Holiday,* and *Travel and Leisure.* A good librarian can also show you how to look up information by specific destinations. Expect articles to be slanted in favor of most destinations. The following magazines offer the most comprehensive information on Caribbean travel and are worth buying if you plan to travel in the region frequently.

Caribbean Travel and Life
Circulation Department
P.O. Box 2054
Marion, OH 43306

Islands
P.O. Box 53717
Boulder, CO 80322
Tel: (800) 284–7958
(303) 447–9330

Tour Companies

The brochures of tour companies are often highly informative. If you read them carefully, they can give specific details that are most useful in planning a trip. By comparing the information from a number of companies, you may decide that a tour is a fine option. Or you may decide to travel independently but see many of the sites or do many of the things suggested in the tour brochures themselves.

Travel Reports and Newsletters

Travel reports can help with trip planning. To find out which of these reports suits your personality, write to each one asking for a sample copy. INT offers a networking service to its readers who can write in asking other readers for information on a specific island (responses generally take several months).

Caribbean Newsletter
c/o GeoMedia
Suite 316
1771 Post Road East
Westport, CT 06880
(no phone)

Great Expectations
P.O. Box 18036
Raleigh, NC 27619
Tel: (919) 846–3600
(Offers networking and
travel advice for a fee.)

Consumer Reports Travel Letter
P.O. Box 53629
Boulder, CO 80322
Tel: (800) 234–1970
(303) 666–7000

International Living
105 West Monument
Street
P.O. Box 17473
Baltimore, MD 21298
Tel: (800) 851–7100
(410) 223–2611

Entree Travel
P.O. Box 5148
Santa Barbara, CA 93150
Tel: (805) 969–5948

*International Travel News
(ITN)*
2120 28th Street
Sacramento, CA 95818
Tel: (916) 457–3643
(800) 366–9192 (to sub-
scribe)

The Affordable Caribbean
P.O. Box 3000
Denville, NJ 07834
Tel: (301) 588–2300

Thrifty Traveler Newsletter
P.O. Box 8168
Clearwater, FL 34618
Tel: (800) 532–5731
   (813) 447–4731

Travel Smart
Communications House
40 Beechdale Road
Dobbs Ferry, NY 10522
Tel: (800) 327–3633
   (914) 693–8300

Networking with Other Travelers

I mention networking several times because it's so important. Keep asking other travelers about their finds, the things they found most interesting or dull, the hotels that may have just been built and are still great buys, restaurants that really met their expectations or didn't, contacts who were most helpful, local tours that turned out to deliver everything they promised—ask, ask, ask. Judge the recommendations by the person you're talking to. If someone has just spent several months traveling through the Caribbean and only mentions one or two hotels, one special experience, and one restaurant, wouldn't you give those special attention? While traveling, I get more useful, up-to-date information from other people than from any other source.

Getting Detailed Maps

Free maps given out by tourist offices and local tour companies are fine for most travelers. Detailed maps are expensive but essential for off-road travel (particularly when hiking on some of the larger islands, although I advise hiring a guide). Following are several companies offering excellent maps as well as numerous publications covering the area. Write each for a catalog with prices.

International Travel Map
   Productions
P.O. Box 2290
Vancouver, BC V6B 3W5
Canada
Tel: (604) 687–3320

Map Link
25 East Mason Street
Santa Barbara, CA 93101
Tel: (805) 965–4402

San Diego Map Center
2611 University Avenue
San Diego, CA 92104
Tel: (619) 291–3830

South American Explorers
   Club
126 Indian Creek Road
Ithaca, NY 14850
Tel: (607) 277–0488

World Aeronautical Charts
U.S. Department of Commerce
National Oceanic & Atmospheric Administration
6501 Lafayette Avenue
Riverdale, MD 20840
Tel: (301) 436–6990

Where to Go

This chapter provides useful information on planning an itinerary. Begin the process of deciding where to go by reading this chapter and the section on Doing Things (pp. 271–308). The latter chapter may sway you to go to a specific island, or it will at least help you narrow your selection to a few potential destinations.

Where Do You Want to Go?

You have the perfect vacation mapped out in your personality—try to match your destination with what you want most from the trip. You may just want warm weather, a nice beach, a good view, and a chance to relax. Or you may want to travel extensively from one island to the next. Perhaps you're focused on special-interest activities. Naturally, if a trip is long enough, you can combine a wide variety of goals. But on short trips this can be quite difficult. Define your goals ahead of time so that your expectations meet reality. The major questions are

- How much time do you have?
- How much money do you want to spend?
- How much energy are you willing to exert?
- What do you really want to do?
- How far are you willing to travel?
- If you have traveling companions, do they agree with you?

Thumbnail Sketches of the Islands

Of course, it's unfair to try to give an impression of an island in a few words, but the following is helpful in leading you in the right direction. I've already given you sources of free information. The following will help you focus on a few islands. Their distance from North America is apparent on the maps in the front of the guide. And that may play a key role in your decision as to where to go. Also, there's something very curious about how people view each island. Ask ten different people how they liked a specific island on the same trip and you'll get ten different answers. Your personality, perceptions, and personal experiences on an island tinge your point of view. Still, you have to start somewhere. And that's all the following information is meant to do.

Island Index

The information on islands is listed alphabetically by island and island groups. The island groups include the Bahamas, British Virgin Islands, Caymans, Grenadines, Turks & Caicos, and United States Virgin Islands. These groups contain islands listed alphabetically under that island group or chain. Some islands go by more than one name, and this can be confusing. Also, some islands are advertised by their main city as if that were the island name. In this list you'll find cross-references to clarify these problems. Here are the islands and where to find them.

Abacos (see **BAHAMAS**)   37
Acklins (see **BAHAMAS**)   37
Andros (see **BAHAMAS**)   37–38
Anegada (see **BRITISH VIRGIN ISLANDS**)   46
ANGUILLA   35
ANTIGUA   35–36
ARUBA   36
BAHAMAS   36–43
BARBADOS   43–44
BARBUDA   44
Bequia (see **GRENADINES**)   53
BERMUDA   44–45
Berry Islands (see **BAHAMAS**)   38
Biminis (see **BAHAMAS**)   38
BONAIRE   45
BRITISH VIRGIN ISLANDS   45–48
Canouan (see **GRENADINES**)   53
CARRIACOU   48
Cat (see **BAHAMAS**)   39
Cayman Brac (see **CAYMANS**)   48
CAYMANS   48–49
Crooked (see **BAHAMAS**)   39
CULEBRA   49–50
CURAÇAO   50
DOMINICA   50–51
DOMINICAN REPUBLIC   51–52
Eleuthera (see **BAHAMAS**)   39–40
Exumas (see **BAHAMAS**)   40
Freeport (see **Grand Bahama** in **BAHAMAS**)   40–41
Grand Bahama (see **BAHAMAS**)   40–41
Grand Caicos (see **Middle Caicos** in **TURKS & CAICOS**)   67
Grand Cayman (see **CAYMANS**)   49

Grand Turk (see **TURKS & CAICOS**)   67
Great Inagua (see **Inagua** in **BAHAMAS**)   41
GRENADA   52
GRENADINES   52–55
GUADELOUPE   55
Inagua (see **BAHAMAS**)   41
ISLA MARGARITA   56–57
ISLES DES SAINTES   56
JAMAICA   57
Jost Van Dyke (see **BRITISH VIRGIN ISLANDS**)   47
LA DESIRADE   57–58
LES SAINTES (see **ISLES DES SAINTES**)   56
Little Cayman (see **CAYMANS**)   49
Little Inagua (see **Inagua** in **BAHAMAS**)   41
Long Island (see **BAHAMAS**)   41–42
MARGARITA (see **ISLA MARGARITA**)   56–57
MARIE GALANTE   58
MARTINIQUE   58–59
Mayaguana (see **BAHAMAS**)   42
Mayreau (see **GRENADINES**)   54
Middle Caicos (see **TURKS & CAICOS**)   67
MONTSERRAT   59
Mustique (see **GRENADINES**)   54
Nassau (see **New Providence** in **BAHAMAS**)   42
NEVIS   59–60
New Providence (see **BAHAMAS**)   42
North Caicos (see **TURKS & CAICOS**)   67–68
Paradise Island (see **New Providence** in **BAHAMAS**)   42
PETIT MARTINIQUE   60
Providenciales or **Provo** (see **TURKS & CAICOS**)   68
PUERTO RICO   60–61
Rum Cay (see **BAHAMAS**)   42
SABA   61–62
SAINT BARTHÉLÉMY   62
SAINT BART (see **SAINT BARTHÉLÉMY**)   62
SAINT BARTH (see **SAINT BARTHÉLÉMY**)   62
SAINT CHRISTOPHER (see **SAINT KITT'S**)   62
Saint Croix (see **UNITED STATES VIRGIN ISLANDS**)   69
Saint John (see **UNITED STATES VIRGIN ISLANDS**)   69–70
SAINT KITT'S   62
SAINT LUCIA   62–63
SAINT MARTIN (also see **SINT MAARTEN**)   63–64
Saint Thomas (see **UNITED STATES VIRGIN ISLANDS**)   70
SAINT VINCENT   64

Salt Cay (see **TURKS & CAICOS**) 68
San Salvador (see **BAHAMAS**) 43
SINT EUSTATIUS 64
SINT MAARTEN (also see **SAINT MARTIN**) 64–65
South Caicos (see **TURKS & CAICOS**) 68–69
STATIA (see **SINT EUSTATIUS**) 64
TOBAGO 65
Tobago Cays (see **GRENADINES**) 54–55
Tortola (see **BRITISH VIRGIN ISLANDS**) 47
TRINIDAD 65–66
TURKS & CAICOS 66–69
Union (see **GRENADINES**) 55
UNITED STATES VIRGIN ISLANDS 69–70
VIEQUES 71
Virgin Gorda (see **BRITISH VIRGIN ISLANDS**) 47–48
Watlings Island (see **San Salvador** in **BAHAMAS**) 43

ANGUILLA
(pronounced "ann-GWILL-uh")

Size: 35 square miles
Population: 10,700
Highest point: 213 feet
Language: English
Currency: Eastern Caribbean dollar, but U.S. dollar readily accepted
Description: This peaceful, quiet coral island lies like a flat pancake in a clear sea. Dry and nearly treeless, it is surrounded by brilliant white beaches—33 in all including those on offshore islets—among the most beautiful in the Caribbean. The island, strangely, has an upscale appeal for those seeking sand, sea, and serenity. Since Anguilla lies only 5 miles north of Saint Martin, travelers go to that island for gambling, golf, nightlife, and shopping. However, the food on Anguilla is excellent, as are some of the accommodations. This is a very popular place with divers, snorkelers, and the yachting set. It is often called the Caribbean's best-kept secret, but that name has been obsolete for years. Get to some of the small islets or cays offshore, including Dog, Flat, Little Scrub, Prickly Pear, Sandy, Scilly, Scrub, Seal, and Sombrero. These are favorite areas for birding, diving, and snorkeling, as well as for phenomenal stretches of white beach.

ANTIGUA
(pronounced "ann-TEE-guh")

Size: 108 square miles
Population: 75,000

Highest point: 1,360 feet
Language: English
Currency: Eastern Caribbean dollar, but U.S. dollar widely accepted
Description: Antigua is a major center for yachting in the Caribbean. English Harbour is a safe and excellent port. Cruise ships find it equally inviting. The island claims to have 365 beaches, with the most tranquil on the southern coast, but the "official" count may be a bit of poetic license. Some beaches are accessible by boat or hiking only. This is a limestone and coral island of gently rolling hills with limited vegetation. Some people may find it a bit bleak or austere. There are many coves or scalloped bays, and the beaches are excellent. The island is protected in many areas by coral reefs. The pace on the island is relaxed with modest nightlife. The food is quite good. The festival of Antigua Sailing Week in late April and early May requires reservations months in advance, and you will need coat and tie or comparable dress for women to get into parties. Hike up the path to Shirley Heights during the day for a view of Guadeloupe and Montserrat or come here late Sunday afternoon for a barbecue and a chance to hear reggae and steel bands. Otherwise, do not hike in this area at night, as it is unsafe.

ARUBA

Size: 70 square miles
Population: 72,000
Highest point: 617 feet
Language: Dutch, Papiamento, Spanish, with English widely spoken
Currency: Aruban florin or guilder, but U.S. dollar widely accepted
Description: Aruba lies 15 miles off the coast of Venezuela and is noted for its dry, sunny climate and its location outside the hurricane belt. This is really a desert island, somewhat barren and bleak, with one excellent beach. It is quite commercial, with most of the hotels along the best beach. The island is noted for its lively nightlife. Some describe Aruba as a huge cruise ship—lots of action, safe, and friendly. Actual cruise ships come into the port of Oranjestad. The island is a favorite place with honeymooners. It is also good for someone who just wants to relax in the sun and is willing to pay a little extra for rooms with "no surprises." Enjoyable is the Bonbini Festival on Tuesday nights at the Fort Zoutman Museum.

BAHAMAS
(pronounced "buh-HAH-mahs")

The Bahamas consist of a 750-mile chain of over 700 islands, most of which are tiny and uninhabited. The Turks and Caicos are really a part of this chain, although they are covered under their own heading because they are a separate political entity. If you live in the Bahamas, you are a Bahamian (pronounced "buh-HAY-mee-uhn"). English is the language used on all the islands, but some of the dialects can be difficult to understand. The smaller islands are known as the Out Islands and can be difficult to reach. There are scheduled flights to these, but charters are equally popular. You can also reach the Out Islands by mailboat from Nassau in New Providence (see pp. 237–238).

Abacos (BAHAMAS)
(pronounced "A (as in apple)-buh-cohs")

Size: 650 square miles
Population: 10,000
Highest point: 120 feet
Language: English
Currency: Bahamian dollar, but U.S. dollar widely accepted
Description: The Abacos are a 130-mile chain of islands, shaped in a boomerang cluster. The main islands are Great Abaco (Marsh Harbour), Great Guana Cay, Elbow Cay (Hope Town), Green Turtle Cay (New Plymouth), Little Abaco, Man-O-War Cay, Sandy Point, Spanish Cay, Treasure Cay, and Walker's Cay. People come to these islands to get away from it all, fish, and relax. The islands are also popular with yachters because the area to the west of the islands is quite protected. This is a great place to sail. Having your own sail or motor boat in this area is advised.

Acklins (BAHAMAS)
(pronounced "AHCK-lins")

Size: 150 square miles
Population: 430
Highest point: 142 feet
Language: English
Currency: Bahamian dollar; U.S. dollar widely accepted
Description: This isn't just an Out Island, but a "way out" island where you can bird (look for flamingoes on the southern end of Long Cay), fish (bonefishing good), shell (some of the best in the Bahamas), shop for colorful fabrics, snorkel, sunbathe (Mayaguana Beach), and so on. This is for the true escapist.

Andros (BAHAMAS)
(pronounced "ANN-drohs")

Size: 2,300 square miles
Population: 8,200

Highest point: 102 feet
Language: English
Currency: Bahamian dollar; U.S. dollar widely accepted
Description: This is the largest of the Bahamian islands, but mostly unexplored. It is separated into sections by channels (bights) and fringed by mangroves. Inland are 147 blue holes as well as creeks, forests, and freshwater lakes. Offshore lies the world's third largest barrier reef and another 50 blue holes. People come here to dive along the edge of the 6,000-foot Tongue of the Ocean (TOTO) and fish (fabulous bonefishing in Lowe Sound). Locals are known for their lovely batik designs (Androsia), made in Central Andros. Huge land crabs migrate from the forest to the sea from May to August and are delicious to eat. If you are not into scuba diving and fishing, go somewhere else.

Berry Islands (BAHAMAS)
(pronounced as you would expect)
Size: 12 square miles
Population: 650
Highest point: 80 feet
Language: English
Currency: Bahamian dollar; U.S. dollar widely accepted
Description: Many of the Berry Islands are privately owned and may only be visited in an emergency. Most are uninhabited. The few open to visitors are famed for championship sport fishing, great diving, and good yachting. The islands are more relaxed and less hectic than the Biminis. You really need a boat here to enjoy what this chain has to offer.

Biminis (BAHAMAS)
(pronounced "BIH-min-knees")
Size: 9 square miles
Population: 1,650
Highest point: 20 feet
Language: English
Currency: Bahamian dollar; U.S. dollar widely accepted
Description: Only 50 miles off the coast of Florida, the Biminis are a cluster of small islands. Some are private, such as Cat Cay. The islands have a reputation for fabulous deep-sea fishing with tons of tournaments held here each year, including those searching for blue marlin. Boating is almost mandatory for visitors.

Cat (BAHAMAS)
(pronounced as you would expect)
Size: 150 square miles
Population: 1,700
Highest point: 206 feet (highest in the Bahamas)
Language: English
Currency: Bahamian dollar; U.S. dollar widely accepted
Description: This 48-mile-long unspoiled island is one of the most beautiful in the Bahamas, with high bluffs, rolling hills, deserted white beaches, caves, offshore reefs, plantation ruins, bonefishing (great off Devil's Point, Columbus Point, Orange Creek, and the southern tip of the island), fresh pineapples, and snorkeling (Fernandez Bay, Port Howe). Don't confuse this island with Cat Cay in the Biminis. Your pulse will drop below 40 beats a minute here.

Crooked (BAHAMAS)
(pronounced as you would expect)
Size: 92 square miles
Population: 400
Highest point: 155 feet
Language: English
Currency: Bahamian dollar; U.S. dollar widely accepted
Description: This is an island of beautiful deserted beaches, surrounded by 45 miles of fringing barrier reef. Crooked is known as "The Fragrant Island" for the aromatic flowers and spices that grow here. Landrail Point is the main town and most of the residents are Seventh Day Adventists. Everything closes on Saturdays, and there is no pork or alcohol allowed. Bonefishing here can be excellent. You come here to take yourself out of the loop.

Eleuthera (Harbour Island, Spanish Wells) (BAHAMAS)
(pronounced "ee-LUTH-uhr-ruh")
Size: 200 square miles
Population: 10,500
Highest point: 168 feet
Language: English
Currency: Bahamian dollar; U.S. dollar widely accepted
Description: Eleuthera, sometimes called Cigatoo by residents, resembles a 90-mile lobster claw. The island has lovely pink beaches, rugged cliffs, and secluded coves. It's a relaxing place to stay, with lots of water sports and nice hotels. Spanish Wells on offshore St.

George's Cay is famed for yachting. Harbour Island, known as "Briland" by residents, has an old-world, romantic appeal and a wonderful pink beach. Driving around the island is highly recommended with lots to see and do. Eat (freshly cooked chicken from roadside stands, pineapples in season, and bread fresh from "Dutch ovens"), fish (bonefishing at Deep Creek—lots of areas along west coast, grouper is good), golf (Cotton Bay Club), hunt (ask about moonlight duck shoots), shell, sunbathe (Harbour Island's 3-mile pink beach, but sandflies can sometimes be a problem), snorkel (illegal bleaching by lobster fisherman has spoiled many of the reefs on the western side), surf (Current Cut, on east side of island beyond Alice Town, and Surfer's Beach on Harbour Island—one of the best spots in the Bahamas), tennis (many facilities here), and windsurf (Harbour Island). You've got the idea. This is a popular and active island appealing to many personalities.

Exumas (BAHAMAS)
(pronounced "ex-ZOO-muhs")

Size: 112 square miles
Population: 3,500
Highest point: 125 feet
Language: English
Currency: Bahamian dollar; U.S. dollar widely accepted
Description: This 120-mile-long archipelago is made up of more than 350 cays, the largest ones joined by a bridge. This is one of the finest sailing and sea kayaking areas in the world. The islands vary from flat and arid to rolling and green after a recent rain. There are 200 miles of coral reefs to explore. For the most part this is a sleepy, relaxed island chain. It's busy during March and April and also alive during fishing tournaments, so ask in advance about these if you want to avoid crowds.

Grand Bahama (Freeport) (BAHAMAS)
(pronounced "grand bah-HAH-muh")

Size: 530 square miles
Population: 41,000
Highest point: 68 feet
Language: English
Currency: Bahamian dollar; U.S. dollar widely accepted
Description: This is one of the most popular islands in the Bahamas. It's 90 miles long with 65 miles of beach, much of it white. The limestone island is covered with scrub, although there are low-

lying marshes and mangrove swamps in the north. Strangely, under-ground freshwater is abundant. There's lots to see and do, making this a place for active vacationers. Popular are Deep Water Cay, with 80 acres of beautiful sandy beaches, colorful reefs for snorkeling, and 300 species of birds; Garden of Groves for waterfalls, birds, and flow-ers; and Lucaya National Park with the largest underwater cave sys-tem in the world. There are special excursions for divers who want to swim with dolphins and sharks, world class bone and permit fish-ing, gambling, golfing, partying, shelling (Deep Water Cay—ferry out to Gold Rock Beach—excellent at low tide), shopping (Freeport/Lucaya area is a shopper's paradise), sunbathing (Gold Rock Beach, the most beautiful on the island but can have horseflies—bring repel-lent; Lucaya National Park; Smith's Point; Pelican's Point; and Taino beaches—William's Town Beach for seclusion), playing tennis (many facilities), and windsurfing (Coral Beach, Xanadu, and Port Lucaya beaches). Yes, it is touristy.

Inagua (Great and Little) (BAHAMAS)
(pronounced "ee-NAH-gwah")

Size: 645 square miles
Population: 1,000
Highest point: 132 feet highest point of two islands
Language: English
Currency: Bahamian dollar; U.S. dollar widely accepted
Description: These islands are hard to get to and appeal to the diehard birder or avid escapist willing to put up with a lot to get to an arid, undeveloped, and remote island noted primarily for its flamingo refuge with roughly 40,000 birds. The island supports its population through salt production. We're talking dry, desolate, and hot—don't expect too much.

Long Island (BAHAMAS)
(pronounced as you would expect)

Size: 173 square miles
Population: 3,100
Highest point: 108 feet
Language: English
Currency: Bahamian dollar; U.S. dollar widely accepted
Description: Barren, desolate, and 160 miles long with tall white cliffs, caves, and cacti—that's it. The island is rocky on one side and sandy on the other, with crystal-clear water for swimming. Look for straw work at Simms, fish (good bonefishing), snorkel, sunbathe on

snowy white sand (Cape Santa Maria beaches), swim (along the west coast), and windsurf (at Stella Maris Inn). But take local advice about where to get into the water and where not to.

Mayaguana (BAHAMAS)
(pronounced "MAY-yuh-GWAH-nuh")

Size: 110 square miles
Population: 300
Highest point: 131 feet
Language: English
Currency: Bahamian dollar; U.S. dollar widely accepted
Description: The least developed and most isolated of the islands has a large reef around the northwest side. Only people seeking utter isolation would think of coming here.

New Providence (Nassau, Paradise Island) (BAHAMAS)
(pronounced as you would expect)

Size: 80 square miles
Population: 172,000
Highest point: 123 feet
Language: English
Currency: Bahamian dollar; U.S. dollar widely accepted
Description: New Providence is the commercial center of the Bahamas. Nassau, the capital, is a bustling and thriving tourist area with lots of shops and fine hotels. Just off Nassau and connected to the main island is Paradise Island, with fine hotels and a casino. Nassau is a good place to visit if you're looking for lots of dancing, dining out, gambling, and nightlife. As in any large hub, you must be cautious at night. Since this is a major tourist center, there's lots to see and do. There's so much free promotional literature on this island that you'll be inundated with ideas of how to take advantage of sights and activities.

Rum Cay (BAHAMAS)
(pronounced "rum key")

Size: 30 square miles
Population: 90
Highest point: 130 feet
Language: English
Currency: Bahamian dollar; U.S. dollar widely accepted
Description: This island caters to fly-in divers and anglers. It offers one of the most interesting dive sites in the Bahamas, with deep reefs and drop-offs.

San Salvador (formerly Watlings Island) (BAHAMAS)
(pronounced as you would expect)

Size: 63 square miles
Population: 465
Highest point: 123 feet
Language: English
Currency: Bahamian dollar; U.S. dollar widely accepted
Description: This is a rarely visited island with lots of creeks, lakes, and beautiful bays. Deserted white beaches fringe the eastern coastline. Diving and snorkeling is excellent with more than 80 marked sites consisting of many modern wrecks, miles of walls, and virgin shallow reefs. Shell at French Bay and sunbathe on Snow Bay Beach, a deserted area with snow-white sand. Another great island for the true escapist.

BARBADOS
(pronounced "bar-BAY-dohs")

Size: 166 square miles
Population: 280,000
Highest point: 1,115 feet
Language: English (but difficult to understand in rural areas)
Currency: Barbados dollar (best to use as common courtesy), but U.S. dollar widely accepted
Description: This is an island of gently rolling hills and deep red roads running through lowlands covered with sugar cane. There are a few hidden corners reminiscent of the island's lush past, but most of Barbados has been deforested. The coasts vary from rugged rock to gentle, if narrow, strips of pink to white sand, periodically washed away only to be replaced. Barbados is a popular place because there are lots of fine hotels and restaurants on the west coast, which has the best beaches and is often referred to as the "Platinum Coast." The people here are quite friendly and helpful with a good sense of humor. However, it is often difficult for visitors to understand the local English without a great deal of effort. The island is noted for its excellent climate. Swimming is comfortable because the water is warm throughout the year. The island is quite safe with a stable government and genuine British influence. It's one of the most heavily visited islands in the Caribbean. There's lots to see and do. Commonly visited are the Andromeda Gardens (orchids), Animal Flower Caves (sea anemones—call ahead because it's closed if seas are rough), Barbados Museum (formerly a prison), Barbados Wildlife Preserve (birds and monkeys—best to come at feeding time), Careenage (wharf area when fish brought in), Flower Forest (strenuous for

some), Harrison's Cave (touristy, but fun), Mount Gay Distillery, plantation houses, Saint Nicholas Abbey (1834), stately homes (on Wednesdays from January through April—inquire locally), Turner's Hall Woods, Welchman's Hall Gully (lovely tropical setting but can be workout for some—occasional monkeys spotted). Eat local food on seedy, but lively Baxter Road at night and at the Atlantic Hotel for Sunday brunch (reserve far in advance), fish (blue marlin—rather scarce—best in winter), golf (Sandy Lane), hike (organized in the peak season through the Barbados National Trust), party in some of the better discos or nightclubs, play tennis (dozens of spots), relax with a local drink and look for the Green Flash as the sun sets and listen to the whistling frogs as it turns dark, ride horses, snorkel (Folkestone Underwater National Park to Dottins Reef with boat), sunbathe and body surf on Crane beach, surf , take a submarine ride on the Atlantis, take tea (at better resorts, Cunard's Mansion, Maryam's), view the stars through a 14-inch telescope at Harry Bayley Observatory (Friday evening), walk through Bridgetown (free-walking maps), or windsurf (one of top places in the Caribbean).

BARBUDA
(pronounced "bah-BEW-duh")

Size: 62 square miles
Population: 1,400
Highest point: 143 feet
Language: English
Currency: Eastern Caribbean dollar, but U.S. dollar widely accepted
Description: This is a flat, coral island with little vegetation, few people, and lots of goats—sort of the "Last Frontier of the Caribbean." It's surrounded by 17 miles of isolated pinkish beaches. This is a sleepy, laidback place popular with birders, divers, shellers, snorkelers (much of the reef is close to the surface), sunbathers (try Palmetto Point—11 miles of pure isolation), and travelers looking for total escape. Fishing (hire a local for bonefishing, snook, or tarpon; bring your own gear) and hunting enthusiasts also fly in. Some would say the island is scruffy; others, starkly beautiful.

BERMUDA
(pronounced "burr-MEW-duh")

Size: 22 square miles
Population: 60,000
Highest point: 260 feet
Language: English
Currency: Bermuda dollar

Description: Bermuda is in the Atlantic, about 600 miles east of Cape Hatteras, North Carolina. Unlike the islands in the Caribbean (1,000 miles to the south), it is most popular from April to late September. The winter months are cool, rarely into the 50s, and ideal for golfing and tennis. The island, in fact, is subtropical because it is warmed by the Gulf Stream. While this is not a high island, the terrain is often hilly. The topography is somewhat strange, like being in Canada one moment, the tropics the next. The irregular coastline has many secluded coves lined by gorgeous beaches varying in tone from light pink to pure white. This is a sophisticated island, really a series of small, connected islands with a strong British influence making it quite formal. The main island is actually the center of an archipelago of roughly 150 tiny islets. The island is clean, usually safe, and particularly popular with young and old from the East Coast. It is also one of the more popular stops for cruise ships because of its shopping. This is a very friendly and orderly island with lots to see and do.

BONAIRE
(pronounced "bow-NAIR")

Size: 122 square miles
Population: 12,900
Highest point: 784 feet
Language: Dutch officially; also English, Spanish, Papiamento
Currency: Netherlands Antilles florin or guilder; U.S. dollar widely accepted
Description: Bonaire is one of the finest scuba diving areas in the Caribbean. Just off the main town of Kralendijk (pronounced "KRAH-len-dike") is Klein Bonaire, a 3-square-mile atoll, also surrounded by spectacular dive sites. Much of the colorful coral reef is close to shore, and its easy accessibility is a tremendous asset. Bonaire is arid, sunny, sleepy, almost barren. Some would call the island ugly. There's little nightlife or glitz or lush flora. Instead, you'll see fields of cacti appropriate for an island receiving less than 20 inches of rain a year. Although stark, the island is clean and safe. The island does have a large flock of flamingoes, approximately 7,000, but you are not allowed to get close to it. However, you will see a few of these birds scattered throughout the island.

BRITISH VIRGIN ISLANDS (BVI)

The British Virgin Islands is a 70-mile-long archipelago consisting of 100 cays, islands (only a handful inhabited), and tiny volcanic rocks covering approximately 60 square miles altogether. The islands are almost all (Anegada excepted) the peaks of drowned mountains. It is one of the main yachting centers in the Caribbean with Sir Francis Drake Passage a favorite day sail. The islands are not nearly as populated as the U.S. Virgin Islands. Expect things to be laidback, casual, friendly, and safe. The islands are noted for superb diving, snorkeling, and yachting (as outlined earlier). All three of these are highly regulated. The common motto of "leaving only bubbles, taking only memories" applies strictly here. There are even special moorings with fees for boats (yellow for commercial boats, white for scuba divers, and red for snorkelers). Nearly half of the visitors to these islands are traveling and sleeping on yachts. There is no better way to get to know the islands than this. All yachts must clear customs if coming from other islands. There is a daily cruising fee per person. The amount varies by season. Clearing customs is routinely described by most as annoying and time-consuming, so avoid going in and out of the territory as much as possible. To make things worse, officials can be officious and demand bond on expensive items. You get your money back when you leave. In general, these islands are aimed at people who love water. Forget about gambling, high-rise hotels, and nightlife. Following are descriptions of the main islands. Some private islands are covered in the section on Where to Stay (see p. 165). Many of the uninhabited islands are delightful for day sails. You'll get lots of tips locally about these.

Anegada (BRITISH VIRGIN ISLANDS)
(pronounced "ahn-ay-GAH-duh")

Size: 15 square miles
Population: 250
Highest point: 28 feet
Language: English
Currency: U.S. dollar
Description: This is a low-lying coral atoll, an island completely surrounded by reef. If you've got agoraphobia, don't come here—it's flat, open, and arid with cacti and sage growing freely, although it does have its own water supply from wells dug directly into the coral. Here you're more likely to encounter a goat than another traveler. Since the entire island is surrounded by reef, it is superb for diving and snorkeling. Roughly 300 wrecks lie offshore. Bonefishing is also exceptional. Don't even think about coming here without a reservation since rooms or tent sites are really limited. Finally, don't approach this island by yourself on a bare boat. The reef is treacherous and requires extreme skill to pass through the one channel to the island.

Jost Van Dyke (BRITISH VIRGIN ISLANDS)
(pronounced "yost van dike")

Size: 4 1/2 square miles
Population: 150
Highest point: 1,054 feet
Language: English
Currency: U.S. dollar
Description: Come to this mountainous island for a day just to enjoy the feeling of being deserted in a tropical paradise. The beaches are lovely (Great Harbour, White Bay) and surrounded by water more green than blue. Hike, relax (on a hammock), snorkel (White Bay), yacht (the island has two nice bays for anchorages—Great and Little harbours). Make reservations well in advance if you intend to eat here, since restaurants prepare only enough food for expected guests.

Tortola (BRITISH VIRGIN ISLANDS)
(pronounced "tore-TOE-luh")

Size: 21 square miles
Population: 13,000
Highest point: 1,780 feet
Language: English
Currency: U.S. dollar
Description: Tortola is a friendly island noted for its great beaches, which are best on the north side, and for seclusion. The hills are covered with terraced gardens and wandering animals. The air smells sweet. From the tops of hills the surrounding islands spread out as if on a living canvas. Tortola bills itself as the "yachting capital of the Caribbean," which makes it an ideal starting point for those who want to get to know the numerous islands by water.

Virgin Gorda (BRITISH VIRGIN ISLANDS)
(pronounced "virgin GORE-duh")

Size: 15 square miles
Population: 2,000
Highest point: 1,500 feet
Language: English
Currency: U.S. dollar
Description: This is a lovely, hilly island on its northern end and flatter in the south with 20 white beaches and protected lagoons. The pace is slow, slower, and slowest. Everything is geared to water sports. Dive (get to Chikuzen, P.O.S. near the Dogs, Paramatta

wreck—need to go out with a boat), ride horses (O'Neal & Sons), snorkel and swim around the Baths (huge boulders surrounding salt-water pools in a 4-acre area) and in the Blue Lagoon on North Sound, hike up Gorda Peak (strenuous and for the serious hiker only), yacht (anchor in the North Sound), and windsurf.

CARRIACOU
(pronounced "car-ee-ah-COO")

Size: 13 square miles
Population: 8,000
Highest point: 955 feet
Language: English
Currency: Eastern Caribbean dollar, but U.S. dollar widely accepted
Description: This little island, which turns a lush green after rains, lies just northeast of Grenada. Carriacou is surrounded by stunning white beaches and is a center for boat building with inhabitants known as "kayaks." Visit offshore islets, such as Frigate, Jack-A-Dan, Large, Mabouya, Mushroom, Palm (popular with cruises), Saline (superb reefs), Sandy (not to be missed for snorkeling, but flooded with cruise passengers on some days), and White (great reefs—popular with cruises).

CAYMANS
The Caymans lie 200 miles northwest of Jamaica. They are noted for exceptional diving. Since the islands are practically flat, being the tops of mountains in the ocean, there is little chance of any runoff during sporadic rains to muddy the water. These islands have instituted strict regulations regarding protection of marine life and reefs. These include a ban on spearfishing (including Hawaiian slings); controlled fishing; fixed moorings for dive boats, which you must use; and rules for snorkeling, which include the use of a marking buoy. The islands are clean and safe.

Cayman Brac (CAYMANS)
(pronounced "CAY-mun brahk")

Size: 14 square miles
Population: 1,300
Highest point: 140 feet
Language: English
Currency: Cayman dollar, but U.S. dollar widely accepted
Description: A dry island with a rural feel, Cayman Brac is truly laid-back and isolated. Some people claim this is the prettiest of the three islands. There may still be goats grazing around the landing strip.

Grand Cayman (CAYMANS)
(pronounced "grand CAY-mun")
Size: 76 square miles
Population: 24,000
Highest point: 60 feet
Language: English
Currency: Cayman dollar, but U.S. dollar widely accepted
Description: Grand Cayman is the most sophisticated of the Cayman islands with many places to stay and eat as well as limited nightlife. Still, the main focus of the island, other than an obsession with money with 500-plus banks, is its incredible diving and snorkeling. It's also a safe island and suited for family travel if water and sun are your focus.

Little Cayman (CAYMANS)
(pronounced "little CAY-mun)
Size: 10 square miles
Population: 70
Highest point: 40 feet
Language: English
Currency: Cayman dollar, but U.S. dollar widely accepted
Description: You come to this bare, laidback island to get into the water. Here you'll feel isolated and alone—the way some people love it. Don't expect much on land except peace and quiet. Dive at any of 40 sites, including Bloody Bay—rated one of the best dives in the Caribbean with virtually every type of coral and sponge imaginable. Visit Owen Island for a picnic on its lovely beach.

CULEBRA (off PUERTO RICO)
(pronounced "coo-LEE-bruh")
Size: 21 square miles
Population: 2,000
Highest point: 650 feet
Language: Spanish, limited English
Currency: U.S. dollar
Description: This gently rolling island, one in a tiny archipelago, is extremely dry and desert-like. It's calm, unspoiled, and truly rustic. If you're looking for isolation and great beaches, this is a hidden gem. Off the island are nearly two dozen smaller islets. The entire area has superb reefs for diving and snorkeling. Bird (thousands of terns pass through here in April), dive, sea sled (ask locally about this—get pulled by boat and snorkel at same time), snorkel off Impact Beach

or around the islet of Culebrita, and sunbathe on some of the Caribbean's finest beaches (Soni—exceptional; Tortuga; and the beaches surrounding the islets of Culebrita and Luis Pena).

CURAÇAO
(pronounced "ker-uh-SOW-oh")

Size: 180 square miles
Population: 200,000
Highest point: 1,238 feet
Language: Dutch, Papiamento
Currency: Netherlands Antilles florin or guilder, but U.S. dollar widely accepted
Description: This dry island lies 35 miles north of Venezuela and doesn't gear itself to mass tourism. It carries on an independent life of its own. In a way, the island suffers from an identity crisis in that it's difficult to explain what it really is other than a commercial hub. In fact, it has good restaurants and hotels, some excellent dive sites, and good weather. It also is undergoing a renaissance, as older buildings are being restored, particularly those in Willemstad, which is reminiscent of Amsterdam. Don't miss the floating market (Ruyterkade) with produce and fish from Venezuela.

DOMINICA
(pronounced "doh-min-KNEE-kuh")

Size: 290 square miles
Population: 73,000
Highest point: 4,747 feet
Language: English, Créole
Currency: Eastern Caribbean dollar
Description: "The Nature Island," devastated by a hurricane in 1979 when 80 percent of its palms were destroyed, is again lush and lovely with 365 streams; tropical flora, including giant ferns, 7-feet-wide gommier trees, and carrapid trees so hard they break an axe; and a myriad of exotic birds. The mountainous island, covered with rain forests where it rains up to 350 inches per year, is one of the most dramatic in the Caribbean. Black beaches, with Picard one of the best, surround the island, but these are not the island's attraction. The following activities are: Bird (160 species, including the world's largest parrot, best seen in April and early May during the breeding season in the Syndicat Area of the northwest), boat up Indian River (be rowed; don't use an engine or you scare off wildlife), dive and snorkel in one of the best but least-known areas in the Caribbean (February through April when water is clear), hike (guide needed on

almost all hikes, especially to the 200-foot-wide cauldron known as Boiling Lake—a strenuous 6-hour hike), and swim in the rapidly flowing Layou River or through the Titou Gorge through a series of rooms to a small waterfall at the end.

DOMINICAN REPUBLIC
LA REPUBLICA DOMINICANA
(pronounced "lah ray-POO-blee-kuh doh-mean-knee-KAHN-nuh")

Size: 18,704 square miles
Population: 7,600,000
Highest point: 10,417 feet (highest in Caribbean)
Language: Spanish
Currency: Dominican Peso
Description: The Dominican Republic covers the eastern two thirds of the island of Hispaniola (the other third is Haiti). The topography of this country is one of the most diverse in the Caribbean, with 1,000 miles of coast, some of it incredibly beautiful, and five mountain ranges. Here you'll see sugar cane fields, mountain forests, desert areas covered with cacti, banana plantations—you name it. The tourist comes here for great beaches and low-cost travel. The traveler comes to explore the countryside as Europeans have been doing for years, but it's helpful to speak Spanish. The country has an extensive national park system, and if that's your interest, you should plan on spending several weeks here. Poverty is evident throughout the island, but, ironically, crime is not as prevalent here as on many other islands. Here are a few pointers on the main tourist destinations and a few off the tourist track. **Altos de Chavón:** Picturesque town with cobblestone streets; a must-see at night when lit by lanterns. **Boca Chica** and nearby **Juan Dolio**: Popular with tourists for fabulous white beaches and reasonably priced accommodations—a good place for people to meet people. **Cayo Levantado:** An islet lying off Samaná; a little paradise with magnificent beaches. **Las Terrenas:** Superb beach area but without many of the hassles of the more popular destinations. **Puerto Plata**: Very popular with its mountain backdrop and fine beaches—many charters and cruises come into this touristy town. Visit the Amber Museum (Museo de Amber). Don't miss the view from 2,600-foot Mount Isabel de Torres (take cable car—get there early to avoid wait). **Punta Cana:** Location of a Club Med and noted for a 20-mile beach and 300,000 coconut palms; referred to as the "Coconut Coast." **Samaná Peninsula**: One of the most photogenic areas in the country, lush and lovely with coconut and banana plantations. The town (Samaná) is laidback and quiet. **Santiago de los Caballeros:** Well worth seeing for anyone willing to get off the beaten tourist track—his-

toric and high in the mountains. **Santo Domingo**: This is a huge, extremely lively city (oldest in the New World with ties to Columbus, who is buried in the huge lighthouse El Faro a Colón) of great historical interest because of its colonial buildings and ancient streets, but it has horrible air pollution. **Sosúa:** Close to Puerto Plata, but more European in feel—somewhat artsy with good nightlife. Also recommended: Bird, dive (off Isla Catalina), drive (any of the high mountain roads for spectacular views), dance (bolero or merengue—in many nightclubs but especially along the Malecón in Santo Domingo), fish (Boca de Yuma, the best point in the Caribbean for blue marlin—contest in June), gamble in Playa Dorada (use dollars to get dollars in local casinos), golf (Casa de Campo in La Romana—courses among the most beautiful and challenging in the world), hike (to top of Duarte Peak— takes 2 to 4 days with a guide; the area around Jarabacoa has lots of good hikes and rustic inns), shop (Santo Domingo), ride, snorkel (Isla Catalina best, but coral reefs off Costambar okay), sunbathe (Bayahibe, Bávaro, Boca Chica, Dorada, Juan Dolio, Grande), surf (Güibia Beach, Macao, Playa), turtle watch (Parque Nacional Jaragua—green, hawksbill, leatherback, loggerhead), whalewatch, and windsurf (Cabarete is considered the top spot for this in the world).

GRENADA
(pronounced "gruh-NAY-duh")

Size: 133 square miles with all offshore islets
Population: 120,000
Highest point: 2,757 feet
Language: English, French patois
Currency: Eastern Caribbean dollar, but U.S. dollar widely accepted
Description: There are some who would say that this mountainous, lush island is the most beautiful in the Caribbean. Known as the "Isle of Spice" or "The Spice Island," it is flower-filled and offers 28 tropical fruits and 12 spices with a third of the world's nutmeg produced here. Along the Atlantic you'll find black-sand beaches; along the Caribbean, gold to white. The heavy rains in the mountains may hit 150 inches per year, creating numerous rivers and waterfalls. Along the coast the rainfall is less. It is not a touristy place. Not a place to come for nightlife, but for laidback living. There are lots of small inns with none taller than a palm tree.

GRENADINES
(pronounced "GREN-uh-deans")
The 32 tiny islands, not counting dozens of minuscule islets, known as the Grenadines cover the 65-mile stretch of sea between Saint Vin-

cent in the north and Grenada in the south like a series of stepping stones. In total the islands and islets cover a mere 35 square miles. These islands are noted for their isolation and unspoiled beauty. Only a few of them are inhabited (two are covered in the Where to Stay section on p. 165 since they are private). Each offers a great deal of privacy and intimacy, although they are now being visited routinely by cruise ships. This is snorkeling and yachting heaven, since all of the islands in this group are surrounded by colorful coral in crystalline water. Their popularity is cause for concern, as some people have been treating the area badly by damaging coral and leaving behind garbage.

Bequia (GRENADINES)
(pronounced "BECK-wee" or "BECK-way")

Size: 7 square miles
Population: 5,000
Highest point: 881 feet
Language: English
Currency: Eastern Caribbean dollar, but U.S. dollar widely accepted
Description: This is a small, intimate island, once a whaling center, which some consider a must-see. It's a lovely and lively place with good beaches and food. Geared mainly to yachters, the island is still a find for those seeking sophisticated, but casual fun in the sun. It draws a great crowd of experienced and interesting travelers. The island is hilly with varied vegetation and acres of coconut palms. Admiralty Bay is charming with the many moored yachts—a photographer's dream.

Canouan (GRENADINES)
(pronounced "CAN-oh-wahn")

Size: 3 square miles
Population: 1,000
Highest point: 877 feet
Language: English
Currency: Eastern Caribbean dollar; U.S. dollar widely accepted
Description: This is a brown, barren island that turns green only after sporadic rains. It's very arid but with stunning beaches—white and ever so long and ever so deserted much of the time. A gem. Snorkel in the area known as The Pool, and sunbathe at Mahault Bay beach.

Mayreau (GRENADINES)
(pronounced "MY-row")

Size: 1–1/2 square miles
Population: 400 people
Highest point: 280 feet
Language: English
Currency: Eastern Caribbean dollar; U.S. dollar widely accepted
Description: This tiny island lies next to the Tobago Cays with a lovely, but expensive resort in an ideal location. Yachters come into Salt Whistle Bay. The island is really geared to seafarers. Just enjoy the sand, serenity, and sea. Swim at Salt Whistle Bay beach, which may well be the loveliest in the Grenadines, and definitely take a boat to the Tobago Cays.

Mustique (GRENADINES)
(pronounced "moo-steeck")

Size: 2 square miles
Population: 750
Highest point: 495 Feet
Language: English
Currency: Eastern Caribbean dollar; U.S. dollar accepted
Description: A place favored by the rich and famous, Mustique has been labeled as the jetsetters hideaway. Here you'll find lots of privately owned homes and villas, most of which are for rent, and two hotels. The island is truly isolated with 12 secluded beaches lining lovely coves. The roads are paved and wind through gentle hills with a somewhat manicured feel. Dive, play tennis or ride a horse (go to the Cotton House), snorkel (Britannia Bay, northern end of Galliceaux Bay, and Lagoon Bay), swim (Macaroni Beach), sunbathe (Sandy Bay), and windsurf—most of these arranged through the Cotton House.

Tobago Cays (GRENADINES)
(pronounced "toe-BAY-go keys")

Population: Uninhabited
Language: NA
Currency: NA
Description: These 4 tiny islands (Barabel, Jamesby, Petit Bâteau, Petit Rameau) are uninhabited but extremely popular among yachters. Do not expect to find yourself alone in the best anchorages. The cays lie just barely above the water line. Cruise through the tiny islands and snorkel at every chance. This is one of the best snorkel-

ing areas in the Caribbean. Avoid illusions of total isolation during the peak season. It's rarely going to happen. The area has been written up numerous times, so there will be tons of boats for diving and snorkeling. Never leave any trash behind or touch the coral reefs—this area is being damaged by misuse.

Union (GRENADINES)
(pronounced as you would expect)

Size: 3.2 square miles
Population: 2,500
Highest point: 999 feet
Language: English
Currency: Eastern Caribbean dollar, but U.S. dollar widely accepted
Description: All of these islands are isolated and small. If any of them could be called developed, then it would be this one. The island is quite dry and unappealing overall but is the beginning of yachters' paradise and acts like a hub to the rest of the Grenadines. It is quite hilly and walking can be difficult. Hike into Chatham Bay to sunbathe and swim, snorkel off Frigate Island off the southern shore, and take a trip to the Tobago Cays.

GUADELOUPE
(pronounced "guah-duh-loop")

Size: 530 square miles
Population: 387,000
Highest point: 4,813 feet
Language: French, Créole
Currency: French franc
Description: Guadeloupe consists of two very different islands connected by a bridge, which runs over La Rivière Salée, not a river, but a 4-mile saltwater band between the islands. The island has two nicknames: "Emerald Isle" for its lush tropical scenery and the "Cuisine Capital of the Caribbean" for its 100-plus restaurants offering varied, topnotch dishes. Basse-Terre (312 square miles) is volcanic and lush. Much of it is covered in rain forest, the rest in banana plantations. Black beaches, often rocky, surround it. Grand-Terre (218 square miles) is a flat, limestone plateau with plains, rolling hills, sugar plantations, and a varied coast—cliffs and mangroves to lovely white beaches, some of which are "clothing optional," a politically correct way of saying nude. Don't miss the tallest fall in the Caribbean, the 300-foot Les Chutes du Carbet, a drive through the National Park, and a hike through rain forests with a guide to locate rare orchids.

ILES DES SAINTES (LES SAINTES)
(pronounced "eel day saunt")
Size: 9 islets cover 6 square miles
Population: 3,350
Highest point: 1,020 feet (most areas under 100 feet)
Language: French
Currency: French franc
Description: This strange, little archipelago of 9 tiny islands, no more than the tips of submerged volcanic mountains, lies just south of Guadeloupe and appeals primarily to adventurers seeking isolation and to yachters. The two main islands are Terre-de-Bas (largest) and Terre-de-Haut (second largest). Once heavily fortified, the islands are called the Gibraltar of the West Indies. The villages are photogenic, the beaches nearly deserted, the seafood excellent on Terre-de-Haut. Nude bathing is common. Visitors fluent in French have an edge, but you'll get by if you don't. Cruise through the little islets of Grand Ilet, Ilet à Cabrit, La Coche, La Redonde, Les Augustins, and Le Pâté. These are beautiful, uninhabited, and peaceful. Picnic on any one of them for an unforgettable experience. Bathe nude at Anse Crawen beach, camp out at Pont Pierre, eat seafood on Terre-de-Haut, hike, snorkel, sunbathe at Pain de Sucre beach fringing a lovely, hidden cove, and take photos of local inhabitants wearing *salakos*, a flat straw hat.

ISLA MARGARITA (off VENEZUELA)
(pronounced "eel-luh mar-gah-ree-tah")
Size: 360 square miles
Population: 200,000
Highest point: 2,900 feet
Language: Spanish
Currency: Bolívar (bolivares)
Description: This island is popular with Venezuelans for shopping, Germans for sun and windsurfing, and Canadians who are experts at seeking out the best value for their weak dollar. It's a dirty, dry, and lackluster place that makes up for its lack of aesthetic appeal with good food and lively nightlife at the right price—low. Beaches are okay but not great. However, windsurfing is indeed terrific. Isla Margarita, simply called Margarita by Venezuelans, makes a good hub for excursions to the mainland. Frankly, the mainland can be dangerous so that using a hub like Margarita or Aruba for flights in and out with guides is a very good idea. Other special-interest excursions include trips to Islas los Roques for superb snorkeling and some of the best bonefishing in the world (bring your own gear) or to Islas las Aves

(Archipelago of the Birds) for great diving and lovely beaches. It really helps to speak Spanish if you plan to visit Margarita. Pack plenty of patience; you'll need it.

JAMAICA
(pronounced "juh-MAY-kuh")

Size: 4,411 square miles
Population: 2,500,000
Highest point: 7,402 feet
Language: English
Currency: Jamaican dollar, but U.S. dollar widely accepted (unofficially)
Description: Jamaica is an enormous island. To get to know it well would take months. The terrain is hilly to mountainous, vegetation lush, and beaches fair to excellent. The most popular tourist destinations (populations in parentheses) are **Kingston** (900,000—for art, business, and dance), **Mandeville** (14,000—bamboo avenue, hiking, and off-beat travel), **Montego Bay** (44,000—golf, nightlife, shopping), **Negril** (1,200—beach, marijuana, meeting people, sunsets), **Ocho Rios** (6,000—passable beach, Dunn's River Falls, fern gully, nightlife, shopping), **Port Antonio** (11,000—fishing, rafting on the Rio Grande, yachting), and **Runaway Bay** (3,000—family vacations, riding at Chukka Cove). The island is popular as a cruise line destination, with nearly a dozen lines arriving in Montego Bay, Ocho Rios, and Port Antonio each week. Since distances are great and travel difficult, match your selection of things to see and do to the time you have on the island. Resorts dot the island, and they are like little cities or enclaves to themselves. Many of the most popular are on the stretch from Montego Bay past Ocho Rios along the coast. Marijuana is just about everywhere, one reason that the majority of travelers to Jamaica are now under 25. However, it is illegal to possess. The fact that marijuana is in the air and smoked by a good percentage of the locals doesn't change that fact.

LA DÉSIRADE
(pronounced "lah day-zee-rahd")

Size: 12 square miles
Population: 2,000
Highest point: 900 feet
Language: French, Créole
Currency: French franc
Description: This desert island, once a leper colony, floats in the ocean like a 7-mile block of arid limestone. It's as if someone has

taken a bite out of the Wild West and dropped it here. There are a few sheep, lots of cactus as a cash crop, and fishing. Two tiny islets off the coast are Terre-de-Bas and Terre-de-Haut, not to be confused with larger islands of the same names listed under Iles des Saintes (Les Saintes). Bask in the sun at one of the beaches; eat seafood; look for agoutis (like guinea pigs) and iguanas in the steeper, rocky areas; and relish the isolation.

MARIE GALANTE
(pronounced "mah-ree gah-lawnt")

Size: 58 square miles
Population: 19,000
Highest point: 670 feet
Language: French
Currency: French franc
Description: A limestone and coral plateau just south of Guadeloupe, "The Sombrero Isle" or "The Island of 100 Windmills," offers a rocky landscape with cliffs along the shore. These encircle beaches, most of which are deserted. The sand on some is pure white and truly stunning. Inland you'll find sugar cane fields and some distilleries. Overall this is a dry, mild place not really geared to tourism and, therefore, highly desirable to some. Eat seafood in one of the island's few but good restaurants, relax, take a ride in an oxcart, and get on a boat to see the Devil's Hole grotto.

MARTINIQUE
(pronounced "mar-tea-kneeck")

Size: 425 square miles
Population: 360,000
Highest point: 4,586 feet
Language: French, Créole
Currency: French franc
Description: "The Isle of Flowers" lives up to its name with lush and diverse flora. Tropical rain forests cover the volcanic, mountainous island ringed by white to black beaches, the latter mostly in the north. The island is a favorite with Europeans, cruise ships, and those looking for a truly tropical setting with terrific beaches. Its port serves as a major hub for yachters heading into the Grenadines. While beautiful overall, this is not an island without some scruffy areas. Visitors speaking French have a distinct advantage. Drive along the northwest coast, eat fabulous French food in any of 200 local restaurants, golf at the club in Trois Ilets, hike on numerous trails, ride horses through fabulous terrain, sunbathe on some of the finest and most isolated

beaches in the Caribbean (many of the best require hikes of 15 minutes to an hour—don't miss those on the southern tip of the island just east of Sainte Anne), surf off the northeast coast where it really gets rough, take a boat out to Les Fonds Blancs from François (these are large, shallow sandbars surrounded by reefs), visit the fishing village of Tartane, and have a drink at Leyritz Plantation, one of the prettiest places to stay on the island. Another fun fishing village to visit is Grande Rivière.

MONTSERRAT
(pronounced "mont-sir-raht")

Size: 40 square miles
Population: 12,000
Highest point: 3,002 feet
Language: English
Currency: Eastern Caribbean dollar, but U.S. dollar widely accepted
Description: "The Emerald Isle" is a lush volcanic island with rain forests and waterfalls. It is surrounded by small gray and black beaches. This is a quiet place with a private feeling, relatively undiscovered and uncrowded. It still exudes an aura of being undisturbed by commercial tourism. It has bounced back from extensive hurricane damage in 1989, but check on volcanic activity before making plans to travel here. It is not a place favored by beach lovers or divers. It's an ideal place to relax—very safe and peaceful, when the active volcano is not playing tricks. Bike (extremely popular here; for athletic bikers—mountain trails), bird, buy the most beautiful stamps in the Caribbean at the Philatelic Building, eat a local barbecue or mountain chicken (huge frogs' legs), feed iguanas (some are nearly tame), hike to a 70-foot waterfall or to an active volcano that still bubbles and gurgles, and visit the Saturday morning market in Plymouth.

NEVIS
(pronounced "KNEE-vuhs")

Size: 36 square miles
Population: 10,000
Highest point: 3,232 feet
Language: English
Currency: Eastern Caribbean dollar, but U.S. dollar widely accepted
Description: A lovely island, covered with rain forest, Nevis is intensely green with mountains shrouded in mist, but there is still damage from recent hurricanes. The island is the tip of a volcanic cone covered in a rich soil, resulting in great gardens and luxuriant

flora. People come here for its peace, privacy, and good beaches. Some of the sugar plantations have been converted into wonderful inns, truly characteristic of the Caribbean. Bathe in hot springs at the Bath Hotel and Spring House, once a spa but now in ruins; hike through rain forests with guides—especially when climbing into the crater on vines; ride horses through mountains or plantations; shop for lovely stamps at the Nevis Philatelic Bureau in Charlestown or for pottery at the Newcastle Pottery Works; snorkel at Newcastle Bay, Oualie Beach, or Pinney's Beach; sunbathe at Pinney's Beach—4 miles long and one of the best in the Caribbean; surf at Windward Beach; visit the Saturday morning market in Charlestown; and wind-surf at Oualie Beach.

PETIT MARTINIQUE
(pronounced "pity mahr-tee-NEEK")
Size: 486 acres
Population: 600 feet
Highest point: 745 feet
Language: English
Currency: Eastern Caribbean dollar, but U.S. dollar widely accepted
Description: This lovely volcanic cone lies just a few miles northeast of Grenada and is surrounded by reefs. Inhabited by boat builders and fishermen, it's known for its great beaches. You come here to lie in the sun and enjoy snorkeling in the sea—that's it. However, check locally about safety since this island has been reported as potentially dangerous to tourists recently. The locals on Grenada will be honest with you.

PUERTO RICO (also see CULEBRA and VIEQUES)
(pronounced "PWEAR-toe REE-coh")
Size: 3,421 square miles
Population: 3.7 million
Highest point: 4,398 feet
Language: Spanish
Currency: U.S. dollar
Description: Puerto Rico is easily and inexpensively reached from many cities in Canada and the United States. It is one of the largest and most diverse islands in the Caribbean, one which would take months to know well. The topography varies from dry, rolling hills (mostly in the south and east) to luxuriant rain forests (mostly in the north). If you're seeking isolation, sun, and water, head immediately to the offshore islands of Culebra and Vieques. However, stay on the main island if you want to be entertained. Puerto Rico is a cos-

mopolitan place geared to hot days and equally hot nights. Food, nightlife, shopping, sightseeing, sports—all are among the Caribbean's best. This is not to say that the island doesn't have its bland or weak spots, but if you seek out the best, it's very good indeed. Visit Old San Juan (7 square blocks filled with historical buildings and museums—takes a couple of days), Spanish colonial towns (Ponce—lots of old buildings and three good museums; San Germán), and typical villages such as Boquerón and Guánica. Bird (Guánica Forest Reserve—dry area with good beaches), dance (dozens of clubs), eat (don't miss the gastronomic inns or *mesones gastronómicos* outside San Juan or seafood in areas where fish is fresh), fish, gamble, golf (terrific courses), hike (El Yunque rain forest—35 miles east of San Juan where it rains 240 inches per year), party, play tennis (100-plus courts on the island), ride horses (Palmas del Mar Equestrian Center or the Hacienda Carabali), snorkel (off Culebra and Vieques on the east coast—not to mention isolated Mona on the west coast), shop (lovely lace, local fashions, and *guayaberas*—embroidered men's shirts), surf (Punta Higuero, Rincón), turtle watch (Mona Island), view wildlife (Cayo Santiago monkey preserve with 900 monkeys or Mona Island off the west coast for birds, beaches, iguanas, and 200-foot cliffs—camping permitted on the latter), and windsurf (off Rincón).

SABA
(pronounced "SAY-buh")

Size: 5 square miles
Population: 1,200
Highest point: 2,855 feet
Language: Dutch, but everyone speaks English
Currency: Netherlands Antilles florin or guilder, but U.S. dollar widely accepted
Description: Saba looms like the top of a lush, green volcanic mountain sticking out from the sea. Landing by plane here is an experience with sheer cliffs at both the beginning and the end of a short runway (more like a sidewalk). This island is a very quiet and secluded place with lots of charm. Its tiny towns have a magical feel. Especially nice is the absence of biting bugs—no mosquitoes or no-see-uhms. But on the flip side—no beaches (well, there is a pebble beach). See lace ("drawn" or "Spanish work") being made, dive and snorkel around the entire island (terrific—best in winter), drink a shot of the 151-proof Saba Spice (spiced rum), fish (charter a boat to take you to the shallows known as the Saba Bank 3 miles to the southwest), hike for fabulous views (climb 1,064 steps to the top of

Mount Scenery from the town of Windwardside), and shop for the island's beautiful stamps.

SAINT BARTHÉLÉMY (SAINT BART, SAINT BARTH)
(pronounced "san bart")

Size: 8 square miles
Population: 5,100
Highest point: 938 feet
Language: French (old Norman dialect), but English widely spoken
Currency: French franc
Description: This small island consists of steep hills surrounded by cliffs and a few bays with lovely beaches. The ride in by plane is an experience in itself as you swoop down a hill for a breathtaking landing. The island has become a kind of mecca for jetsetters and people who want to live the good life in villas nestled in the hills and accessible by narrow, winding roads. The island is small, but you need a car to get around easily since public transportation is poor. Many yachters stop here en route from Antigua to the British Virgin Islands.

SAINT KITT'S (SAINT CHRISTOPHER)
(pronounced as you would expect)

Size: 65 square miles
Population: 36,000
Highest point: 3,792 feet
Language: English
Currency: Eastern Caribbean dollar, but U.S. dollar widely accepted
Description: Saint Kitt's is a lush, mountainous island surrounded by white (in the south) and black (in the north) beaches. Although volcanic in the north, it levels off to a plain in the midsection (lots of sugar cane) and becomes hilly in the south. Basically, this is a good destination for privacy. Bird (in salt ponds), dive (April and May best), gamble at the casino, golf, hike (to top of Mount Liamuga), ride horses (on beaches or in banana and sugar fields), snorkel (Banana Bay), sunbathe (Banana Bay is the best white beach; Dieppe Bay , best black), surf (Conaree Bay), tour on sugar train (ask locally about this—fun when not hauling sugar), watch wildlife (search for the Vervet monkey at Monkey Hill west of Basseterre and in the salt pond area), and windsurf (Banana, Dieppe, and Frigate bays).

SAINT LUCIA
(pronounced "saint LOO-shuh")
Size: 238 square miles

Population: 160,000
Highest point: 3,117 feet
Language: English (patois in rural areas)
Currency: Eastern Caribbean dollar
Description: Lush and lovely, Saint Lucia is arguably the most beautiful island in the Caribbean with its mountainous terrain and photogenic peaks (Gros Piton, Petit Piton). Its many coves shelter white to black beaches—all beautiful. In the humid valleys you'll find acres of bananas. Marigot Bay serves as a yacht harbor and is one of the most stunning, secluded coves in the Caribbean. To fully appreciate this island takes more than a few days. Unfortunately, the island is as poor as it is beautiful, and some hostility towards tourists exists. Drive south from Soufrière through the rain forest (stunning flora) to Vieux Fort, join in the Friday-night "jump-up" in Gros Ilet (barbecues, dancing, music), hike through Pigeon Island National Park (connected by a causeway to the main island), relax on lovely beaches (Anse des Pitons, Choc Bay, Rodney Bay), ride horses along the coast, sail around the island for a day and come into Soufrière Bay for a stunning view of the Pitons, take a helicopter tour of the island (fairly reasonably priced), and windsurf (Anse de Sable, Casen Bas, Rodney Bay).

SAINT MARTIN (see also **SINT MAARTEN)**
(ask locally for French pronunciation)
Size: 21 square miles (with Sint Maarten)
Population: 29,000
Highest point: 1,500 feet
Language: French
Currency: French franc
Description: There is a Dutch and a French side to this island—without any borders, however. The French side is mostly rolling hills, forested in the center and steepest on the north. The shoreline consists of deep coves. The French side is often referred to as the Gastronomic Capital of the Caribbean (a title shared with Guadeloupe) and has a slower, more relaxed feel than the Dutch side. Some say that it has an almost Mediterranean feel. Bathe nude (there's even a clothing-optional hotel), eat at a "lo-lo" (local barbecue place), or sip coffee at one of the charming outdoor cafes (Grand Case is the best town overall for eating), hike (Paradise Peak or Pic du Paradis), ride horses (both along beaches and in the hills), shop in Marigot (some real bargains in luxury goods, especially perfume), snorkel, sunbathe (particularly pleasant with the absence of beach vendors on Cupecoy Beach; Long Beach; Orient Bay—one of the finest clothing-optional

beaches in the Caribbean; Prune Bay for seclusion), take a daytrip to Anguilla for its beautiful beaches and isolated islets, and windsurf (Orient Bay).

SAINT VINCENT
(pronounced as you would expect)

Size: 133 square miles
Population: 115,000
Highest point: 4,048 feet
Language: English
Currency: Eastern Caribbean dollar, but U.S. dollar widely accepted
Description: This is a rugged, relatively undeveloped island with jagged peaks and steep hills dropping into the sea. Much of its area is covered in forests and lush growth. It is surrounded by gold to black sand beaches, mostly the latter. Baleine and Trinity Falls are worth the effort to see. Bird (search for the island's elusive parrot in the wild—best chance in the upper part of the Buccament Valley in early morning or late afternoon), go to church on Sunday (wonderful music), hike (Buccament Forest Nature Trail, La Soufrière—go with a guide if you intend to descend the sheer cliff down into this active volcano), shop at the Saint Vincent Craftsmen Centre, and snorkel (The Gardens).

SINT EUSTATIUS (STATIA)
(pronounced "sint you-STAY-shuhs" or "STAY-shuh")

Size: 8 square miles
Population: 2,200
Highest point: 1,969 feet
Language: Dutch (but English common)
Currency: Netherlands Antilles florin or guilder officially, but U.S. dollar in reality
Description: Basically this is a rather flat, dry island with a couple of peaks, one high and containing a lovely rain forest. This peaceful place appeals mainly to divers (the sunken city), hikers (into the Quill, an inactive volcano), and travelers seeking seclusion. Look for blue beads once used in trading (Gallows Bay), snorkel at Crooks Castle, sunbathe (Concordia and Zeelandia bays), and swim at Corre Corre Bay (30-minute hike).

SINT MAARTEN (see also SAINT MARTIN)
(pronounced "sint MARE-ten")

Size: 16 square miles

Population: 34,000
Highest point: 1,200 feet
Language: Dutch, English widely spoken
Currency: The Netherlands Antilles florin or guilder, but U.S. dollar widely accepted
Description: There is a Dutch and a French side to this island, but no borders between them. The Dutch side is livelier but more congested than the French side. The amount of development gives it a busy, sometimes stressful feeling. The number of cruises arriving in Philipsburg adds to this. Body surf (Guana Bay), eat (good), dive (Proselyte Reef), gamble (more than 10 casinos), party (lively nightlife), shop in Philipsburg (excellent duty-free port), sunbathe (Dawn and Mullet beaches), play tennis (lots of places), and yacht (regatta first weekend in March—one of best in Caribbean).

TOBAGO
(pronounced "toe-BAY-go")

Size: 116 square miles
Population: 50,000
Highest point: 1,890 feet
Language: English
Currency: Trinidad and Tobago dollar
Description: Tobago, part of one nation with Trinidad, is only 21 miles northeast of its larger sister island. It's the vacation island for the residents of Trinidad. Its smaller size makes it easier to explore. Although relatively flat in the southern area, Tobago has a hilly central spine. The main attractions of the island are diving with manta rays (base yourself in the Manta Lodge at Speyside—you are very likely to see 1,000-pound mantas, but don't expect water to be clear) and getting away from it all.

TRINIDAD
(pronounced "TRIN-eh-dad")

Size: 1,864 square miles
Population: 1,300,000
Highest point: 3,085 feet
Language: English
Currency: Trinidad and Tobago dollar
Description: Trinidad is the southernmost island in the Caribbean and lies only 7 miles off the coast of Venezuela. Three mountain ranges cross it in the northern, southern, and central areas. The island is a nature lover's paradise with 433 species of birds (41 hum-

mingbirds), 622 species of butterflies, and 2,300 species of flowering plants (700 of which are orchids). While the nature is terrific, expect populated areas to be less appealing. Carnival here is the finest in the Caribbean (lewd, noisy, and generally safe). You must participate to enjoy it. Many say it's better than Mardi Gras in New Orleans and Carnival in Rio de Janeiro. Get here by the Friday before Ash Wednesday, even earlier if possible, and make reservations a full year in advance, expecting to pay triple the normal price for rooms. Visit the Asa (pronounced "OH-suh") Wright Nature Centre and Lodge (for birding, flora, and hiking), the Caroni Bird Sanctuary to see scarlet ibis known locally as flamants, and the Nariva Swamp (red howler monkeys). Explore the north coast if you have time. Seek out secluded and tiny inns there (some aren't even marked).

TURKS & CAICOS
(pronounced "turks and CAY-ih-cohs")
The Turks and Caicos lie 30 miles south of the Bahamas and are really just an extension of that chain of islands, but politically separate. This is a group of 8 larger islands (6 inhabited) and 40 small cays (2 inhabited). The two island groups are separated by a 22-mile passage. The Turks (Grand Turk and Salt Cay) on one side; the Caicos on the other. The islands in total are surrounded by one of the longest coral reefs in the world. The islands themselves are for the most part flat, dry, and scruffy. Some of the hotels are also scruffy, but others are elegant in a relaxed, rustic way. The islands bask in sun; boast the clearest turquoise water, colorful coral, and 230 miles of the most stunning white beaches imaginable; and are about as laidback in atmosphere as anyone could ask for. In the flats you'll find incredible bonefishing. On the coral reefs you'll enjoy incomparable snorkeling. Farther offshore lies some of the best scuba diving in the world. But getting just about anywhere takes perseverance and patience. In this way the islands are vestiges of the old Caribbean. Islanders call themselves "belongers" and are very friendly. Camping is allowed on most beaches throughout the chain, but there are few facilities. Many of the uninhabited cays are known for various activities: Dellis Cay (shelling—you can be dropped off and picked up here by ferry), East Caicos (diving and snorkeling), French Cay (birding—frigates and ospreys; diving—superb wall), Great Sand Cay (iguanas, nurse sharks by the thousands in shallow lagoons, turtles), Little Island Cay (iguanas), Little Water Cay (connected to Pine Cay—can be dropped off here by ferry for a day), West Caicos (possibly best bonefishing in world off West Caicos Bank), and so on. However, many areas fall within a park system, and permits may be required to visit them. Following are sketches of

the main islands in this group (a couple of others are private and included in the section on Where to Stay p. 165).

Grand Turk (TURKS & CAICOS)
(pronounced as you would expect)

Size: 7 square miles
Population: 3,700
Highest point: Less than 45 feet
Language: English
Currency: U.S. dollar
Description: Grand Turk is the business and government center for the Turks and Caicos. Cockburn Town (pronounced "cob'n") is also sometimes referred to by the island name Grand Turk. This is a dry island covered with salt pans and white powdery beaches. It's a funky, little island, which doesn't exactly hum with activity, but is one of the best places to dive in the region. Go to church on Sunday night in Cockburn Town (like a reggae concert with outsiders entirely welcome—come and go as you please); relax; snorkel and swim on Governor Beach; ride in a donkey cart in the main town (fun); take excursions to Gibb's, Pennington, and Round cays—all nature preserves.

Middle Caicos (Grand Caicos) (TURKS & CAICOS)
(pronounced "middle or grand CAY-ih-cohs")

Size: 48 square miles
Population: 300
Highest point: Less than 45 feet
Language: English
Currency: U.S. dollar
Description: This is the largest and least developed of the islands. There are dramatic, tall limestone bluffs along the northern coast. There's a large wetland area as well along the south. The island has a desolate, but quiet beauty. Ask someone to guide you to extensive, cathedral-size caves (Conch Bar). This is truly an offbeat destination.

North Caicos (TURKS & CAICOS)
(pronounced "north CAY-ih-cohs")

Size: 41 square miles
Population: 1,300
Highest point: Less than 45 feet
Language: English
Currency: U.S. dollar

Description: North Caicos is more lush and fertile than the other islands, with mangrove-lined swamps in the south and beaches on the north. The island's main activities are farming (fruit trees) and fishing. The entire island is surrounded by good snorkeling areas.

Providenciales (Provo) (TURKS & CAICOS)
(pronounced "PRO-vih-den-see-AHL-liss")

Size: 38 square miles
Population: 6,000
Highest point: Less than 45 feet
Language: English
Currency: U.S. dollar
Description: The most developed of the islands, Provo is still a land of peaceful, rolling green hills. It has a deep harbor called Leeward Going Through at the northeast end. Although the liveliest of the islands, it's certainly not to everyone's taste. Dive off Northwest Point in the marine park (one of the finest dives in the world), fishing (excellent bonefishing at Chalk Sound, Sapodilla Bay—May prime— and superb blue marlin fishing offshore), snorkel (just east of Turtle Cove), visit the Northwest Point Marine Park, and walk Grace Bay Beach on the north coast (one of the finest you'll see, but come with lots of water).

Salt Cay (TURKS & CAICOS)
(pronounced "salt key")

Size: 4 square miles
Population: 210
Highest point: Less than 45 feet
Language: English
Currency: U.S. dollar
Description: Harsh and desolate, but still austerely beautiful, this island was once the world's prime salt producer. Now only skeletons of this industry remain as old windmills. The island has no fresh water (the hotel collects it in cisterns) but is bug free. Bird, rest, shell, snorkel, swim, and take a trip out to see whales (from January to March, 2,500 humpback whales pass by here on their way to breed north of the Dominican Republic).

South Caicos (TURKS & CAICOS)
(pronounced "south CAY-ih-cohs")

Size: 8 square miles
Population: 2,000

Highest point: Less than 45 feet
Language: English
Currency: U.S. dollar
Description: This island is geared mainly to the harvesting of conch (3 million per year) and lobster (800,000 pounds per year). However, some of the best scuba diving in the region is found off its shores. You may not want to stay, but you'll certainly want to dive here.

UNITED STATES VIRGIN ISLANDS (USVI)

The United States Virgin Islands consist of nearly 50 islands (100 if you include tiny islets), but only three of them are major tourist destinations. The three will appeal to different tastes as outlined below.

Saint Croix (UNITED STATES VIRGIN ISLANDS)
(pronounced "saint croy")
Size: 84 square miles
Population: 55,000
Highest point: 1,096 feet
Language: English
Currency: U.S. dollar
Description: Saint Croix is an island of varied terrain and equally varied attractions. It is not as commercial as Saint Thomas. It offers an interesting botanical garden (850 species of plants) in Saint George and many historic buildings with a Dutch influence in Christiansted and Frederikstad. Bird (Caledonic Valley, Great Salt Pond), drive the Mahogany Road through the rain forest, fish (Lang Bank for kingfish), hike (the 15-acre rain forest area), golf (Carambola), ride horses (through the rain forest—best way to see it), watch wildlife (go to Limetree Beach to see large iguanas), shell (Northside, Rainbow, and Sprat Hall beaches), shop (Christiansted), snorkel, sunbathe (Buck Island beach—get there by boat), surf (Davis Beach), and windsurf (Reef Beach).

Saint John (UNITED STATES VIRGIN ISLANDS)
(pronounced as you would expect)
Size: 26 square miles
Population: 3,500
Highest point: 1,277 feet
Language: English
Currency: U.S. dollar
Description: This is an ecological gem of an island, just a short ferry ride from Saint Thomas. Rolling hills with coves lined by lush vegeta-

tion and some of the loveliest beaches in the Caribbean draw an interesting combination of travelers, from the yachting and upper-crust set to those seeking camping in screened enclosures. Most of the island and surrounding reefs are protected as part of the National Park system. People come here to relax and snorkel. This is not a lively or wild place. Crisscross the island in one of the open-air jit-neys. Hike on any of 22 trails, the most popular being Reef Bay, relax, shop in the little port of Cruz Bay, snorkel, sunbathe on the more popular or isolated beaches (Honeymoon Beach, Jumby Bay), and windsurf (Cinnamon Bay).

Saint Thomas (UNITED STATES VIRGIN ISLANDS)
(pronounced as you would expect)

Size: 32 square miles
Population: 51,000
Highest point: 1,550 feet
Language: English
Currency: U.S. dollar
Description: The main port Charlotte Amalie (pronounced "Char-lotte ah-MAHL-yuh") lies in the more densely populated southern part of the island and spills down the hills to the port where cruise ships come in by the dozen to take advantage of the island's repu-tation as one of the best duty-free ports in the Caribbean. The town offers lots to see, good places to eat, and a number of lively night spots. The island itself is hilly, with potholed roads climbing up and around steep hills. From their summits you'll see an irregu-lar coastline with many bays lined with 44 white sand beaches. Visit the Aquarium, known as Coral World with the largest reef exhibit in the world near Coki Beach, and the old buildings in Charlotte Amalie, but follow local precautions as to which areas are safe to visit even in the day. Drive Route 40, known as Skyline Drive, for lovely vistas; fish (ask for free pamphlet showing you where to fish from shore for free) or go out for game fish with a charter; ride up the 700-foot gondola for a good view of the town; shell at Brewer's Beach; shop (remember you have double the allowances normally allowed for importation of goods back into the United States); sunbathe at Magens Bay, which is often crowded but one of the loveliest spots in the Caribbean, or Lime-tree Beach, which is more tranquil; take a ride on the submarine Atlantis, which goes once a week for a dive off Saint John—take a night dive if possible; surf at Hull Bay; and windsurf at Bluebeard's, Great Bay, or Sapphire beaches.

VIEQUES (off **PUERTO RICO)**
(pronounced "vee-AY-case")

Size: 51 square miles
Population: 7,500
Language: Spanish
Currency: U.S. dollar
Description: This is a very sleepy little island only 9 miles off the coast of Puerto Rico. People come here to get away from it all. This is strictly a place for people who like sun (it only rains 47 inches a year) and water (lots of good coral) and an extremely laidback atmosphere (simple inns with decent food). Listen to the frogs (*coquí*) at night, relax, snorkel, and swim (Sun Bay is one of the best beaches).

When to Travel

When people think of the Bahamas, Bermuda, and the Caribbean, they dream of good weather. Many travelers say that warmth and sunshine are among their highest priorities. The reality is that weather is fickle, but these areas do have many months of idyllic weather. The problem is predicting when those months or weeks will be. Naturally, if you're on a week's or two vacation as most people are, you'd like to put the odds in your favor. Most travel brochures talk about sun and warmth when describing the islands. There are two other factors that hardly anyone discusses. These are humidity and wind. Some people thrive in high humidity; others find it unbearable. Windsurfers and yachters like wind, but many travelers find constant wind annoying. So when talking about weather, you're really talking about sun (versus rain), temperature, humidity, and wind. And then, of course, storms. Most guides do bring up the topic of hurricanes, and tips concerning these are covered in detail.

You may not have much choice as to when you can travel. If you do, however, the following information will be helpful. If you're primarily interested in special-interest travel, read the section on Doing Things (see pp. 271–308) before deciding when to travel. Timing can be critical for such activities as birding, fishing, turtle watching, windsurfing, and so on. Some of these take place during the off-season, often in less than ideal weather.

Weather

This guide covers a wide range of islands with completely different weather patterns. In fact, on some of the larger islands such as Jamaica and the Dominican Republic, you'd have to break these countries into sections to explain the varying weather patterns. The problem with any discussion of weather is that you're talking about patterns, not the specific week or two you'll be traveling. The reality is that scientists have proven that we are in a period of extreme instability in regard to weather, and this has been proven out over the past few years. The point is for you to keep your expectations in line with reality, but to place the odds in your favor if weather is one of your primary concerns. Since this guide covers islands in the Atlantic as well as in the Caribbean, I've broken the discussion of weather into three broad-brush strokes moving from north to south.

Bermuda

Bermuda lies in the Atlantic far to the north of the Caribbean. However, it is lucky in that it is warmed by ocean currents giving it a subtropical climate. In general Bermuda is quite warm from late April to mid-October. This is the peak season on the island, even though early fall is the prime time for hurricanes. This is when you would want to swim and sunbathe. Since the island is low-lying, humidity is generally tolerable. The off-season begins in November and runs to mid-April, give or take a week or two depending upon the year. The off-season is cool and can be sunny or cloudy (rainy) and occasionally windy. This is a popular time for people who like to golf or just get away from the much colder temperatures in the north. The Bermuda Tourist Office is well-organized and will be glad to send you tables on temperature and rainfall on a month-to-month basis.

The Bahamas
(and the Turks and Caicos Islands)

The Bahamas and the islands to their south known as the Turks and Caicos also are in the Atlantic. They cover many hundreds of miles in an arc heading south from southern Florida. Here you have the reverse of Bermuda in terms of seasons. The peak season runs from mid-December to mid-April. The most northern islands have weather somewhat similar to that of Key West at the southernmost tip of Florida. The farther south you go, the more reliable the sun and warmth. However, in general these islands are quite warm and sunny during the winter months. They are also low-lying and do not have a lot of rain at this time. Humidity is tolerable but does increase later in the season. The off-season runs from late spring to late fall. The heat and humidity can be stifling. The greatest chance of hurricanes runs from late summer through early fall. Winds are very unpredictable and can be annoying even in the peak season.

The Caribbean

The peak season in the Caribbean is essentially the same as for the Bahamas. The majority of travelers looking for warmth and sun come between mid-December and mid-April. Since the area is so large, it's easiest to deal with the varying elements in general tips:

AIR TEMPERATURE

In general, the winter temperatures on most Caribbean islands will vary between 70 and 80 degrees F. with higher temperatures the closer you get to the Equator. During the summer they may rise by 5 to 10 degrees or so, but this is highly variable. The "feel" of these temperatures is related to humidity and wind.

WATER TEMPERATURE

If you're interested in diving, snorkeling, or swimming, water temperature is a major concern. As you would expect, water temperature does rise with air temperature from early summer to late fall. However, the farther south you go in the Caribbean, the more likely you'll find warm water (even in the middle of winter).

SUN (RAIN)

Many travelers lose their sunny disposition under what islanders refer to as "liquid sunshine." The patterns of rainfall throughout the region are extremely complex, but the following tips generally apply.

- Most rain falls from May through November, which is why most travelers come to the area in the winter. Few people really want to exchange snow for rain no matter how warm it is.
- Higher islands (volcanic) tend to be wetter than low-lying ones. See island-by-island descriptions on pp. 32–71.
- Rainfall is much higher in the upper regions of volcanic islands. You might see 150 inches per year at high elevations, 50 inches at lower points along the coast.
- Although most rain occurs in the summer and fall, sporadic rains are not uncommon throughout the entire year on the more lush islands. Little bursts of rain even occur on dry islands, but these are actually refreshing.
- The farther west you go in the Caribbean, the greater your chance of finding dry islands (Aruba in the south, the Caymans farther north—both dry).

HUMIDITY

As you would expect, humidity is highest on islands with lots of rain and lush growth (the higher islands). Islands covered in rain forests and luxuriant vegetation are obviously humid. A person's reaction to humidity varies. Some people enjoy it, others detest it. Generally, as people get older, they become more sensitive to humidity (more annoyed by it). A few tips:

- If humidity really bothers you, go to more arid islands that offer activities you enjoy. Arid islands are usually low and lack some of the beauty of the more lush islands, but they are much drier.
- If you really want to visit a lush island, go in the peak season. It will be drier, but, of course, you'll pay more for the room.
- On more lush islands you can often escape the effects of humidity by going higher up (which can be wetter but often cooler).
- If you want to be on a beach on a lush island, make sure your room has air conditioning even in the peak or so-called dry season.

- Different areas on islands vary in humidity. Ask about this when making a hotel reservation.
- Some little towns are notorious for being in stifling locations where there is little air circulation and horrendous humidity even in the dry season. They are known locally as humidity hellholes. They are usually in the lee and protected from breezes by hills. So they are most common on hilly or mountainous islands.

WIND

A windsurfer considers the prevailing wind an ally, as do most yachters. Wind serves as natural air conditioning and is a welcome relief for many of the inhabitants during torrid periods. However, some people do not like wind and find it annoying over a period of days (or weeks). Here are a few basic tips.

- The Caribbean is windy.
- The wind is generally stronger in the winter (the peak season) than in the summer.
- The wind generally comes from the northeast in the winter.
- Hotels often are built in areas protected from the prevailing winds. If so, make sure they have air conditioning.
- Other hotels are built on high ground to take advantage of these winds for cooling effects. This includes some of the most beautiful hotels in the Caribbean, but for someone who doesn't like wind, they can cause anxiety.
- Whenever you make reservations for a hotel, ask about wind or protection from it if wind is a concern.
- Wind is probably the least discussed subject in travel brochures and guides, and yet it can ruin a vacation for travelers who do not see it as a plus.

HURRICANES

Most of the Caribbean islands lie within the hurricane zone. There are usually about 10 hurricanes or tropical storms each year. In some years there are many more, and some of these can be furious. Individual islands within hurricane zones generally experience about 4 hurricanes per century. Hurricanes are tropical storms with winds from 74 to 200 miles per hour. They cover areas from 60 to 1,000 miles wide. Hurricanes occurring in June, July, October, and November usually last about 7 days. Hurricanes in August and September may last up to two weeks. The course of hurricanes is impossible to predict, but you will often have several days warning to evacuate an island as one approaches. A hurricane watch indicates that the storm may hit within 36 hours; a warning means that a storm is likely to hit within 24 hours. Get out of the path of a hurricane if possible since they can be extremely serious. Here are the general guidelines.

- Hurricanes can occur from June through December.
- Hurricanes are most common from late summer to mid-fall.
- The worst months for hurricanes are August and September.
- If you're traveling during the hurricane season, consider staying on islands rarely hit by them (islands far to the south and as far to the west as possible).
- Consider trip cancellation insurance if you're traveling during peak hurricane months. Make sure it covers cancellation of the trip and evacuation in case of an approaching storm. Read the fine print carefully. Since this kind of insurance is difficult to get, here's a good lead. Call Travel Guard and ask about their "Cruise, Tour, and Travel" package (800) 826-1300.
- If you're caught in a hurricane, follow local advice. Get plenty of food and water since these can be scarce.
- If special shelters are provided, go to them.
- Once a hurricane is over, devastation can make leaving an island difficult. It can also be quite dangerous getting to the airport. Ask locals for help.

Using Time Wisely

This section gives you a few tips on how to take advantage of whatever time is available for your trip, whether it's just a week, or much longer.

How Long Can You Travel?

The length of your trip may be predetermined, so you may feel you have little leeway in this regard. However, extend your trip to the maximum length possible. Employers will often bend a little with enough advance notice. Following are some tips to keep in mind.

- Subtract two days of the overall trip as wasted (travel days)—the first and the last. If you're traveling for a week, that leaves only five days of real vacation.
- If you're traveling by charter, you have little control over when a plane leaves and returns. However, if you are making your own arrangements, leave as early as possible from your home and as late as possible from the island.
- When you travel between islands, simply write off one full day unless the island is just a short ferry ride away. You will simply not believe the delays and cancellations in regard to air travel.

Structuring Short Trips

The shorter the trip, the more organized it must be. Every phase of the trip should be planned to help you avoid waits (you'll still have some anyway). You should have reservations for plane flights, all reservations for hotel rooms, and reservations for fancier restaurants made well in advance of arrival. If you plan to attend any possible tourist activity that could be sold out, get reservations in advance if possible.

- Limit yourself to one carry-on bag. This will save you time in countless ways.
- You'll often pay a little more for a structured trip, but it will be worth the extra cost.
- Consider taking a tour for special-interest activities. These tend to be more expensive than individual travel, but highly organized to take advantage of limited time.

Structuring Long Trips

Plan long trips in the peak season as if they were short ones, because hotels will be packed and planes booked solid. During the off-season you can be more relaxed about reservations.

- The big advantage of off-season travel is that you have a choice: You're never bound by a prearranged schedule; you can shift travel plans daily (and often do); you can move out of a hotel you don't like; you can seek out regional restaurants on your own—in short, you can do just about anything at whim.
- Loosely structured trips have another great advantage over structured travel: They can be less expensive. When you get through reading this book, you'll have discovered many ways to cut costs if you begin to think like the local residents and are willing to bend and bargain.

Whom to Go With

Should you make a trip by yourself, with a friend or spouse, or with a group of people you like? Should you take the kids or a baby? There's no easy answer, although the answer's often taken for granted—especially in the case of couples. The hints in this chapter should be helpful to you, not only in making your decision but also in living with it.

Solo Travel

There are many advantages to traveling alone: You can do as you damn well please, when you damn well please, at your own pace, with or without someone else along, as you choose. In short, you have total freedom. On the other hand, you pay for such freedom. If you go on a tour, you may be socked with a single surcharge. If you're totally on your own, you will have no way of sharing expenses at mealtimes, in the hotel, and for personal transportation. It's all out of your pocket and only your pocket. You may also be lonely—but loneliness can be converted into an advantage, as it will force you to get to know local residents and other travelers. You may also put yourself in danger, but much of this can be avoided by following basic safety guidelines (see p. 225).

Traveling Alone and Liking It

- The cost of a single room is often just a little less than that of a double. Therefore, many travelers on a budget hook up to share room costs. If you're worried about sharing a room with a stranger, leave all valuables in the hotel safe.
- If you're adventuresome, stay with locals. You practically become part of the family and often learn about things other travelers miss.
- Use public transportation whenever possible. It's extremely inexpensive.
- As a loner, take advantage of short and inexpensive tours to popular tourist sights. You'll not only meet people but also keep your costs down.
- When faced with the prospect of eating alone, bring a newspaper, a book, or a journal with you to the restaurant. If you meet someone interesting, fine; if not, you'll catch up on your reading or note taking.

- Ask about popular, casual eating places where it's easy to meet people. Many of the islands have restaurants or hotels with happy hours or informal parties.
- Go a little before or after the peak dinner hours in fancier places to avoid running into poor treatment at the hands of waiters, as solo travelers sometimes do.

Single but Looking for Company

Singles who would rather not be alone can check into resorts and organizations catering to them. If this doesn't appeal to you, begin travel and hook up spontaneously with other singles, as outlined earlier. This is often quite easy to do, because people feel safer traveling with another person and like to share costs.

CRUISES

Cruises are a natural for someone looking for a travel partner, but ask many questions about the available cruises to match them to your personality and age (see p. 96).

RESORTS

There are numerous resorts throughout the Caribbean catering to singles. Your travel agent can be helpful in booking these for you. Hedonism II and Jack Tar Villages on Jamaica are examples.

CLUB MEDS

Club Meds, oriented to singles, couples, and families, are world-famous and located in beautiful settings. The two most popular with singles are on Guadeloupe and Martinique.

Club Med (Head Office)
40 West 57th Street
New York, NY 10019
Tel: (800) 528–3100
    (212) 750–1670

AGENCIES SPECIALIZING IN MATCHING SINGLES

A number of companies set up tours for single people or arrange to get singles together. Each agency is unique. Ask lots of questions about how the agency works, what group it aims at, its costs, and so on. The companies vary from simply putting two people together to organizing special cruises for ballroom dancing. Following are some of the main companies specializing in single travel or matching travelers.

Gallivanting
515 East 79th Street
Suite 20F
New York, NY 10021
Tel: (800) 933–9699
  (212) 988–0617

Gramercy Singleworld
444 Madison Avenue
New York, NY 10022
Tel: (800) 223–6490
  (212) 758–2433

Marion Smith Singles
611 Prescott Place
North Woodmere, NY 11581
Tel: (516) 791–4852

Mesa Travel Singles Registry
P.O. Box 2235
Costa Mesa, CA 92628
Tel: (714) 546–8181

Partners-in-Travel
11660 Chenault Street
Suite 119
Los Angeles, CA 90049
Tel: (310) 476–4869

Singleworld Cruises and Tours
P.O. Box 1999
401 Theodore Fremd Avenue
Rye, NY 10580
Tel: (800) 223–6490
  (914) 967–3334

Society of Single Travelers
3000 Ocean Park Boulevard
Suite 1004
Santa Monica, CA 90405
Tel: (213) 450–8510

Travel Companion
  Exchange
P.O. Box 833
Amityville, NY 11701
Tel: (516) 454–0880

Travel Companions
Atrium Financial Center
1515 North Federal High-
  way
Suite 300
Boca Raton, FL 33432
Tel: (800) 383–7211
  (407) 393–6448

Travel in Twos
239 North Broadway
Suite 3
North Tarrytown, NY 10591
Tel: (800) 692–5252
  (914) 631–8301

Travel Mates International,
  Inc.
49 West 44th Street
New York, NY 10036
Tel: (212) 221–6565

Umbrella Singles
P.O. Box 157
Woodbourne, NY 12788
Tel: (800) 537–2797
  (914) 434–6871

Vacation Partners, Inc.
853 Sanders Road
Suite 272
Northbrook, IL 60062
Tel: (708) 205–2008

FOR WOMEN

Women who prefer to travel with another woman or with women alone might consider checking with these organizations.

Jane's International and
  Sophisticated Women
  Travelers
2603 Bath Avenue
Brooklyn, NY 11214
Tel: (718) 266–2045
(Specializing in matching
  single women for travel)

Rainbow Adventures, Inc.
15033 Kelly Canyon Road
Bozeman, MT 59715
Tel: (800) 804–8686
  (406) 587–3883
(Offers a sailing trip through
  the Virgin Islands each year
  for women over 30)

OLDER SINGLES

Some agencies specialize in getting older, single people together.

Saga Holidays
222 Berkeley Street
Boston, MA 02116
Tel: (800) 343–0273
  (617) 262–2262
(Tries to match people up on
  cruises or escorted tours to avoid
  paying single supplements)

Suddenly Single Tours, Ltd.
161 Dreiser Loop
New York, NY 10475
Tel: (800) 859–8396
  (718) 379–8800

Solo Flights
63 High Noon Road
Weston, CT 06883
Tel: (800) 266–1566
  (203) 226–9993

Twosome

The big advantage of staying together are shared company and shared costs. A room for a couple or traveling partners may only be a few dollars more than it would be for a solo traveler. In short, it costs far less for two people to travel together than to go independently. But savings mean nothing unless you're both doing what you really want to do and getting along well.

Traveling as a Twosome

- Discuss the goal of a trip in detail. Don't assume the other person can read your mind. Communicate exactly what your expectations are.
- If you and your partner cannot agree on the purpose of a trip, consider traveling independently. You may prefer completely different destinations or activities, so why not go separate ways?
- Or compromise. You may agree on the destination, but go your separate ways once on the island. You can still share a room to cut costs but get what you want from the trip.
- Carry your own bags, unless you're willing to pay someone else to do it. It is unfair to ask a partner to carry your luggage. If you have one piece of carry-on luggage, this isn't a problem.
- Share all responsibilities with your partner. Anyone who has to make all the decisions shoulders the burden for any mistakes made. That burden should be equally divided.
- Iron out all money matters before you start. This is especially important in the Caribbean where prices vary considerably by island and resort. You and your partner need to discuss your overall budget in detail.
- Each person of a married couple should have control of part of the money, including "mad money" for special occasions. Each person should be responsible for handling part of the payment for everyday expenses.
- Discuss things that really bother you. What may seem petty to one person is particularly annoying to another. For example, does your potential travel partner have to turn the television on, if there is one, the second they enter the room at the very moment you might like peace and quiet? How does smoking affect you? What about a person taking a shower so long you run out of hot water?

Family Travel

Many people enjoy family trips to the Caribbean. The more people involved in a trip, the more complex the planning is going to be. You can't expect to suit all tastes at all times when working with a group.

- Talk about the purpose of the trip. Let each person contribute feelings about what they would like to do. Is the trip for relaxation, stimulation, or some group activity (special interest)? Or is it going to be a combination of these?

- Everyone should have some "mad money." Teach kids about foreign currencies, and let them deal with it on their own. They love it.
- Consider traveling in shoulder or non-peak periods. Yes, take your children out of school. Never let school interfere with your children's education.
- Dress casually. Everyone should wear comfortable, well-worn shoes.
- Since each person will carry his own luggage, the size of the bag must match the size of the person. Backpacks work best for everyone.
- Travel light.
- Pack several days ahead of time. Use a checklist. Let or help each child pack bags. Involve them in pre-trip shopping. This heightens anticipation of the trip and adds excitement.
- Each person should have a map. Kids like to know exactly where they are going.
- Carry plenty of snacks. Lots of individually wrapped or packed items work best. Highly recommended are candy, cheese and crackers (comes in little packets), dried fruit, granola bars, gum, nuts, raisins, and something to drink. Everything should be in little prewrapped packages, not loose.
- If your kids like cameras, radios, or stereos, encourage them to bring inexpensive ones along. Your kids can sell or trade them for items at the end of the trip (kids love to bargain and trade). Trading shirts is one of their favorite pastimes.
- Bring a ball (for catch), books, cards, a Frisbee, and toys. If a blanket or stuffed animal is permanently attached to one of your kids, bring it.
- Prepare for all minor medical emergencies with an appropriate kit containing items used regularly. Always carry this with you onto the plane.
- Gear the pace of the trip to that of the youngest member of the group. Oftentimes less really is more. Keep in mind each person's limitations and needs—both physical and emotional.
- Book flights that include meals. The airlines are cutting back on meals to save money. Flights at normal mealtimes don't necessarily have meals. Ask.
- Select seats as far in advance as possible. Ask to see a seating chart to choose a place on the plane best suited to your family's needs. If you can't choose a seat when making a reservation, get to the airport early to get better seats.
- Travel non-stop whenever possible. At least, fly direct so that you don't have to change planes. Airlines used to have large blocks of

gates all in one area. Many now have blocks to walk between gates. This can exhaust young children and parents, who may have to carry them.

- If plane changes are required after a long flight, consider stopping over for a day before continuing on. Make this stopover part of the fun of the overall trip. Plan something special at the stopover.
- Agree that all responsibilities will be shared. If they're not, one person's always to blame—someone's got to be wrong, right? Actually not, since travel often throws curves, which no one has control over. But that doesn't stop people from getting angry.
- Children need numerous breaks in the itinerary: a trip to the beach, a picnic in a park, a pause for a cold drink. Slow down. Let go.
- Younger children can appreciate markets, museums, and ruins—in small doses. But they really tend to be activity oriented.
- Encourage separation at appropriate times so that each person feels in control and free.
- Some hotels and resorts cater to adults. Keep this in mind when reserving rooms or choosing places to stay. Your travel agent can help you find places that welcome—rather than tolerate—kids. In fact, many resorts have been set up with families in mind. It may be really nice to have the kids off your hands periodically each day. Really nice.
- Don't rule out a yachting vacation just because you have kids. For some families this can be an experience of a lifetime.
- Consider the many advantages of renting an apartment, cottage, home, or villa for a family. Many of these have excellent kitchen facilities (but this doesn't mean you have to eat in all the time). Kitchens are terrific, though, for breakfasts, making sandwiches and snacks, keeping drinks cool, and so on. You cut overall food costs drastically by eating some of your meals in.
- And, numerous restaurants catering to wealthy residents and foreigners detest the presence of small children. Eat outside or in places where noise and dropped food won't create hostility.
- When traveling as a group, always have a plan in case someone gets lost. Giving each child a "get unlost" card is an excellent idea. Explain to them exactly what to do.
- Here's an organization dealing with traveling with children.

Rascals in Paradise
650 Fifth Avenue
Suite 505
San Francisco, CA 94107
Tel: (800) 872–7225

- The following company prints a newsletter, *Family Travel Times,* with tips for traveling with children.

  Travel With Your Children (TWYCH)
  45 West 18th Street
  7th Floor Tower
  New York, NY 10011
  Tel: (212) 206–0688

Traveling with a Baby

- Consider staying in a place catering to families. For instance, Club Med has a program that allows parents plenty of free time by taking care of children off and on during the day. Check on other resorts with similar programs.
- Contact any airline well in advance if you wish to reserve a specific seat with plenty of space.
- Ask the airline about in-flight safety procedures depending upon the weight of your child. A rear-facing (for children under 20 pounds) or forward-facing (for children between 20 and 40 pounds) child-restraint seat is advised. Children above this weight should have their own seat and use the aircraft's seat belts. Ask whether the aircraft has any such child-restraint seats. You may have to buy one. Ask about appropriate sizes of these seats to fit the aircraft.
- If you plan to travel by car on the islands, a safety seat is strongly recommended. Yes, it is a hassle to carry.
- When making reservations for air travel, schedule departure and arrival times so that they do not coincide with the baby's feedings. This is not easy every time; just do it as often as you can.
- Most airlines now offer preboarding privileges to anyone traveling with children as a matter of course.
- Give the baby water (not milk) to drink during takeoff and landing: The sucking will help relieve the pressure that builds up in the baby's ears.
- Bring a towel to cover you during feeding and to place under the baby at changing time.
- Bring baby books, baby wipes, a small blanket, a cloth carrier, disposable diapers, life vest, plastic pail and shovel for beach play, plastic bags for disposable diapers, small toys for the baby to play with, and a folding (umbrella) stroller—the latter is a big help.
- Disposable diapers are sometimes hard to find abroad. When available, they are extremely expensive.
- Baby food is often located in pharmacies if you have trouble finding it in grocery stores. The most common label abroad is Gerber.

Highly recommended besides small jars of baby food are canned milk, canned fruit juices, fresh fruit (readily available everywhere), and powdered formula.

Traveling as a Group

Getting a group together to go to the Caribbean often makes sense. Small to large groups often work out well for chartering yachts or renting apartments, homes, and villas—or even whole islands for those in the upper-income bracket. However, here are a few tips.

- How all bills are to be paid should be worked out in advance.
- Consider taking a short vacation as a group before committing to a longer one. Personality conflicts often emerge in close quarters.
- Discuss at length the purpose of the trip to avoid any hassles once in the Caribbean. The purpose may be as simple as cutting costs.
- When couples travel together, they may have different ideas of what a vacation means. Some people may prefer to eat in; others out. Some may be active, others couch potatoes. Each person or couple must feel free to do what they want with no strings attached or resentment will build up. The best way to avoid this is to talk about this in advance. For example, if you will be eating in, who will be doing the shopping, the cooking, the cleanup? What time will meals be? It's the little things that end up driving people apart.
- People don't change. If you don't like someone or find certain characteristics annoying, things are not going to get better because you're in a romantic or beautiful place. If smoking drives you crazy at home, imagine what it would do to you in the closed quarters of a shared condo or yacht?
- Finally, the assumption that couples who are close friends at home will travel well together is a poor one. There's no way of knowing until you actually do it. By discussing a trip in detail in advance, red flags will often appear. Follow your gut instincts, and be honest with yourself. Feelings should always override logic.

For Older People

The following organizations have lots of information for older travelers. Elderhostel offers courses worldwide for people over 60 and keeps the price manageable. Golden Companions offers a networking system for people over 45 who have common interests. Each of these organizations is unique. Note that the term older may mean different things to different organizations, airlines (always ask for their special-discount booklets), hotels, and so on. Many discounts begin at 50 (or younger). Always ask about discounts when making any kind of reservation once you reach 50. You may be pleasantly surprised.

American Association of
  Retired Persons
601 East Street NW
Washington, DC 20049
Tel: (800) 424–3410
  (202) 434–2277

Canadian Association of
  Retired Persons
27 Queen Street East
Suite 1304
Toronto, ON M5C 2M6
Canada
Tel: (416) 363–8748

Elderhostel
75 Federal Street
Boston, MA 02110
Tel: (617) 426–7788
(Please do not call—write)

Golden Age Travellers
Pier 27
The Embarcadero
San Francisco, CA 94111
Tel: (800) 258–8880
  (415) 296–0151

Golden Companions
P.O. Box 754
Pullman, WA 99163
Tel: (208) 858–2183

Grand Circle Travel
347 Congress Street
Boston, MA 02210
Tel: (800) 248–3737
  (617) 350–7500

Interhostel
University of New
  Hampshire
6 Garrison Avenue
Durham, NH 03824
Tel: (800) 733–9753
  (603) 862–1147

Mature Outlook
6001 North Clark Street
Chicago, IL 60660
Tel: (800) 336–6330

Mayflower Tours
1225 Warren Avenue
Downers Grove, IL 60515
Tel: (800) 323–7604
  (708) 960–3430

Merry Widows Dance Tours
1515 North Westshore
  Boulevard
Tampa, FL 33607
Tel: (813) 289–5923

National Council of
  Senior Citizens
1331 F Street NW
Washington, DC 20004
Tel: (202) 347–8800

Omni Tours
104 Wilmot Road
Deerfield, IL 60015
Tel: (800) 962–0060
  (708) 374–0088

Saga Tours
222 Berkeley Street
Boston, MA 02116
Tel: (800) 343–0273
    (617) 262–2262

Younger Travelers

Generally, you have more time, less money, and more energy than older travelers. If you're willing to trade energy and time for money, you'll be surprised at the possible savings. You will be told by many that the Caribbean is super expensive. It can be. It can also be incredibly inexpensive (in some areas) if you know what you're doing. The tips throughout this guide will save you hundreds of dollars.

- Take more money than you think you're going to need. The Caribbean can be reasonable, but the islands have learned how to add on lots of little costs to up the ante for outsiders.
- Get to the islands on a charter whenever possible (see p. 109).
- Use public transportation where available. Yes, it's crowded and slow, but it costs next to nothing because the locals are dependent on it.
- Hitch only where locals recommend it. Try hitching a ride on a yacht as well (see p. 133).
- Stay in places that are clean, comfortable, and cheap. You can find these on most (not all) islands. The more heavily populated islands like the Dominican Republic have hundreds of places to stay that fall into this category.
- Eat and drink in local places. Use common sense in judging the safety of the food and the surroundings.
- Consider a pre-set time to call home each week, even if just for a few minutes (see p. 122). Faxing is also highly recommended; writing is not (mail often doesn't even get through).

Traveling with Pets

Yes, a few yachters travel with a small dog or cat or canary, but traveling with pets in the Caribbean is a continuous nightmare. Don't do it.

Tours and Cruises

There are a number of ways of seeing the Caribbean and each has its appeal to a certain person. Or each may appeal to the same person at different stages in life. The options are basically these: You travel independently, often working with an agent to make plane reservations and book rooms (although you may do that on your own as well). You work through an agent to come up with a package, generally with the idea of lowering overall costs. A package means that you're buying transportation, accommodations, and sometimes meals at a set price. In a few instances it may include island hopping and be a package tour. You buy a tour for special-interest travel, from bird watching to natural history. You travel by cruise ship. Or you charter a crewed yacht. This chapter does not cover independent travel, since strategies for that are an amalgam of the many tips throughout the entire guide. Nor does it cover hiring a crewed yacht, which is a very specific kind of activity covered in detail (see pp. 126–133). Following are tips on packages, special-interest tours, and cruises:

Packages

Tour packages are really nothing more than a way for an airline and a hotel to cooperate in selling a specific destination. Some islands have lots of packages, some have relatively few, and a few have almost none. Packages may or may not cost less than independent travel arrangements, but, in theory, they should cost less. They are certainly promoted as a way of saving money. However, they are oriented to two people traveling together. Travel agents are familiar with a huge selection of packages in varying price categories. In selecting a package, there are some questions worth asking:

- How many years has the packager been in business?
- Will the packager provide a bank reference?
- How many people has this packager already taken to this destination?
- How many representatives does the packager have on the island?
- Are these representatives part of the overall company or part of a local tour company?

Saving Money Through TourScan

Travel agents are an excellent resource for information on tours to the Bahamas, Bermuda, and the Caribbean. However, some of them do not take the time to compare prices. The following company does nothing but that—comparing hundreds of packages offered by varying tour companies each year and printing out the most favorable ones in a booklet. This is similar to shopping for the best airfare. There's a small charge for the booklet, the cost being offset if you book a package through the agency. For detailed information, contact:

TourScan
P.O. Box 2367
Darien, CT 06820
Tel: (800) 962–2080
   (203) 655–8091

A Sampling of Major Tour Companies

You may want to compare offerings of several companies to get a feel for what's available and at what price. Some of these are affiliated with major airlines. Travel agencies will usually book tours at no extra cost, but if you'd like to do a little independent research before working with an agent, ask for brochures from the following: Alken Tours (800) 538-2553, American Express Vacations (800) 241-7700, Cavalcade Tours (800) 356-2405, Delta Dream Vacations (800) 872-7786, Fly AAway Vacations (800) 433-7300, Friendly Holidays (800) 221-9748, Globetrotters (800) 999-9696, GoGo Tours (800) 526-0405, Haley (800) 232-5565, Horizon Tours (800) 525-7760, Thomson Vacations (800) 222-6400, Travel Impressions (800) 632-6721, and United's Vacation Planning Center (800) 328-6877.

Tours for Students and Young People

Certain companies cater primarily to students. One of the main destinations in the Caribbean for the under–25 crowd is Jamaica. Following are organizations worth contacting.

Student Travel Services (STS)
1344 Ashton Drive
Hanover, MD 21076
Tel: (800) 648–4849
   (410) 859–4200
(Air travel to Jamaica)

Sunburst Holidays
4779 Broadway
New York, NY 10034
Tel: (800) 666–8346
    (212) 567–2050
(Packages into Jamaica—actually,
    for all ages)

Sun Splash Tours
236 West 27th Street
Suite 700
New York, NY 10001
Tel: (800) 426–7710
    (212) 366–4922
(Jamaica—primary desti-
    nation; New Providence
    in the Bahamas—
    usually spring break)

Tours for Singles

Particularly popular with singles is the following.

Windjammer Barefoot Cruises
1759 Bay Road
Miami Beach, FL 33139
Tel: (800) 327–2601
    (305) 672–6453
(Sailing vessels that run weekly from Antigua, Grenada, Tortola in
    the British Virgin Islands, and Sint Maarten. Some cruises are for
    singles only, but others include couples.)

Tours

For the most part people who are traveling to the Caribbean are not
making tours similar to those through Europe or other areas where
you're dealing with land travel in adjoining countries. Tours in the
Caribbean involve detailed exploration of a single island for special-
interest purposes (see pp. 271–308) or limited island hopping to get
to know a few islands at a time. Often, this island hopping is related
to special-interest programs as well. Since most tours are focused on
a particular activity from birding to whalewatching, the following tips
apply mainly to special-interest tours.

Advantages of Special-Interest Tours

- Special-interest tours may require special knowledge, highly-
  trained guides, expensive equipment, pre-arranged permission

from local governments, reservations made far in advance for unique jungle lodges, and so on. The value of these trips is often quite subtle. For example, you might be able to go for next-to-nothing to a good birding area and see next to nothing, whereas with a competent guide who knows the area, the birds, and the right time to look for them, you might see as many as 200 to 300 species. So, if you were really into birding, the difference between total frustration and absolute exhilaration might be worth the extra money. The advantages of working with specialists are numerous. Trips are meticulously scouted and prearranged. Sometimes, the only way to get the very best is to go on one of these tours. In short, if a company offers a great trip, you pay for it, just as you would expect to pay for a vintage wine.

- Tours can be prepaid, allowing you to know in advance how much the trip is going to cost. You can also put off payment by financing the trip.
- Tour packages, which cover all major expenses, allow you to pay in U.S. dollars. In this way you avoid the hassle of currency exchange.
- Tours offer companionship and frequently humor for travelers prone to loneliness.
- Tours help less aggressive travelers cope with the language barrier and avoid embarrassing situations.
- Tours have clout, the ability to get you into a hotel or restaurant in peak tourist seasons. And to get the most that place has to give.
- Tours save you time and energy by preventing potential hassles and knowing how to avoid others.
- Tours are excellent for people who may be physically or mentally exhausted and just don't want to be bothered with details. The resiliency required for independent travel in the Caribbean can be quite high.
- Tours can take you to places that could be potentially dangerous on your own. Skilled guides, proficient in local customs and language, may help you get into an area and out safely, with full enjoyment of the area.

Disadvantages of Tours

- The cost of special-interest tours is often quite high. If you have lots of time and energy, you could make arrangements at a lesser cost in a number of instances. Many local tour companies arrange travel similar to that of companies working out of North America. If you want a list of these, ask for one from the appropriate tourist office. Dealing with foreign travel agents from a distance is not always easy. But you certainly have that option. If you have lots of time, you may want to make arrangements with local companies on arrival. However, anyone with limited time shouldn't even think about this, especially in the peak season.

- Tours can be canceled. If there are not enough people, the company simply says "sorry" and sends your money back. The amount of time left for you to regroup may not be enough to organize the kind of trip you'd really like.
- You pay for a tour sight unseen, which is something like marrying the same way. You don't know what you've got until it's in the boat. There's no real chance for a refund if things go awry.
- Tours are groups of people, people whom you may or may not like. Whatever your feelings, you're stuck with them all the way.
- The words in tour brochures are just that—words. You'd better get references to see whether the tour matches the promise.
- Always take tours that match your physical ability. Some trips are extremely strenuous, requiring excellent physical conditioning. Even some of the trips that are called soft adventure may require stamina in certain segments. Ask about this aspect before joining a tour so that you don't get in over your head. Most tour companies are excellent at matching the abilities and interests of clients to their tours or referring you to another company that will.

Tour Package Checklist

If you take the trouble to consult tour brochures or agents and find answers to the following questions, you will be in a much better position to judge the quality of any tour package you're considering. Most tours to the islands are really packages (transportation to and from the island, plus rooms), but some include much more, especially on special-interest tours. So get specific answers to every imaginable question before signing the dotted line.

- [ ] Is the tour operator a member of the National Tour Association, Inc. or United States Tour Operators Association?
- [ ] How long has the tour operator been in business (the longer, the better)?
- [ ] Will the tour operator give a bank reference (good ones will do this as if by second nature)?
- [ ] How much will the tour cost altogether?
- [ ] Will a service charge be added on? If so, how much will it be? Often you'll find that there is a service charge outlined in very fine print at the end of the brochure. Words like "extra," "optional," and "bonus" should also be red flags to you.

☐ What extra or supplemental charges will apply to you? What will optional packages cost you? How much is the advance deposit?

☐ What are the penalties for cancellation?

☐ Are substitutions allowed on the passenger list?

☐ Can the dates of the tour be changed arbitrarily?

☐ Can the schedule or itinerary be rearranged for any reason?

☐ Can the tour be canceled? How much notice must be given?

☐ Does the tour include transportation to and from the airport near your home? Most tours don't.

☐ Does the tour cost include the full price of airfare to and from your destination? What are the dates and times of flights? Are the flights nonstop?

☐ Does the tour price cover all airport departure taxes?

☐ What kind of ground transportation is provided?

☐ Does it include all transfers from airports to hotels? Does it include the cost of transportation to meals and nightlife?

☐ What kind of transportation is provided: air, boat, bus?

☐ If it's a bus, is it air-conditioned, or is it "air-cooled" (a tour brochure expression meaning that the windows can be opened)?

☐ What is the quality of the bus? Does it have a bathroom? If it does, it's probably a pretty decent bus.

☐ If it's a plane, what class will you be in?

☐ How many nights' accommodation is included in the tour price? Are there any nights where the cost of a room has been left out?

☐ Is there a supplemental charge if you want a room to yourself? How much?

☐ Which hotels will you be staying in? Get the names.

☐ Can other hotels be substituted arbitrarily? If so, get the names.

☐ What's included in the room? Bath or shower? Two beds? Air conditioning? Ocean view? Get exact details.

☐ Where are the hotels located? Ask them to show you on a map.

☐ Are all tips and taxes included in the room price?

☐ Is there any charge whatsoever that's not included?

☐ Are all meals included in the price of the tour? Is any meal not included? If not, why not? Or, if not, where not?

☐ Where will you be eating? In the hotel? In a restaurant? What restaurants?

☐ What's included with the meal? Is wine included? Is coffee included? Is dessert included? Is anything excluded? If so, how much will it cost?

☐ Do you have a choice from the menu at each meal? Can you make substitutions at no extra charge?

☐ Are all tips and service charges for meals included in the tour price?

☐ Who pays the entrance fee to museums, galleries, and events?

☐ What is the pace of the tour? Does it leave you any free time?

☐ Does the tour spend enough time in each city or area to let you get anything out of the visit?

☐ Will the tour have an escort? Will the same escort be with the tour for the whole time? If so, that's an added value.

☐ Will the tour have travel guides for each activity or attraction?

☐ Does the tour include insurance for accidents, health, baggage, and so on? If so, how much? Any deductible? Any exclusions?

☐ Who takes care of the baggage? Is there any extra cost? How many bags are free? Are all tips to porters included in the cost of the hotel room?

Cruises

Cruises are an extremely popular way to travel in the Caribbean. Many new ships have been built as demand has increased in recent years. The islands frequented by cruises include Antigua, Aruba, Barbados, Bermuda, British Virgin Islands, Cayman Islands, Curaçao, Grenada, Grand Bahama, Guadeloupe, Jamaica, Martinique, New Providence (Nassau in the Bahamas), Puerto Rico, Saint Croix, and Saint Thomas.

Advantages of Cruises

• You know what the cost of your trip will be in advance. Most of your expenses are covered in the overall price. You prepay in U.S. dollars and avoid much of the hassle of currency exchange.

• You are insulated from many of the hassles common to land travel.

• Service is usually important and, on some lines, a trademark.

• Most cruises are relaxing and relatively stress-free.

• Food is good and plentiful on most lines.

• You tend to meet people easily.

• Some cruises are geared to special-interest travel and have experts on board who can tell you a great deal about varied topics.

• You get a taste of a few Caribbean islands.

• There is usually lively nightlife and on some lines superb entertainment and even gambling for those inclined.

• If you are ill or disabled, this may be one of the best ways to travel.

• If you are elderly, cruise travel often makes travel possible when it might otherwise be difficult.

Disadvantages of Cruises

- It is critical for you to choose a line that matches your personality.
- The Caribbean islands are not the main focus of most cruises. The cruise is. If you really want to get to know certain islands, this is not the way to do it.
- Space is tight on most cruises. If you want spacious accommodations, the price goes up accordingly.
- Cruises tend to be quite expensive on a per diem basis. The first and last days are generally write-offs.
- Transfers of passengers to islands often takes more time than people realize. Much of the time in port may be wasted if the cruise has not set this up adequately or if the weather is poor.
- Many cruises do not include island tours in the overall price. Always ask about this in advance. And it is common for tours to be scheduled at mealtimes. This forces you to buy your meal on land. It also saves the cruise line a considerable amount of money if many people want to get off and explore an island.
- If you are ill or elderly, the cruise may not be capable of handling medical emergencies as well as land-based hospitals would. A special section on medical considerations follows later in the chapter.
- If you are at all prone to sea sickness, this can ruin a cruise. Medications are helpful, but often make people drowsy or less aware. You don't get sick, but you don't enjoy the cruise either.

Magazines and Newsletters

For general information on cruises there are numerous guides on the market and information from the following:

Cruise Digest Reports
1521 Alton Road
Suite 350
Miami Beach, FL 33139
Tel: (305) 374-2224

Cruise Travel Magazine
P.O. Box 342
Mount Morris, IL 61054
Tel: (800) 877-5983
   (815) 734-4151

Cruises & Tours
Vacation Publishers
1502 Augusta Street
Suite 415
Houston, TX 77057
Tel: (713) 974-6903

Ocean and Cruise News
P.O. Box 92
Stamford, CT 06904
Tel: (203) 329-2787

The Millegram
Bill Miller Cruises Everywhere
P.O. Box 1463
Secaucus, NJ 07096
Tel: (201) 348-9390

The Cruise Line

Cruise lines are as distinctive as hotels. Ask specific questions:

- How many ships does the line operate?
- What is the reputation of the line?
- What personal experience has the agent had with the line? How have clients liked it? And for what reason? Or disliked it? For what reason? Ask for references of people who have been on the ship you might choose.
- What is the cruise line noted for?
- What age group does it normally attract?
- Does it attract a different age group at varying times of year?
- What is the crew-to-passenger ratio? The more crew members there are per passenger affects the overall service.

The Cost

Each cruise line aims its "tours" at a specific price bracket. Some lines offer extremely economical tours, while others are geared to the upper-income bracket. By telling an agent from the start what price category fits into your budget, you'll save lots of time. Here are a few general tips on money.

- The cost of a cruise varies dramatically by line, length of the cruise, and choice of cabin.
- Competition among cruise lines is going to be tremendous in the coming years. Too many ships have been built, and this should lead to significant savings for people who enjoy cruises—at least, for the short term.
- If you're older, always ask about discounts. The age cutoff may be lower than you think.
- Check on cruise prices by proposed sailing dates. Perhaps by changing your travel plans slightly, you might get an extremely favorable price.
- When comparing cruise lines and prices, always ask how long the price is guaranteed. Some lines will change fares on a moment's notice; others guarantee rates until a specific date. Ask about these cutoff dates. If you wait too long, you may have to pay extra.
- Ask whether there are any incentives or special rates—two for one prices, upgrades on the best rooms with early booking, coupons to cut the costs of on-board services from massages to drinks, and so on. If you don't ask, no one hears.
- The lowest-priced cabins on most cruises go first.
- If money is a major consideration, ask whether there are any ways to reduce the cost, such as agreeing to standby status.
- Outside cabins are more expensive than inside ones. Windows

are more expensive than portholes, but both up the price of a room because they provide a view. If you're willing to forego the view to lower cost, do your sightseeing from a chaise longue on deck.

- Cabins higher up on a ship are generally more expensive than ones lower down. The closer you get to the bowels of a ship, the more noise. To get people to overlook such things, cruises offer incentives—a lower price for less desirable rooms.
- The larger the cabin, the higher the price. Space is a major consideration on board. Such things as a bath rather than a shower can add significantly to price because this takes up so much room. If you're willing to be somewhat cramped in your sleeping quarters, you'll save considerably on the cost.
- You have the right to know what the specific price for the cruise will be. Ask what is included in the price and what is not. Be specific.
- Does the price of the cruise include airfare to the port of embarkation?
- For an additional fee can you stay extra nights at the port of embarkation at a discounted price in a specific hotel?
- Does the overall price include all tips?
- Wine, beer, cocktails—all may cost extra. On some lines you'll get complimentary wine with a meal. But you must ask about this in advance to avoid surprises.
- Any land tours or excursions to the mainland cost extra on almost all cruise ships. These can be quite expensive, especially if they include a guide and transportation. However, if they are included in the overall price, that's an important consideration—ask.
- If the price does not include shore excursions, can you pay only for a transfer to shore at ports of call instead of paying for the full price of a guided tour?
- Does the price include all entry and exit fees from ports of call?
- Is there anything at all that the price does not include?
- Is the price the same throughout the year, or are there special offers at off-season periods? When are these periods?
- Some cruises offer reductions of up to 50 percent for extremely early bookings. A few lines that offer extremely good rates for early bookings include Carnival at (800) 327–9501, Holland America at (800) 426–0327, Norwegian at (800) 327–7030, and Royal Caribbean at (800) 327–6700. Since early-bird specials change frequently and are offered by a number of lines, work with a cruise-oriented agency. It does not cost you any more.
- Will the line guarantee the lowest cost to the earliest person booking a room or match discounted fares offered to latecomers?

Agencies That Can Reduce Costs

Some cruises do try to fill all cabins by offering discounts for reservations made at the last minute or during less popular periods. The following organizations, some of which are fee-based, specialize in regular and discounted cruises.

Caribbean Travel Service
Cruise Department
1203 Southwest 41st Court
Fort Lauderdale, FL 33315
Tel: (800) 709–1414
  (954) 359–7000

INFINET Travel Club
P.O. Box 1033
186 Alewife Brook Parkway
Cambridge, MA 02140
Tel: (800) 883–4482
  (617) 553–4300

Cruises of Distinction
2750 South Woodward
Bloomfield Hills, MI 48304
Tel: (800) 634–3445
  (810) 332–2020

Spur of the Moment Cruises
411 North Harbor Boulevard
Suite 302
San Pedro, CA 90731
Tel: (800) 343–1991
  (800) 427–8473 (CA only)
  (310) 521–1070

The Cruise Line, Inc.
150 Northwest 168th Street
North Miami Beach, FL 33169
Tel: (800) 777–0707
  (305) 653–6111

Vacations To Go
1502 Augusta Drive
Suite 415
Tel: (800) 338–4962
  (713) 974–2121

The Itinerary

Where you go may be extremely important if you're on a special-interest cruise, but far less important if the main purpose of your trip is rest and relaxation. If you're into birding or wildlife, you want to be in areas where you can come in close contact with animals and sea life. You'll want to make sure that smaller boats are provided for excursions to islands and hard-to-get-to lagoons and sanctuaries. In general, however, the islands are merely the backdrop for a cruise, not the main performance. Most cruises give you little time to appreciate any specific destination. Much of the orientation of larger cruises is towards shopping in port. Yes, you're in the Caribbean, but you are not on the islands. You're on a ship, which becomes its own island—one you either love or despise.

The Purpose

Each cruise line tries to satisfy a need in the marketplace. Some cruises are blatantly aimed at people who like to party, others are geared strictly to eco-tourism, and others just for relaxation and sun. On a few you'll actually be put to work rigging sails and doing chores. Unless you know the exact type of cruise you're going on, you could be disappointed. Match the cruise to your personal needs. The range in cruises is remarkable. Here are special-niche cruises: educational (either you're learning about the islands or you're studying something on board, such as cooking); group cruises (swinging with other singles, nude bathing, and so on); professional cruises (taking a vacation while learning about your career—often tax deductible); theme cruises (solving a crime, listening to specific music, playing bridge, ballroom dancing)—and on and on.

The Ship

Ships that ply Caribbean waters vary from old-fashioned sailing ships with real sails to modern luxury liners with enormous and lovely cabins offering all of the accoutrements of a fine hotel. Match the ship to your personality. Here are some questions worth asking about.

- How large is the ship? You'll usually have a good idea from the gross registered tonnage (grt). Grand Circle Travel (see p. 88) classifies ships into intimate (10,000 or less grt), small (10,000 to 20,000 grt), medium (20,000 to 30,000 grt), and large (anything above 30,000 grt).
- How old is the ship? When was it last renovated? Is it presently being renovated? (Beware if it is.)
- Smaller ships have fewer people. This is a major advantage for anyone interested in hassle-free shore excursions.
- Smaller ships can often get into places where larger ships can't.
- Smaller ships may be oriented to special-interest groups, such as natural history tours.
- On the flip side, smaller ships can be hard on you in rough seas.
- Larger ships are ideal for people interested in meeting other people. The more people, the better your chance of meeting others with similar interests and personalities.
- Larger ships generally offer smoother sailing in rough weather as implied earlier.
- Larger ships are less desirable for those interested in shore excursions and in the more intimate atmosphere of smaller ships where there may be just one seating (not two) for dinner—as one example.
- On larger ships you often end up waiting for just about everything, including leaving port on time. The more people, the more problems, the more delays at every stage of the trip.

The Cabin

For some people the cabin in which they'll be staying is extremely important, while to others it is of little importance, since they don't plan to spend much time there. Here are a few tips.

- Ask to see a layout of the ship. Know exactly where your cabin will be.
- Ask to see an exact layout of your cabin with specific dimensions.
- Just because you choose an outside cabin does not mean that you'll have a terrific view. By checking the layout, you'll have a much better idea of what you'll really be seeing. Who wants their window or porthole to be looking out to a busy deck or to lifeboats dangling from their supports? Don't assume anything.
- Expect there to be some noise no matter where you're located. Bring earplugs. Ships vibrate, groan, and make strange noises. It's all to be expected.
- If you're prone to sea sickness, ask which cabins are the most stable. And, of course, take medication for this illness, which for the most part can be avoided.
- If you're particular about specific things, say so. Example: Does the room have a television set?
- If you have trouble getting the layout of a specific ship, contact the Cruise Lines International Association (CLIA), which provides these.

CLIA
500 Fifth Avenue
Suite 1407
New York, NY 10110
Tel: (212) 921–0066

Food and Drink

Most cruises try hard to provide good to excellent food for passengers. Some lines do a much better job than others. Almost all serve food from morning to night, from snacks and teas to midnight smorgasbords. If food is really a major concern, get on a ship noted for quality cuisine and be willing to pay extra for it. Here are a few other tips.

- All ships have special dining hours. Inquire about this in advance so as not to be surprised.
- Some ships schedule shore excursions during dining hours. Ask about this in advance.
- On larger ships, there may be more than one seating for each meal. Ask about the hours, and choose the seating that best suits your needs.

- Each seating has its advantages and disadvantages, and they are related more to personality than anything else. Early seatings tend to be more rushed but are fine for people who like to eat quickly and get on with things—like other activities on the ship or on shore.
- If the hour you eat is important to you, get your seating assignment immediately once on board. Don't wait. Find out who's in charge of seating and get to that person as quickly as possible.
- On many ships you'll be assigned to a specific table. If you do not like the people you're with, let this be known after the first meal. The sooner you request a change, the likelier it will be made.
- If you have specific requests in regard to eating (no smoking, for example), make this clear from the start.
- On many cruises, wine is not included with the meal. You must order and pay for this as an extra. If you order wine, order enough so that the people sitting with you can have a glass. If they accept the offer or vice versa, they or you should pay for wine the following evening.
- If you are uncomfortable with this, you might ask about ordering wine by the glass.
- Bring a bottle of your favorite booze on board. This makes you less dependent on overpriced and often undersized or watered-down drinks. The quality and size of drinks is highly variable.
- On most cruises there are so many free snacks and edible extras on board that someone may whimsically remark that you board as a passenger, disembark as cargo.

Sanitation

The United States Public Health Service keeps records on health violations. While it is difficult to predict outbreaks of disease caused by poor sanitation, it is certainly worth the time to rule out ships with a poor record in this regard. The reports on individual ships are known as Green Sheets. Write the following office for a free Green Sheet on any ship you're considering.

Chief Vessel Sanitation Program
National Center for Environmental Health
1015 North America Way
Suite 107
Miami, FL 33132
Tel: (305) 536–4307

Dress on Board

For many people on vacation, being able to relax means never having to dress up at all. For others gala events and dances requiring tuxedos and evening dresses are enjoyable. Before booking any cruise, ask about dress requirements. Don't ask whether things are formal or informal; ask exactly what the dress requirements are. Informal on some ships means coat and tie instead of a tuxedo, while to you it may mean a shirt and a pair of slacks. If you want to eat in shorts or a bathing suit, ask about this in advance. Don't assume anything.

Booking a Cabin

Travel agents specializing in cruises are your best resource. Booking a cruise is really booking a tour—the very heart of travel agency business. For information on agents specializing in cruises only, send a stamped, self addressed envelope to the National Association of Cruise Only Agencies (NACOA), which represents approximately 700 agencies throughout the United States. Each of these must meet the association's standards, a form of protection for you. You may request information on agencies in any two states for free.

NACOA
3191 Coral Way
Suite 630
Miami, FL 33145
Tel: (305) 446–7732

Cruises for Ill People

If you have a chronic health problem, check with the following company for cruises specially geared to you.

Crossroads Travel
(University Hospital of Cleveland)
15294 Pearl Road
Strongsville, OH 44136
Tel: (216) 238–7015

If Traveling Alone

- A number of cruise lines now offer a program that guarantees you'll get a roommate if you want to keep costs down.
- If they don't find a match, you'll be given a single room without supplemental charges.
- If a cruise does not offer such a program, ask whether it's possible to book a room without a supplement. If you book a room far in advance, some cruises will not charge the supplement. This works best in non-peak periods. If you don't ask for this charge to be waived, it won't be—I can assure you.
- Some cruises even offer single rooms at no extra charge if they're having trouble filling the ship.

If Traveling with Children

- Some cruises are suited to families with young children; others are not. Ask in advance. Often children travel free or at reduced cost depending upon age, but you must ask to take advantage of this very special incentive.

Length of the Cruise

- Most cruises last 1 or 2 weeks, providing adequate time for rest. Whenever possible, take a cruise at least a week long.
- A few cruises offer 3- and 4-day voyages. The first and last days are often write-offs.

Tipping on Board

- Ask about the company policy on tipping before you buy a ticket. Tips may be included in the ticket price. If they are, the ticket is really costing you considerably less than a comparable ticket on a line where tips are not included.
- If tips are not included, tip room stewards, waiters, and other service staff for special services. The more service you ask for, the more you should expect to tip. Tips are best given immediately for such services as bringing late-night snacks.
- One very effective way of tipping: Hand the room steward or waiter an amount adding up to half the tip you expect to give him altogether. Tell him exactly what you expect. And tell him that you will give him the other half of the tip at the end of the trip (the day before you disembark). This is upfront bargaining for good service. And does it work!

Medical Emergencies

Whether you have chronic health problems, are elderly, or just happen to get sick at sea, you should know ahead of time what kind of health care is available on any given cruise. Medical problems are much more common than you might think.

- Ask about medical facilities on board. Here are the basic questions: On the most remote part of the voyage how long will it take to get to a land-based hospital? Will the ship automatically change course in a life-threatening situation? How many doctors and nurses will be on board? What did the doctor or doctors specialize in (hopefully emergency medicine)? Does the doctor have certification for Advanced Cardiac Life Support (ACLS) and Advanced Trauma Life Support (ATLS)? What kind of equipment is available on board for tests and x-rays? Does the ship have a respirator, a cardiogram machine, and so on? Can surgeries be performed on board?

- You may also want to check on the type of pharmacy on board. How extensive is its supply of medications? Are these U.S. or foreign products? If you're on a particular medication, you might specifically ask whether it's available.

Special Problems

Following are some of the more common problems possible with taking a cruise. The key tip is to read the fine print, even if it takes a magnifying glass, and to ask lots of questions. Your attitude must be that if it isn't in writing, it may not happen or be true.

- Cruise lines have the right to cancel cruises. If they do, you should get a full refund.
- Cruise lines have the right to change itineraries. This is reasonable since the weather in the Caribbean is impossible to predict. If you happen to miss an island on the original itinerary, that's too bad, but that's the way it is. And no, you will not get a refund.
- As mentioned earlier, islands are a backdrop to a cruise vacation, not the main stage. If you absolutely must see a specific island, then skip a cruise.
- Cruise lines may have the right to change dates arbitrarily. Check the fine print before signing on. If you're traveling by air on a restricted ticket to the port of embarkation, this could be a real problem. Ask if you can't find anything in the literature offered to you about the cruise line's policy. Get the statement in writing.
- If you do not make it on time to get on a cruise, it's your responsibility to get to the next port of call at your expense. Always call the line to let them know what happened and that you intend to catch up with the cruise at a later time.
- If you cancel a cruise, the penalties can be stiff. Ask about this in advance. You can get insurance in case of unexpected illness, injury, or death in the family. But, as always, read the fine print of each policy, especially if you have a pre-existing illness that could cause you to cancel.

Getting to the Islands

Plane travel is the fastest and most convenient way to get to many islands in this region. In some instances, it can be quite inexpensive, if you take advantage of charters and discount fares. You can also reach the islands by boat, either sail or power.

Plane Travel

Following are some tips about getting to the islands. These will help you avoid some irritations and save money. This subject is fairly complex, and you should be aware of all the options. The more time you have to plan and study the options, the more likely you are to save money.

Saving Money by Comparison Shopping

Flying is often the only practical way of getting to many islands. Yet, on every flight, some passengers end up paying as much as 3 or 4 times what others pay. Smart travelers know this and learn strategies to keep costs down.

- Call a local travel agent and ask what airlines fly to your destination. Ask the agent to come up with the lowest possible fare to that city. This information is computerized. A good agent can do this quite quickly.
- Make sure that the agent does not charge a fee for this service. Airlines have reduced their payments to agents in recent years, and a number of agencies are now charging ticketing fees to make up for this loss.
- While the agent checks on prices, spend some time on the telephone comparing offers of different airlines. Use their 800 numbers to save money. Ask whether there are any unadvertised specials.
- Call the same number twice to get different airline agents. They will often work differently. One may offer you information that the other doesn't. This tip may seem absurd, but I cannot tell you how many times I've come up with better fares by doing it.

- Caribbean, European, and North American scheduled airlines fly into the area. Check with these on current offerings: Air Aruba, (800) 827–8221; Air Canada, (800) 776–3000; Air France, (800) 237–2747; Air Jamaica, (800) 523–5585; American, (800) 433–7300; AVENSA, (800) 428–3672; Bahamasair, (800) 222–4262; British Airways, (800) 247–9297; BWIA, (800) 538–2942; Cayman Airways, (800) 422–9626; Continental, (800) 231–0856; Delta, (800) 221–1212; Dominican, (212) 765–7310; Iberia, (800) 772–4642; LACSA, (800) 225–2272; Lufthansa, (800) 645–3880; Northwest, (800) 447–4747; TWA, (800) 892–4141; United, (800) 241–6522; USAir, (800) 428–4322; and Viasa, (800) 327–5454.
- Airlines advertise their offerings from specific destinations in Sunday papers in all major cities. Libraries often carry papers from other cities. Read these to find about offerings from varied points of origin. You might save a substantial amount of money by arranging a trip from a different city than the one you live in.
- Watch for introductory fares or special coupon offers. As airlines open up new routes, they offer incentives to new customers in the form of temporarily reduced rates. These tend to be heavily advertised in local newspapers—so stay alert to the possibility of coming up with a once-in-a-lifetime bargain.
- Once the travel agent has quoted you a price, ask whether there are any ways of reducing the price. Keep notes.
- If you live near Canada, consider flying from there. You may be able to save money by taking advantage of the weak Canadian dollar.
- Always ask about special passes. Both domestic and foreign airlines often have unusual fares that must be requested. They may go under odd names. It is not unusual for these passes to go unmentioned unless you ask. Ask airlines and travel agencies about these. They may give you numerous stopover privileges on more than one island at greatly reduced rates. Naming passes is a waste of time since they change constantly. Knowing that they often exist is the important tip (see p. 125).

Asking the Right Question

- Let the person on the other end of the telephone know immediately that you're bargain-hunting by asking for the lowest fare from A to B.
- Ask if there are any incentive fares.
- Find out if there are reductions for midweek flights.
- Find out about reductions for night flights—they're often offered out of main cities.

- Try to buy tickets with small cancellation fees. Unfortunately, the lowest priced tickets often have the highest cancellation fees.
- Even after you've arranged for a flight, continue to watch for better deals. If a bargain pops up, turn in your ticket and go with the better fare if the total cost will be less after deducting any cancellation fees.

Special Tour Rates on Scheduled Airlines

In most areas there are specialized tour companies that buy blocks of seats on regularly scheduled airlines. In some cases, these seats are sold at rates far below those offered by the airline itself. This is most common with flights to major destinations such as the Dominican Republic, Jamaica, Puerto Rico, Saint Croix, and Saint Thomas.

- Get familiar with the companies in your area that specialize in low-cost airfare. They tend to advertise heavily in Sunday papers.
- Call and ask them about any upcoming offerings. You sometimes have to get an inside edge to know when specials will be advertised. That means getting to know an agent well enough so that they will go out of their way for you.
- Since these companies usually advertise on Sunday, they set their rates on Thursday. The day to call is Thursday, since the lowest price seats are often gone by the time you get through on Monday. *This is an extremely important tip.* The bargain rates are often limited to just a few seats as a come-on to potential travelers, but there are always a few available to the first callers.

Comparison Shopping: Charters

Tour and charter companies rent planes to take passengers to specific destinations. These rented planes are called charters. In a few cases the company actually owns the planes and virtually runs a sort of mini-airline. By reading papers from larger cities, you'll often see advertisements for charters.

- Charters often save you money, because seats are usually offered at a discounted rate as an incentive to use the nonscheduled plane in the first place.
- Charters often leave at weird times and are rarely on a tight schedule, but if you're trying to save a buck, they can really make sense.
- Charters must now advertise the full price of a ticket. It can't go up or down according to the number of seats sold.
- On any contract with a charter company, the escrow bank and bonding company must be clearly stated.
- Charter companies must state clearly what the itinerary will be and stick to it.

- Charter companies cannot cancel a flight within 10 days of the intended departure—they used to do this regularly, leaving passengers with no way of getting to where they were going.
- There are stiff cancellation penalty clauses on most charter airlines. You cannot just turn in your ticket for a refund. It doesn't work that way. You're saving money because you're guaranteeing the airline that you're going. You can take out cancellation insurance, available from charter companies and independent brokers, but read the fine print.
- There are dozens of companies capable of getting you on charter flights. Here's just a sampling.

Carnival Airlines
1815 Griffin Road
Suite 205
Dania, FL 33004
Tel: (800) 824–7386

DER Tours
P.O. Box 1606
Des Plains, IL 60017
Tel: (800) 782–2424

Council Charter
205 East 42nd Street
New York, NY 10017
Tel: (800) 800–8222

Maverick Airlines

Small airlines come and go. Their offerings also come and go. The tip is that maverick airlines often exist, sometimes fleetingly, but are not highly publicized. Ask about these. Here are examples.

Pan Am AirBridge
(formerly Chalk's)
1000 MacArthur Causeway-Watson Island
Miami, FL 33132
Tel: (800) 424–2557
     (305) 371–8628
(From Fort Lauderdale to Bimini in the Bahamas, and from Miami to Bimini and New Providence in the Bahamas)

Gulfstream
P.O. Box 777
Miami Springs, FL 33266
Tel: (800) 992–8532
     (305) 587–8076
     (305) 871–1200
(From Fort Lauderdale and Miami to the Bahamas—Abaco, Eleuthera, Grand Bahama, New Providence)

Tower Airline
Hangar No. 17
JFK International Airport
Jamaica, NY 11430
Tel: (800) 221–2500
(From New York to Puerto Rico)

Packagers

A packager offers airfare plus a hotel room and possibly food or sightseeing at a discount. You may want to contact the following for current offerings. Actually, most travel agents are familiar with numerous packages and can use their computer to find offerings by specialized companies, but comparison shopping never hurts if you have the time and energy.

Cosmos
5301 South Federal Circle
Littleton, CO 80123
Tel: (800) 221–0090

GWV International
300 First Avenue
Needham, MA 02194
Tel: (800) 225–5498
    (617) 449–5460

Wholesalers

Wholesalers set up packages with travel agents. To keep costs down ask your travel agent to check the computer for current offerings from wholesalers. Most do this immediately for budget-minded customers, but some are beginning to charge a booking fee since airlines and packagers are offering less incentives to agents than they used to. Ask about any potential fees in advance and work with companies dealing primarily in budget travel with no booking fees whatever. Following is just a *sampling* of the many companies working with agents throughout the United States on highly discounted travel including both airfare and accommodations.

Apple Vacations, (800) 727–3400
Friendly, (800) 221–9748
FunJet Vacations, (800) 558–3050
Haley, (800) 262–6123
Inter-Island, (800) 245–3444
M.K. Travel, (800) 344–4532
Travel Charter, (800) 521–5267
Travel Impressions, (800) 284–0044

Consolidators (Bucket Shops) and Discounters

A number of companies can get you tickets at reduced rates. What they call themselves is less important than what they can do for you as a consumer. When working with agencies specializing in discounted fares, be wary.

- These companies or individuals sell tickets at wholesale prices. Look for them in travel sections of Sunday newspapers. Large cities, such as New York, often have the largest number of consolidators (bucket shops).
- Work through a travel agent whenever possible. They often know whether a certain company has been selling fraudulent tickets.
- Always pay for tickets with credit cards.
- Tickets do not qualify for frequent-flyer miles.
- In the case of a canceled flight, most other airlines will not honor your ticket for one of their flights. You'll have to wait for the next available flight on the airline originally booked.
- You must use all legs of the ticket or it can be invalidated or confiscated.
- Expect flights to have many stops or more connections than you might get on more costly tickets.
- Understand exactly what the small print says on your purchase through a consolidator. Restrictions can be extremely tight in exchange for drastic price reductions. If you want flexibility, this isn't the route for you.
- Although there are many consolidators throughout the United States, here are a few for you to start with.

Air Travel and Tours
5 West 36th Street
Suite 304
New York, NY 10018
Tel: (800) 938–4625
   (212) 714–1100

All Continents Travel
5250 West Century Boulevard
Suite 626
Los Angeles, CA 90045
Tel: (800) 368–6822
   (310) 337–1641

Austin Travel
7512 West Grand Avenue
Elmwood Park, IL 60635
Tel: (800) 545–2655
   (708) 452–1010

BET World Travel
841 Blossom Hill Road
Suite 212C
San Jose, CA 95123
Tel: (800) 747–1476
   (408) 229–7880

Carefree Getaway Travel
701 North Walnut Street
Roanoke, TX 76262
Tel: (800) 969–8687
   (817) 430–1128

Consumer Wholesale
   Travel
34 West 33rd Street
Suite 1014
New York, NY 10001
Tel: (800) 223–6862
   (212) 695–8435

Council Charter
205 East 42nd Street
New York, NY 10017
Tel: (800) 800–8222
    (212) 661–0311

International Adventures
60 East 42nd Street
Suite 763
New York, NY 10165
Tel: (212) 599–0577

Magical Holidays
501 Madison Avenue
New York, NY 10022
Tel: (800) 228–2208
    (212) 486–9600

Northwest World Vacations
5130 Highway 101
Minnetonka, MN 55345
Tel: (800) 800–1504
    (612) 474–2540

Overseas Travel
16740 East Iliff Avenue
Aurora, CO 80013
Tel: (800) 783–7196
    (303) 337–7196

Panda Travel
1311 East Northern Avenue
Phoenix, AZ 85020
Tel: (800) 447–2632
    (602) 943–3383

Pennsylvania Travel
15 Maple Avenue
Paoli, PA 19301
Tel: (800) 331–0947
    (610) 251–9944

Royal Lane Travel
8499 Greenville
Suite 100
Dallas, TX 75231
Tel: (800) 329–2030
    (214) 340–2030

Skytours
26 Third Street
Suite 460
San Francisco, CA 94103
Tel: (800) 246–8687
    (415) 777–3544

TFI Tours
34 West 32nd Street
12th Floor
New York, NY 10001
Tel: (800) 745–8000
    (212) 736–1140

Travac
989 Sixth Avenue
New York, NY 10018
Tel: (800) 872–8800
    (212) 563–3303

Travel Network
13240 Northup Way
Suite 4
Bellevue, WA 98005
Tel: (800) 933–5963
    (206) 643–1600

Travel Time
1 Hallidie Plaza
Suite 406
San Francisco, CA 94102
Tel: (800) 235–3253
    (415) 677–0799

Tulips Travel
420 Lexington Avenue
Suite 2738
New York, NY 10170
Tel: (800) 882–3383
  (212) 490–3388

WBT Tour and Travel
26 West Boylston Street
West Boylston, MA 01583
Tel: (800) 300–6727
  (in MA)
  (508) 835–6727

Unitravel
1177 North Warson Road
St. Louis, MO 63132
Tel: (800) 325–2222
  (314) 569–0900

- The following publication specializes in information on low-cost flights. Ninety percent of its information is on consolidators. The rest is on charters.

Jax Fax
397 Post Road
Darien, CT 06820
Tel: (203) 655–8746

Comparison Shopping: Clearinghouses and Clubs

Clearinghouses and special airline travel clubs offer reduced tickets to countless places in the world. Basically, they pick up spaces on tours and flights that are not sold out. They also may work with hotels to set up packages. Some even offer rebates on packages as well.

- Most of these clubs charge a membership fee.
- Most of your reservations will be made through a toll-free number, and waits can be quite long.
- Some of these clubs are geared to spur-of-the-moment travel. You may have to make up your mind within only a few days of the planned trip—for a discount, of course.
- A few can plan a trip well in advance and still save you money.
- When dealing with a club, ask how long it's been in business and how many members it has. Here are the clubs:

All-American Travel Club
2150 Goodlette Road
Suite 102
Naples, FL 33940
Tel: (800) 451–8747
  (941) 261–3279

Discount Travel
  International
114 Forrest Avenue
The Ives Building
Suite 203
Narberth, PA 19072
Tel: (215) 668–7184

Encore's Short Notice
4501 Forbes Boulevard
Lanham, MD 20706
Tel: (800) 638–0930
    (301) 459–8020

Hotline Travel
3001 East Pershing Boulevard
Cheyenne, WY 82001
Tel: (800) 543–0110

INFINET Travel Club
P.O. Box 1033
186 Alewife Brook Parkway
Cambridge, MA 02140
Tel: (800) 883–4482
    (617) 553–4300

Last Minute Travel Club
1249 Boylston Street
Boston, MA 02215
Tel: (800) 527–8646
    (617) 267–9800

Spur of the Moment Tours
    & Cruises
411 North Harbor Boulevard
Suite 302
San Pedro, CA 90731
Tel: (800) 343–1991
    (310) 521–1070

The Travel Club
P.O. Box 705
Plymouth Meeting, PA
    19462
Tel: (800) 292–9892

Traveler's Advantage
3033 South Parker Road
Suite 900
Aurora, CO 80014
Tel: (800) 548–1116
    (303) 377–3247

Traveler's Advantage
CUC Travel Service
P.O. Box 5250
Glen Allen, VA 23058
Tel: (800) 835–8747
    (615) 320–0752

Vacations to Go
1501 Augusta Drive
Suite 415
Houston, TX 77057
Tel: (800) 338–4962
    (713) 974–2121

Worldwide Discount
    Travel Club
1674 Meridian Avenue
Suite 206
Miami Beach, FL 33139
Tel: (305) 534–2082

Using Travel Agents

It costs no more to buy a ticket through a travel agent than to buy one directly from the airline. Unfortunately, though, many agents do not like working with discounted fares, because the airlines have cut their commissions drastically in recent years.

• Use agents that do not charge fees upfront. With lowered commissions, a number are now charging $25 or more just to make reservations. If someone is planning and making reservations for a complicated trip including many hotel reservations, the fee is reasonable. But no fee should be involved for simply reserving a seat on a plane and a room in a hotel.

- Don't be afraid to comparison shop with travel agents. Make it clear to each one that you want to know the best deal to get you from A to B.
- A few agencies (not many) now guarantee that they will come up with the lowest possible rate or refund any overpayment you've made.
- Sometimes a good agent will come up with a tour fare that will cost you less than comparable airfare. This is getting very hard to do now, but it does happen.
- Agents who really know how to wring fares from the computer can be invaluable to their customers. Once you've found a good agent, reward them with your business.

Companies Offering Rebates

Following is a sampling of companies that offer rebates on airline tickets (note that some clubs also do this). For example, Travel Avenue charges a set fee per person, so the more complicated your itinerary, the more valuable the service. However, it refunds from 5 to 23 percent of the fare as a way of covering this expense. It also searches for the lowest possible fares, including charters for your trip. The Smart Traveler offers rebates only to those who have done their homework and planned their own itinerary, but it offers rebates on all aspects of travel—not just air. BET is a discounter and a rebate agency and has been around for years.

BET World Travel
841 Blossom Hill Road
Suite 212C
San Jose, CA 95123
Tel: (800) 747–1476
    (408) 229–7880

Travel Avenue
10 South Riverside Plaza
Suite 1404
Chicago, IL 60606
Tel: (800) 333–3335
    (312) 876–1116

The Smart Traveler
P.O. Box 330010
3111 Southwest 27th Avenue
Coconut Grove, FL 33133
Tel: (800) 448–3338

An Agency Specializing in Cutting Airline Costs

Travel For Less specializes in keeping costs down for travelers who have to travel on a specific schedule but do not know how to jump through all of the hoops to make substantial savings.

Travel For Less
1301 47th Street
Brooklyn, NY 11219
Tel: (800) 223–6045

Student Discounts

These are not readily available in the region. However, you should contact local student offices or organizations catering to students to see whether special charters are being organized during school break periods.

Senior Coupons

Senior coupons are presently one of the great travel bargains. These coupons are available for a set number of flights for a deeply discounted rate. Some of the major airlines have included Puerto Rico and the U.S. Virgin Islands in this unique program. The age limit is presently 62 in the United States.

Barter or Trade Exchanges

In most Sunday newspapers there is a section dealing with the sale of plane tickets. Many of these come from individuals who can't use up their frequent flyer coupons. The legality of all this is highly questionable, especially on international flights. However, thousands of people have bought tickets in this manner. Be wary. Only buy a ticket if it can be issued in your name.

Free or Discounted Travel Through Courier Services

Look for *Air Courier Service* in the Yellow Pages. These companies pay for all or part of your fare. Many books, magazines, and newsletters have named specific companies, only to have them inundated with inquiries. The companies then have no need for additional couriers. Major libraries have Yellow Page directories for most major cities. Librarians can help you get the addresses of courier companies. Write as many as you have the patience and stamina to try. Getting a job as a courier is not easy. Also check with major companies in your area to see whether they ever need courier services. A few points about courier services that are important.

- You have to be incredibly flexible.
- You will travel alone.
- You will probably be traveling with carry-on baggage only.
- You'll have to show up early at the airport.

- Your stay in the islands may be highly restricted, possibly to no more than a week, sometimes longer.
- And your fare may not be reduced as much as you might like considering the restrictions.
- This was at one time a true travel bargain, but once exposed to too much sunshine, it dried up—not completely, but almost. Personally, I'd look for a charter or highly reduced rate on a scheduled airline before going this route these days. The following company is just one of many with lots of information on discounted airfares, but it also will match potential couriers with companies looking for them, for a fee.

Discount Travel International
169 West 81st Street
New York, NY 10024
Tel: (212) 362–3636

Money-Saving Strategies

No matter how you decide to travel, whether by tour, scheduled airline, or charter, you can usually save money by following certain strategies.

Buy Tickets in the United States

- Buy as many of your plane tickets as possible in the United States (or Canada). If you buy tickets abroad, you'll have to pay for them in foreign currency, often at a pre-set and unfavorable rate of exchange. Also, you may have to pay a high VAT (Value Added Tax).
- An airline in the United States cannot raise the price of a ticket once you've paid for it. However, simply making a reservation does not guarantee the price. Until paid for, the price of a ticket can go up.
- Hard to believe, but true: A round-trip ticket may be less than one-way fare. Always ask about this if you're traveling only in one direction.
- When getting a quote on an airline ticket price, ask if it includes all fees and taxes for international travel, including inspection fees and departure taxes on all legs of the flight. Often, certain fees are not included, and it helps to know ahead when and where they aren't.

Frequent Flyer Programs

The airlines have teamed up with numerous organizations, such as credit card companies, telephone companies, travel clubs, and so on, to offer you free miles depending upon membership and purchases made through their sponsors. Normally, there is an airline in your area that you're most likely to use for both domestic and international flights. First, join that airline's frequent flyer program. Secondly, find out which companies it works with for additional free miles. These programs may also have other incentives, such as reduced hotel or car rental rates.

Buying Tickets in Advance

Since only a certain number of seats are allotted for highly reduced fares on any given flight, you can save hundreds of dollars by buying a ticket far in advance of a planned trip. In short, the early bird does get the worm. The exceptions to this have already been noted in the section on travel clubs and clearinghouses (pp. 114–115), where the last in may get the best buy. Also, risk takers often steal tickets on charters by waiting until the last minute to buy a ticket in the off-season (see later in the chapter).

Keeping Flexible About Travel Dates

- Be as flexible as possible in your travel plans so that you can take advantage of lower rates. What if you have to leave on a Thursday instead of a Friday or return on a Monday instead of a Sunday? Isn't it worth $100?
- Ask about excursion rates with minimum and maximum lengths of stay. It may be that by adding or subtracting a few days from your planned trip, you can save yourself a good deal of money.
- Ask the airline whether a standby fare exists on the route you're planning to take. This will make sense in the not-so-popular vacation periods. Standby status is for flexible travelers who will do anything to save a buck.

Stopover or Extension Privileges

Whenever buying a ticket to any destination, ask about possible stopover privileges. Perhaps you can see more than one island for the same price. If you don't ask, they're unlikely to mention this.

Off-season Travel

In the Caribbean the off-season runs from mid-April to mid-December. This is a rough guideline, since there are a few slack periods even during this time frame. In Bermuda the off-season runs from late November to mid-April. Again, this is a rough guideline. The off-season in the Bahamas is similar to the Caribbean.

- Check with the airline to see exactly when rates will drop for the off-season. Maybe you can take advantage of lower rates by changing your trip dates by no more than a week or two.

- Note the earlier tip regarding charters. Some of these fly in the off-season. If you're extremely flexible and patient, you can sometimes come up with a steal to a popular tourist destination by waiting to buy your ticket at the last minute.

- There are also discounts on what agents refer to as shoulder seasons. Check with your agent or airline on exact cutoff dates for each type of fare. I like traveling in shoulder seasons a great deal because airline rates are reasonable, rooms readily available, and the weather fairly reliable.

Trouble-savers for Booking Your Own Flight

- Call before 7 A.M. or after 7 P.M. to get through to the airline without a long wait.

- Make a point of being very specific. Repeat the day and date several times to avoid mix-ups. Get the name of the person helping you. Mark down the date and time of your call along with the information concerning your flight.

- Early flights are less frequently delayed. The earliest flights rarely suffer from the cumulative effects of mounting earlier delays.

- Flights originating from your city are subject to fewer delays.

- Try to book nonstop flights whenever possible.

- Direct flights are second-best. A direct flight means you do not have to get off the plane when it makes a stopover. Ask how many stopovers there will be on the direct flight.

- If you cannot fly non-stop or direct, try to stay on the same airline to avoid long walks and check-in hassles at the connecting airport. Airlines usually have a block of gates in each terminal; if you fly with one airline, you'll have only a short walk to a connecting flight.

- There are exceptions to the above rule, especially in the United States. Smaller carriers don't carry the same clout as larger ones, so choosing a powerful airline puts the odds in your favor that you won't have a long walk from one gate to the next.

Tips on Using Credit to Purchase Tickets

- Get credit cards that charge minimal interest on monthly debt. The difference between cards can be incredible.

- If you use credit cards but pay off debt immediately, get a cash-back card, which refunds you a portion of your total purchases each year.

- Some of the lesser known cards are fine to use for the purchase of airline tickets but not easily used in the Caribbean. Having several cards to use for different purposes does make sense.

- Before charging your airline ticket on a credit card, compare finance charges with rates available from your bank on a short-term loan to come up with the most favorable terms (lowest interest rate).
- If you have a certificate of deposit at a bank, remember that almost all banks will loan you money against these certificates at a rate of about 2 percent above what they are paying on the certificate. Your certificate acts as collateral for your loan. Compared to the high interest rates charged by most credit cards, this is a steal.
- Also, if you're strapped for vacation money and have a life insurance policy, don't forget that you can take out its cash value at whatever interest rate has been established by your policy. That rate is often much lower than the one charged by credit card companies.

Special Meals

Scheduled airlines often offer special meals to passengers with specific dietary restrictions, either for cultural, health, or religious reasons. Ask about these meals when making a reservation. Specify your needs at that time. Charters may or may not have special meals available. Either carry appropriate food and drink with you, or eat before or after your flight. I recommend carrying snacks and something to drink at all times for everyone. Also, when you reconfirm your flight, specify once again that you have ordered a special meal.

Picking Up Tickets

- Pay for and pick up tickets in advance to avoid the crush at the airport. It's a good feeling to have the tickets in your pocket, an assurance that now no one will be able to bungle your important reservation.
- If your agent is not close to your home and if you have time, have them send out tickets to you in the mail to save time and energy.
- When you get your tickets, check the dates, flight times, and flight numbers for accuracy. Read all materials closely so that you know your rights.
- Check to see whether all taxes and fees, including departure taxes have already been paid. If you're not sure, ask.
- Count the flight coupons to make sure there are enough to cover all legs of your flight. Usually, they're all there. However, I have had missing coupons on occasion. Without the coupon (slip of paper denoting a certain leg), you can't get a boarding pass.
- Photocopy all of the coupons twice. Leave one copy at home with family or friends and take one with you—just in case you lose your tickets.

Selecting a Seat

Find out about available aircraft and best seats at the time you pick up or pay for your ticket—don't wait until you're in the hurried atmosphere of the departure lounge. Ask to see a seating chart, choose where you'd like to be, and reserve a seat right away if you can. If you can't, mark down your preferred seats and several alternatives on your ticket folder so that you can ask for them when checking in.

Traveling by Private Plane

Most of the popular islands are accessible by private plane. Flying in this area must be done carefully with regard to all local regulations. Part of the reason is obviously related to the problem of drug running.

Getting Information

If you're planning extensive travel throughout the region, consider membership in the following organization and buying a copy of the *Bahamas & Caribbean Pilot's Aviation Guide* from Pilot Publications.

Aircraft Owners and
  Pilots Association
421 Aviation Way
Frederick, MD 21701
Tel: (800) 872–2672
  (301) 695–2000
(Produces flying kits
  for its members)

Pilot Publications
102 Nightingale Lane
Brunswick, GA 31525
Tel: (800) 521–2120
  (912) 264–4195
(The guide covers the
  Bahamas, Caymans, the
  Dominican Republic,
  Jamaica, Puerto Rico,
  Turks & Caicos, and the
  Virgin Islands.)

Getting to the Islands by Boat or Yacht

While most people get to the Bahamas, Bermuda, and the Caribbean islands by plane, a number travel by boat (either power or sail). Yachting is extremely popular from Florida to the Bahamas. You might be able to hitch a ride with one of these boats by checking into yacht clubs along the Eastern coast, especially those in Florida. You might also want to advertise or look for help-wanted ads in yachting magazines. It helps to have sailing experience, references, and the ability to do some sort of work. Especially helpful is a background in cooking, because good food is one of the primary concerns of people at sea. Always remember that this is truly a free-floating lifestyle. Schedules and destinations may change at whim, much like the wind. If you're not flexible, fly.

Transportation Between the Islands

This chapter covers planning for travel between the islands. There are basically three ways to do this: by boat (ferry), by plane, and by yacht (bareboat or crewed). Additional information is given on pp. 232–238, which covers advice once you arrive in the area.

Plane Travel

Plane travel is the fastest and most convenient way to get to most of the islands. Obviously, some remote or extremely small islands don't even have an airstrip, but these are the exceptions to the rule.

Basic Tips on Plane Travel

- There are numerous inter-island airlines that seem to come and go. Main ones at the moment are Air Anguilla, Air Guadeloupe, Air Martinique, Air St. Kitt's/Nevis, ALM, American Eagle (affiliated with American), Bahamas Air, BWIA, Carib Aviation, Cayman Airlines, Charles Air Service, Jamaica Airline, LIAT, Montserrat Airways, Mustique Airways, Turks & Caicos Airways, and WINAIR. But this is strictly a partial list. And, as underlined, these come and go, change names, merge, and so on. American Eagle and LIAT are the main players in the region. The latter once stood for Leeward Islands Air Transport. It is now said to mean Loyalty Is Always There. Tourists more often refer to it as Leave Island Any Time or Luggage In Another Town. In fairness to LIAT, schedules are not exactly tight on any of the inter-island airways. And luggage does have a way of getting lost or misdirected on the other larger inter-island airlines just as frequently.
- Scheduled or chartered planes serve most of the islands. There are a few that you can reach by boat only.
- The prices to each island vary by line. Scheduled airlines usually offer lower prices than specially chartered planes, but this is not always the case (especially if you can get enough people to fill all seats on a charter).

- Travel agents are excellent resources to get up-to-the-minute prices on scheduled airlines, but they may not be able to come up with fares on all of the smaller companies operating in a particular area. You may have to do that in person.
- Here are some names of the inter-island charters in the Bahamas: Abaco Air in Abaco, (809) 367–2266; Bahamas Air Charter in New Providence, (809) 327–8223; Four Way in New Providence, (809) 327–5139; Nixon Aviation in Exuma, (809) 366–2104; Pinders in New Providence, (809) 327–7320; and Trans Island Airways in New Providence, (809) 327–8777. See p. 225 for safety concerns.
- A number of airlines in the region offer special passes that allow you to visit a number of islands over a certain period of time. An example would be the inter-island pass offered by LIAT, which allows you to visit all of their destinations during one month for a set price. Other airlines may also be offering passes (BWIA, for example). The LIAT pass has so many restrictions that in my opinion it's next to useless. A true pass is one that allows you to travel to a set number of destinations on your own schedule as long as space is available.
- *Important:* If you lose one of these airline passes, you often will get no refund. Consider these tickets as you would cash.
- Since passes vary constantly, check with a travel agent to get current rates and information. Read the fine print with a magnifying glass.
- Regional airlines often do not meet FAA standards. If a line flies in and out of the United States, it must meet these standards. But the FAA does not have jurisdiction over inter-regional lines.
- You must inquire locally about the safety record of these lines. The local people are well aware of which ones are most reputable.
- Throughout the Caribbean, flights can and often are canceled on the flimsiest excuses, especially on regional carriers.
- Bumping is also very common and doesn't carry with it the penalties it would in the United States. It can be quite frustrating, especially when you look around at the people who have been bumped and notice that they are all tourists, not locals. I'm not saying that it is this way on all of the islands, but I am saying that discrimination is blatant on some of the islands.

Reservations

- Make reservations for flights in the United States whenever possible. If this can't be done, see pp. 232–236.

Boats (ferries)

You can get to many islands by boat. Some restaurants and lodges are accessible by boat only. Generally, you make arrangements locally for these trips, which rarely last more than a few hours. Boats range from frail, tipsy dugouts to large ferries capable of loading numerous cars and trucks. See pp. 236–238 for additional tips. In almost all instances you'll buy your tickets locally or bargain on boat transportation with the locals. If you're planning a fishing or scuba diving trip, see the appropriate sections in the chapter on Doing Things, pp. 271–308.

Yachting

Yachting is placed in this chapter because it can be one of the easiest ways to island hop in the Bahamas or Caribbean. However, it could just as easily be viewed as a private, free-floating, all-inclusive hotel, sampling the best of land and sea. It may be one of the best-kept secrets in the travel business. Many people spend the entire season cruising through these waters. The most popular areas include Antigua, the Exumas in the Bahamas, Grenada (gateway to the Grenadines), the Grenadines, Martinique (another point of origin for the Grenadines), and the Virgin Islands (both British and United States). However, the entire string of islands from Puerto Rico to Trinidad are wonderful for yachting.

The Pros and Cons of Yachting

Yachting can be the most wonderful or the absolutely worst of vacations. You may want to try it for a day before deciding on a full week or longer. Be honest with yourself. If you know in your soul this isn't for you, don't pretend just to make someone else happy, because you won't. You'll just make yourself and others miserable. However, for many people this type of vacation is the epitome of relaxation and high adventure. And don't for a second think that age is a barrier. There are 10 year olds who turn on to yachting as if it were first love. And there are elderly people who find it just as exhilarating. Following are many tips to help insure a great trip and to avoid some of the most common pitfalls that could turn potential nirvanas into nervous breakdowns. A few things to consider:

- Yachting is enjoyable for people who really love to sail. The process of sailing the boat is relaxing for some people.

- You can island hop without the hassles involved with planes and ferries. You, therefore, see a number of islands with the minimum of inconvenience.
- You can get to many remote islands where you're virtually on your own. You can dive reefs with no one else around. You escape the islands when you want to, moving back close to shore when the time is right.
- You see or experience many things that would be impossible to do on shore.
- But yachting can be expensive for a single person or couple. ›
- If you're prone to sea sickness, yachting may be a poor choice.
- Accommodations can be crowded, the toilet, or "head," minuscule, and the shower a dribble. Although this varies by boat.
- Loners may dislike being in confined quarters.
- If you don't like your captain or crew (if not bareboating), you're stuck.

The Pros and Cons of Bareboating

Bareboating refers to renting a boat without a crew. Here are a few tips to keep in mind.

- Bareboats are usually a bargain in the off-season. They may be just as expensive as crewed boats in the peak season when you add in all additional fees to the base price, such as insurance, food and drink, mooring fees, sporting equipment, rental of a dinghy, hotel stays, and so on.
- Ask about the types and sizes of boats available. Ask for an exact layout.
- Get prices in writing.
- Get any regulations and conditions set out in writing.
- Most bareboat rental companies want you moored one hour before sunset at the latest.
- If you want provisions, you get them yourself or hire a provisioner to do this for you.
- Get appropriate insurance. This can be difficult if you plan to visit some areas (the Dominican Republic, Grenada, Jamaica, and islands just off South America).
- Be prepared to prove you're capable of handling whatever boat you rent. You can understand why any company would not hand over a bareboat to an inexperienced sailor. But this forces you to stay in a hotel the first night until you are "okayed" to set sail the next day. Sometimes you're forced to stay in a specific hotel at an inflated rate. Always check on this ahead of time.

IMPORTANT INFORMATION

If you plan to bareboat, then the following information is especially important. Even if you're not, reading publications may give you a feeling for what yachting may be like if you've never done it before.

- Buy yachting guides well in advance to decide on appropriate routes. They contain a wealth of information on possible choices.

Cruising Guide Publications
P.O. Box 1017
Dunedin, FL 34697
Tel: (800) 330–9542

Tropic Isle Publishers, Inc.
P.O. Box 610938
North Miami, FL 33261
Tel: (305) 893–4277
(Recommended are the *Yachtsman's Guide to the Bahamas* and Turks and Caicos and the *Yachtsman's Guide to the Virgin Islands*)

- **Get charts before leaving Canada or the United States.**

Armchair Sailor
126 Thames Street
Newport, RI 02840
Tel: (800) 292–4278
  (401) 847–4252

Bluewater Books & Charts
1481 Southeast 17th Street
Causeway
Fort Lauderdale, FL 33316
Tel: (800) 942–2583
  (305) 763–6533

General Tips on Bareboating

Bareboating can be an excellent choice for anyone with lots of sailing experience and a desire to be totally independent. While it's a misconception, a number of people believe that only wimps get on crewed yachts. And if that's your overall feeling, then a bareboat is certainly your best choice. Contrary to what most people think, the less experienced you are, the bigger the boat you should rent. As you gain skill, you can go down in size. Actually, it's less a question of skill than it is a sense of comfort with confined space.

- Work with a dependable company. Get references. Following are two with excellent reputations.

Ed Hamilton & Company
Route 1, Box 430
Whitefield, ME 04353
Tel: (800) 621–7855
  (207) 549–7855

(An independent broker with over a quarter century of experience in matching customers to just the right bareboat. Totally independent of any specific company, although works extensively with The Moorings, Ltd.)

The Moorings Ltd.
19345 US 19 North
Fourth Floor
Clearwater, FL 34624
Tel: (800) 535–7289
     (813) 535–1446
(One of the best companies in the business with a fleet of over 600 bareboats. A limited number are available for one-way charters where you rent a boat on one island, leave it off on another.)

- Book yachts far in advance for the peak season.
- Get exact layouts of any potential boat you'll be renting.
- Get information on all costs, not just the base price. Shopping for bareboats is similar to renting a car sight unseen. Don't assume anything.
- Ask about basic rates by number of people. Find out costs for security payments, any special sporting gear, mooring fees, and so on.
- Since deposits are non-refundable and up to 50 percent of the cost of a trip, always get cancellation insurance in case you can't go. Read the fine print to make sure it covers all potential contingencies, including any pre-existing medical conditions.
- Many bareboats must be returned to the place where they are first rented. This is inconvenient for someone who would like to sail along a string of islands and leave the boat at another destination.
- Some boats are not available during the off-season, but those that are offer deep discounts.
- Study sailing guides carefully before you arrive to know about local idiosyncrasies that could result in heavy fines or problems with the police. For example, dealing with immigration just going from the British Virgin Islands to the United States Virgin Islands can cause enormous delays and be a kind of surrealistic nightmare for the uninitiated.
- These guides also have detailed information on harbors, moorings, supplies, weather, and so on. The subject is so involved that you really need a full book for this kind of vacation.

General Tips on Packing

- Travel as light as possible. All things should be in duffle or sea bags—preferably waterproof.

- Bring just the basics: bathing suit, blouse (long-sleeved), earplugs, hat (wide-brimmed), pants (cotton and long), scuba gear (only regulator and mask—not tanks or weight belts), shirt (cotton and long-sleeved), shorts, snorkeling equipment, sunglasses, sunscreen, T-shirts, underwear, and wind jacket—and the obvious extras, medications, and toiletries.
- Anyone renting a bareboat should consider bringing a few extra items that may or may not be on the boat: bottle opener, heavy-duty can opener, cassette player with ear phones, duct tape (for every imaginable use), ice chest (made of waterproof fabric), flashlight (tiny pen kind with extra batteries), netting (the lightweight kind to cover any holes in the boat), plastic bags (locking kind), rope (there's rarely enough on board), sheets (ask supplier what's on board), Swiss Army knife (sharp), tool kit (screwdriver with varying heads, penetrating or lubricating oil, pliers, wire, wire cutter), trash bags (heavy, black plastic), and water jug (collapsible with a spigot). A few of these items can be found only at stores specializing in yachting supplies.
- *Essentials:* Your passport, the up-to-date vessel's license (certificate), clearance documents from the last port, and appropriate flags.

The Pros and Cons of Crewed Yachts

There are many misconceptions about crewed yachts. One of them is that they are necessarily more expensive than bareboats. Yes, in the off-season they are, but in the peak season the total costs of a bareboat may be similar to that of a crewed yacht. Crewed yachts may be less expensive for couples and travelers wanting to travel in one direction only (not returning to the point of departure). Following are the advantages and disadvantages of booking a crewed yacht.

- Crewed yachts may be comparably priced or even less expensive than bareboats in the peak season. The extras added to the base price of bareboats are usually included in prices quoted for crewed yachts. Ask about any potential extras.
- You will not have to stay on shore. You can arrive on an island and be on the boat that same day.
- The purpose of yachting for many is to get away from any worries. Not cooking, not clearing customs, not dealing with paperwork, not having to think about anything—from something that breaks on board to shopping in a local market (although the latter can be enjoyable and lots of fun for photographers). The crew takes care of this for you.

- The crews of yachts are often couples. Many have sailed around the world. Some several times. They can teach you how to sail, if you're interested. It is very common for people on crewed yachts to sail the boats. Some guests actually sail more on crewed yachts than on bareboats. Having someone experienced by their side gives guests of all ages the confidence and knowledge necessary to sail the yacht safely.
- Each member of a crew specializes in activities varying from great cooking to local knowledge of fauna and flora. Individuals may be experts on astronomy, birding, fishing, locale lore, marine ecology, scuba diving, snorkeling, water skiing, windsurfing, and many other activities. Many crewed yachts include the costs of such things as fishing tackle and scuba equipment in their quoted price (you'll pay for lost gear and filling tanks with air, but not for the use of the equipment).
- Crewed yachts know the best to see and do in any area from years of experience. They also know what places to avoid. In short, you don't just see the tip of the iceberg, but know what's underneath the surface.
- The pace is set by the guests. Whether you want to lounge in the sun or be super active, that's your choice. The crew is there to help you get as little or as much from the vacation as you want.
- Yachts vary greatly in layout and size. Virtually all have brochures and flyers that show the layout and amenities on board. Get these in advance. For example, it's nice not to have to share the bathroom (head) with the crew. It's also nice to have plenty of deck space for lounging around (this is often overlooked).
- If this is your first time on a yacht, rent the largest one you can afford. As you gain experience, move down in size according to what feels comfortable to you.
- Always get references from previous guests. Good crewed yachts provide them readily. Follow up on the references with calls.
- If you're allergic to pets, ask whether any are on board. If you intend to bring pets (a real hassle), ask whether this is allowed.
- Trouble on crewed yachts can come up when the personalities of the guests and crew don't match. Be honest in what you expect and are looking for. Neither you nor the crew are to blame. It's just that certain people blend better with each other.
- Worse problems come from guests who aren't matched to each other. Sail only with people you really like and who have similar interests. The wrong partners can make heaven into hell. Or, as one operator put it, never suffer the company of fools. You know in your gut whether you want to be with certain friends or relatives—follow that instinct as if it were law.

- A corollary to this tip is to travel in a small group. This isn't D-day. Most companies suggest that an ideal number is 4. True, you may cut costs somewhat with larger groups, but is it worth it if there are interpersonal problems that turn a daydream into a nightmare?
- The one thing that almost all guests remember about any yachting experience is the food. If food is a top priority, make this clear when booking a yacht. Some of the cooks are excellent and cater to specific tastes or dietary needs.
- If you're a non-smoker and smoking bothers you, make sure that the crew are non-smokers as well. You may even ask whether smoking is ever allowed on board to weed out yachts that could be impregnated with smoke from previous guests.
- Since deposits are non-refundable and up to 50 percent of the cost of a trip, always get cancellation insurance in case you can't go. Read the fine print to make sure it covers all potential contingencies, including any pre-existing medical conditions.

Companies Renting Crewed Yachts

Working through a company that specializes in crewed yachts has many advantages. Ask the company how long it has been in business, whether it has sailed the recommended yacht, whether it is familiar with the crew (so that you can get a good match), how much repeat business the yacht has, and so on. In return, reputable companies will grill you with questions, many of which may seem extremely personal. The more questions they ask, the better. Be totally honest. This questioning is essential for the agency to do its job of matching you to the right crew and yacht. Yachting is not just a question of getting a good boat at a fair price; it's more like arranging a good marriage. Working through these companies costs you no more than booking yachts directly. It saves you a lot of time and trouble. Following are companies noted for finding excellent crewed yachts.

Ann-Wallis White
P.O. Box 4100
Horn Point Harbor
Annapolis, MD 21403
Tel: (800) 732–3861
   (410) 263–6366
(Represents numerous crewed yachts and knows each extremely well. Will match you to just the right crew. Inspects boats regularly. One of the best in the business.)

Interpac
1050 Anchorage Lane
San Diego, CA 92106
Tel: (619) 222-0327
(Another terrific broker who personally inspects hundreds of
    yachts each year. Much of her expertise comes from years of on-
    board experience.)

Sail Vacations Ltd.
P.O. Box 823
Roadtown
Tortola, BVI
Tel: (800) 368–9905
    (809) 494–3656
(Offers a boat crewed by three people which can accommodate up
    to four couples. You do not have to book as a group. Individual
    couples can book a single room independently of others, but, of
    course, you will share the yacht with others.)

Tom Collins Yachts Worldwide
400 South Hibiscus Drive
Miami Beach, FL 33139
Tel: (800) 637–5407
    (305) 673–5400
(Once a captain himself, Tom Collins knows the Bahamas and
    Caribbean well. He handles both sail and power boats through-
    out the region. He's expert in matching clients not only to the
    right crew, but to the right area as well.)

Yacht Hopping

Some people get around the Caribbean by hitchhiking on private
yachts. Not all yachters are willing to take strangers on board, but
some will. You have a much better chance of getting on board if you
have references indicating specific skills (such as being a dynamite
cook). You may also be asked to produce proof of your ability to get
home (such as an airline ticket). Finally, never get off on an island
with the intention of not getting back on the yacht without notifying
the captain. This can cause a great deal of trouble—as can any con-
cealed weapon or drugs of any kind unless accompanied by a prescription and in a properly labeled container. Best places to hitch a
ride are the yacht clubs or harbors in Antigua, the Bahamas, the
Grenadines, Martinique, Saint Lucia, and the United States Virgin
Islands.

Transportation on the Islands

This chapter is meant only to give you an overview of what to expect concerning travel on the islands. It tells you what you can do before going to the Caribbean to get the most value for your dollar and how to avoid common pitfalls. Detailed information related to what to do concerning local travel on the islands once you're there is in a second chapter (pp. 239–245).

Plane Travel

Some of the larger islands have several airports. Getting around these by plane can make sense. For example, traveling long distances by car on Jamaica is extremely tiring and frustrating. Every time you go through a town you must honk your horn incessantly to avoid hitting pedestrians. It gets old. Plane travel for longer trips on the Dominican Republic may be advisable as well.

Bus Travel

You'll find buses available on most islands in the Caribbean. The quality of bus service varies greatly by island.

Car Travel

Car travel is for people willing to pay a price for freedom. And that price is often worth it in the Caribbean. Cars are available on most (but not all) Caribbean islands. Cars cannot be rented by tourists on Bermuda. For even more detailed information on car travel, see pp. 239–242.

Advantages of Car Travel

- Cars can get you just about anywhere. Occasionally, there are a few hidden corners accessible only by boat or walking, but you can reach most places by car.
- Cars get you to places much faster than buses. You're never tied to someone else's schedule. This gives you a great sense of freedom.
- You don't have to worry about reservations, tickets, and ticket lines.
- You don't have to travel light unless you prefer to.
- When you travel by car, you can stop whenever you like. You can take a break for a picnic, stop for a pee, pause for a truly great photo—do whatever you like, when you like, pretty much as you damn well please.

Disadvantages of Car Travel

- Car travel is expensive. Rental rates are exorbitant.
- The cost becomes more manageable as the number of passengers increases.
- Car travel can be dangerous. Local drivers, especially bus drivers, are terrible.

Travelers Who Don't Need Cars

- If your travel is limited to one resort with an excursion or two, a car may actually be a burden and a pointless luxury.
- You can always supplement inexpensive public transportation with more expensive taxis—more expensive, yes, but still cheap compared to the high cost of car rental.

Who Can Rent a Car

- To rent a car in the Caribbean you need: proof that you're not too young or too old (according to company rules), a valid driver's license, a passport for identification, and a major credit card (or a large chunk of cash).

Reserving a Car in Advance

- The major U.S. car rental companies operate in many, but not all of the Caribbean islands. Some islands allow only local companies to rent cars.

- You can find out about all of these local companies by requesting a list from the National Tourist Offices (see pp. 18–26). Tell them to send you a complete list with addresses and local phone numbers.
- You can make reservations with major companies by calling their toll-free 800 numbers. Or you can have a travel agent do this for you.
- Make reservations far in advance for peak season travel from mid-December to mid-April.
- Cars are at an even higher premium during Christmas, New Year's, Carnival, and Easter. Plan ahead.
- When you make a car reservation, always get the name of the person you're talking to. Ask for a confirmation number so that you have proof that the reservation has been made. Then ask for a written confirmation.
- Have the exact address where you are to pick up the car. Ask the person to send you a map, if one is available, pinpointing this location. Get specific hours when the agency is open. They often close on the flimsiest excuse.

What Kind of Car Should You Rent

- Try to get by with the smallest car possible. Streets can be narrow, torturous, and steep. Small cars can go almost anywhere. They guzzle less gas, are roomy enough if you're traveling light, can weasel into tiny parking spots, and cost less for ferries.
- *Important:* Ask the company or travel agent to request a car in the best possible condition. Many of the vehicles are so badly abused that there is no way you won't suffer a breakdown.
- I wish I could tell you that there would be some way to guarantee that you'll get what you ask for, but I can't. By working with major companies, you may lower the odds of getting a lemon.

Stick Shifts

- If you don't know how to operate a stick shift, you should learn. Even if you reserve a car with an automatic shift, there is no guarantee that you'll get one. Furthermore, in an emergency you should be able to drive any car that's available. A competent driving instructor can teach you how to use a stick shift in 6 hours or less—from the basics to starting on a 45-degree incline.

Car Rental Costs

Car rental is much more expensive on Caribbean islands than in the United States or Canada, so much more expensive that you may figure the price isn't worth it. The overall cost includes the basic charge, supplemental costs for air-conditioning or automatic transmission, insurance premiums, mileage charges, gas refill charge, a tourist tax, and special driving permits (see p. 240)—more about each of these later.

SHOPPING AROUND FOR THE BEST BASE RATE

- Travel agents use computers to compare rates. Using an agent not only saves you money but also time.
- Sometimes companies will give you a price break for a guaranteed reservation made far enough in advance. There's usually a cancellation penalty for this special offer. Ask for full information on potential savings, restrictions, and penalties.
- If you prefer to shop around on your own, do it. Using the toll-free 800 numbers in your telephone book, call major car rental firms, such as Avis, Hertz, and National. Ask these companies to send you their free worldwide directories listing current car rental locations. Once you know locations, ask for prices. They have deleted these from directories to make comparison shopping more difficult.

THINGS THAT UP THE BASIC RATE

- All car rental rates are related to the model and size of the car you rent. Rent the smallest car that will accommodate your party. The many advantages of small cars have already been given.
- Most cars have stick shifts. You'll pay a surcharge if you want a car with an automatic transmission. However, do not assume that you'll get an automatic car simply because you reserved one. It just doesn't work that way.
- During the sticky summer heat of the tropics you'll want air-conditioning—but it's an option for which you often pay a surcharge. During much of the year it's really not necessary. In some cases, air is included in the base rate.
- Cars with 4-wheel drive are always more expensive and in great demand during peak seasons on islands where off-road travel is common. Such travel voids your insurance, as outlined later.

THE MILEAGE CHARGE

Many rental agreements add an additional charge for miles driven. The extra charge may be per kilometer, roughly 6/10 of a mile. You can double the kilometer charge for a rough estimate of the per-mile cost—and it's steep.

AVOIDING THE MILEAGE CHARGE

If you rent a car for more than three days (in most areas), you can get a car at a set price per day or week without paying an additional charge for mileage. This is an *unlimited mileage agreement*. Ask about these in advance.

INSURANCE PREMIUMS

- As in the United States and Canada, insurance charges jack up the total bill of a car considerably. Sometimes insurance is included in the quoted rate. Ask to be sure.
- *Note:* Almost all car rental insurance has a deductible for which you're responsible. This applies to partial theft, glass breakage, and collision. So your insurance is really only partial insurance—a rip-off by anyone's standards.

COMPARING DEDUCTIBLES

Car rental companies make as much money selling insurance as they do renting cars. Without insurance, your deductible can be thousands of dollars. Get a company with as good a base rate as possible but also one with the lowest possible deductible. Have your agent shop around.

COVERING YOUR DEDUCTIBLE

Once you've established the deductible on a car, you now want to cover it as inexpensively as possible.

- In theory, many credit card companies claim that they will cover this deductible if you use their card when renting a vehicle abroad. In reality, this is partially true.
- They will cover certain cars driven on *paved* roads. If you drive on a dirt or unpaved road, the coverage is void. Some credit card companies say this directly; others do it dishonestly by saying that cars must be driven on federally-maintained roads, a euphemism for paved roads.
- Many of the roads in the Caribbean are unpaved. So, you've just had an accident and are on a dirt road—guess who pays the deductible? You do, even though you thought your credit card company would pick up the tab.
- That's not all the bad news. Many credit card companies do not cover open vehicles, 4-wheel drive vehicles, or trucks.
- Some companies will cover 4-wheel drive vehicles if the car is covered, not open the way so many cars are in the Caribbean. Again, coverage is for 4-wheel drive vehicles driven only on *paved* roads.
- *Tip:* Following is a company that will cover vehicles used on designated highways (paved or not) as long as the vehicle is rented

from a licensed auto rental company and not used for off-road travel. No one will cover you for off-road use.

Travel Guard International
1145 Clark Street
Stevens Point, WI 54481
Tel: (800) 826–1300
    (715) 345–0505

DROP-OFF CHARGES

Drop-off charges are only a major consideration on the larger islands such as the Dominican Republic and Jamaica.

- In most instances, you cannot rent a car in one town and drop it off in another without paying a charge for this service. The charge is usually related to the distance between the two cities.
- Always ask about drop-off charges in advance, and make sure to get the charge in *writing* before renting the car.

THE VALUE ADDED TAX

On all of your rental car expenses, you'll pay a government tax (IVA or VAT). Keep this in mind. Ask what the tax will be and whether it's included in the price being quoted. Get this in writing.

Boats

In a few areas, tourist spots or lodges are accessible by boat only. This can be lots of fun. Generally, you make arrangements locally for these short trips, which rarely last more than a few hours. Boats range from frail, tipsy dugouts to large ferries capable of loading numerous cars and semi trucks. In the Bahamas and the British Virgin Islands, consider renting a boat and using it as you would a car for inter-island transportation. In even the most remote places, you can often find a local with a boat. He'd be delighted to earn extra cash for special trips and often knows the waters better than anyone. The way you find out about these people is to be friendly and willing to ask for information and help.

Reservations

In almost all instances, you'll buy your tickets locally or bargain on boat transportation with the locals. If you're planning a trip out to a fishing lodge or to a dive site, see the appropriate sections in the chapter on Doing Things.

Motorcycling

Getting around by moped, motorcycle, or scooter is highly recommended on many of the islands (see p. 243).

Biking

Biking is an excellent way to see some of the islands. On others, it should be viewed as a sport. On a few, it really is impractical (see p. 239). If you do bike, always wear an ANSI- or Snell-approved helmet. It reduces the risk of serious injury by 85 percent. Bring it with you if you'll be doing lots of biking.

Hitchhiking

Hitchhiking is generally not recommended, but there are enough exceptions that this cannot be ruled out (see p. 242).

Where to Stay

You'll want to match the wide variety of accommodations to your budget and preferred style of travel. Please read the chapter on Hotel Strategies (pp. 205–214) before going to the Caribbean. It may help you ask additional specific questions that will make your trip more enjoyable. Following are the basic questions.

- How much are you willing to spend per night?
- Are you looking for a place with a totally island or Caribbean feel, or are you more interested in creature comforts (like air conditioning)?
- How heavily will your vacation revolve around a specific activity or sport?
- Do you want to be on a specific island, or are you flexible in this regard? See the chapter on Where to Go, pp. 32–71.
- If you're traveling with children, will the hotel accept them?
- Are you looking for a place that is conservative (people acknowledge but rarely talk to you) or wild (just about anything goes, including people's clothes)?
- How important is food? Are you interested in *haute cuisine*, creole (Caribbean), or American foods? There are even hotels catering to vegetarians or people on macrobiotic diets.
- How important is the location? Do you want to be right on the beach? In the hills with a great view and nice breeze? Next to a golf course? Where?
- How important is peace and quiet?
- Do you prefer large resort complexes with lots of activities or more intimate hotels?
- Do you like to dress up for evening meals, or do you want to be casual the whole time? Some places require jackets (and ties) and comparable dress for women in the evening.
- Do you want to eat in the hotel or be free to eat in local restaurants? Some hotels insist that guests pay for certain meals in the peak season?
- Do you want to avoid places that allow conventions, cruise-ship passengers, and meetings? These can be very distracting if you're into peace, quiet, or seclusion.
- How important is a pool? Some areas are fine for sunbathing but not good for swimming.

Information on Where to Stay

Following are some ways of getting good information on possible places to stay. No matter what you want to spend, there's usually something available if you dig hard enough. In a few areas, hotels may close down for a month or two during the off-season, either for renovation or simply because there is a shortage of guests. Always find out about this in advance if you're traveling in non-peak periods.

Travel Agents

Travel agents specializing in the Caribbean are excellent resources for current information. They can often get you better rates than you could on your own, particularly in the peak season. Good agents have learned how to negotiate, have often visited specific properties, and may know of special places suited to your personality and price range. They may also be able to come up with "packages" offering a combination of airfare and accommodations at a substantial discount. Many of them have libraries of offbeat or relatively unknown books that they will let you look through to find places with special appeal to your interests or peculiarities. They also have books describing hotels that might appeal to you. Ask to read through them. They are extremely expensive and aimed primarily at specialists in travel. These specialized books cover many hotels on each island but tend to leave out any that will not pay a commission or are extremely inexpensive. They also grade hotels as deluxe, first-class (superior or standard), moderate, and tourist. Each book may have its own rating system. Do not be fooled by these ratings. Some hotels with quite a high rating may be lousy. The better books give detailed descriptions and will often admit that the classification given to the hotel is off the mark. The classification may come more from the local government than the books themselves.

TOURSCAN, INC.

TourScan, Inc., is one of the largest travel agencies in the world. It specializes only in the Caribbean and promises to come up with the best package rate possible for any hotel you choose to stay in. Its computers sift through thousands of potential packages (travel jargon for a combination of airfare and hotel costs) to save you hundreds of dollars at any time of year. Write or call:

TourScan, Inc.
P.O. Box 2367
1051 Boston Post Road
Darien, CT 06820
Tel: (800) 962–2080
    (203) 655–8091

Travel Guides

There are dozens of general and specialized travel guides to the Caribbean. These vary from well-known to obscure. The value of the guidebook depends on the following factors:

- Is the book aimed at your needs? If you're looking for an intimate inn, then a book just on inns in the Caribbean makes good reading.
- Are evaluations made by on-site inspections. This is an expensive and time-consuming process. Imagine the difficulty in visiting hundreds of places each year—not to mention the many new places being built each year.
- How often is the guide updated? The average is every two years with the better guides, but updating may or may not include thorough on-site inspections.
- How extensive are the descriptions of the properties? Do you feel like the person actually stayed there or not?
- Is the price clearly stated? Doing this is risky because costs change each year, but if prices are listed you can at least get a feeling for the general cost of an island and the difference between the properties. You can verify the current price through an agent or by fax or phone.
- Are the fax numbers of the properties listed? This is helpful in making and confirming reservations.

Tourist Offices

Tourist offices are excellent sources of general information. Ask for a list of all properties on the island. Specify the price range you're most interested in. If you want to stay in someone's home or are looking for extremely low-cost places to stay, specify this, because these places rarely can afford to advertise and are sometimes not included in general accommodation lists published by these offices. Many tourist offices offer specialized brochures on unique places to stay. An example: the British Virgin Islands *Inns and Villas,* (800) 888–5563, ext. 857. Remember that some of the tourist offices are next to useless or underfunded and may not respond to this request (see pp. 18–26).

Special Accommodation Hotlines

Some islands have toll-free numbers for hotel reservations. The companies represent a wide range of hotels, but certainly not all of them. Examples would be the Barbados Reservations Service, (800) 822–7223 and Bermuda's Small Properties, (800) 637–4116. The tip is that you can contact the appropriate tourist office (see pp. 18–26) and ask whether there are any toll-free hotel reservation services operating for that island at that time. In some instances, they may give you more than one number, since different companies may represent different hotels.

Island Hotel Associations

The island hotel associations try to get information to potential travelers about the available range of accommodations on their island. They can be an excellent source on some islands, a little less so on others. Give them a try. Call them to see whether they'll send you a listing of hotels: **Anguilla** (809) 497–2944, **Antigua** (809) 462–0374, **Aruba** (297) 82 26 07, **Barbados** (809) 426–5041, **Barbuda** (809) 462–0374, **Bonaire** (599) 75 134, **British Virgin Islands (BVI)** (809) 494–3514, **Cayman Islands** (809) 947–4057, **Curaçao** (599) 963–6260, **Dominica** (809) 448–3288, **Dominican Republic** (809) 532–2907, **Grenada** (809) 440–1353, **Guadeloupe** (590) 88 59 99, **Jamaica** (809) 926–3635, **Martinique** (596) 76 27 82, **Nevis** (809) 465–5304, **Puerto Rico** (809) 725–2901, **Saint Bart's** (590) 27 64 80, **Saint Christopher** (see **Saint Kitt's**), **Saint Croix (USVI)** (809) 733–7117, **Saint John (USVI)** (809) 774–6835, **Saint Kitt's** (809) 465–5304, **Saint Lucia** (809) 452–5978, **Saint Martin** (590) 87 56 85, **Saint Thomas (USVI)** (809) 774–6835, **Saint Vincent** (809) 457–1072, **Sint Maarten** (599) 52 23 33, **Tobago** (809) 624–3065, **Trinidad** (809) 624–3065, **Turks & Caicos** (809) 946–2232.

Varieties of Lodgings

Following are some suggestions on the variety of places to stay in the Caribbean as well as some tips on making reservations before your trip. For more information on reservations and places to stay once abroad, see pp. 205–214.

Apartments, Condos, Houses, Villas

There is an enormous range of apartments, condos, homes, and villas available to travelers in the islands. These vary from simple, inexpensive accommodations to the most luxurious imaginable with a staff of cooks, gardeners, maids, and pool attendants. These can be an excellent value for couples, families, and groups. It is a wonderful way to get to know an island. It is especially convenient and economical in keeping food costs down—breakfasts are a snap, picnics are easy to make for lunch, and dinners are much less expensive than those in most restaurants.

**The key tip is to match the place you rent to your tempera-
ment and pocketbook. Couples and families should discuss
goals at length to choose the right island and the right place on
the island to best suit varied needs.**

While many places are advertised by owners in travel magazines
and newsletters, consider working through an agency rather than
renting directly. An agency has more clout in case things go wrong—
and, unfortunately, they easily can. Often, properties are offered by
an absentee owner without proper recourse if problems arise. If you
do deal directly with an owner, bear this in mind.

When you rent an apartment, condo, home, or villa, you need lots
of information to make an intelligent choice. You need answers to
specific questions. If a company can't answer them to your satisfac-
tion, move on to another company. Always work far in advance (one
year is ideal) to get the best value during the peak season. If you
wait too long, you'll often be given inferior accommodations at
inflated prices. Following are a few tips.

- Has the company personally inspected the property? How long
  ago? It's impossible for a company to give accurate information if
  they haven't been to a property recently. Some companies are a
  lot more particular about the places they represent than others.
  And, some are a lot more religious about personal inspections
  than others.
- Is the property aimed at couples, families, or groups? What kind of
  people would like the place and why?
- Exactly where is the apartment, condo, house, or villa located? Ask
  the company to pinpoint this location on a map. Ask them to
  describe the location in detail. Ask them whether there are any
  safety problems: Can you walk in the area at night, for example?
- What is the floor plan? Ask to see it. It should include actual
  dimensions of all rooms—not just be a general brochure. If it's in a
  group of similar properties, have the company pinpoint the location of your specific unit so that you know whether it will be
  quiet, have a view, be suited to your age, and so on.
- Is there a local contact who can help you with any problems
  should they come up? Get the name and telephone number. **The
  presence of a local property manager is critical since things
  do break or go wrong.**
- Is service of any kind included in the base price? Exactly what service—anything from cleaning to cooking to driving you around
  the island. Ask.
- Is transportation provided to and from the airport at no charge?
  Or, is it available at all?

- Are the kitchens fully supplied with utensils and cooking gear? Ask exactly what appliances are in the kitchen. Suggestion: Always bring snacks and favorite liquors since they may not be available locally or can be extremely expensive.
- Will the kitchen be supplied with basics? How is this done? Is there someone available to do local shopping?
- Are any bikes included with the rental? Or, any other mode of transportation? Is public transportation close by?
- What kind of amenities are on the premises? Dishwasher, washer and dryer, pool, air conditioning, and so on?
- What kind of activities are readily available, from windsurfing to jet skiing or sailing. Properties vary enormously in what they offer.
- What are the answers to detailed financial questions: Is there a deposit? What is the refund policy if you have to cancel? Does the stated price include government taxes and service charges? Is there an extra charge for housekeeping and other provided services? Are tips included? Even if they are, tip 7 to 15 percent extra since companies may not give the staff appropriate tips. Is there an extra deposit required for anything at all, such as for a phone or long-distance calling? Keep asking!
- Finally, once you've decided on a place and have answers to your questions, get a confirmation in writing just as you would for a hotel. If you do have a staff, you are rarely expected to feed them, but you are expected to give them one night off per week at a minimum. Again, this is something worth discussing with the rental company so that no misunderstandings occur.
- Just as you should expect direct answers to all of your questions, you should be willing to go through a gentle grilling from the rental company. They need to know who you are in order to match you to a specific place and to a specific island. In talking to you they may suggest a different destination than you first had in mind. Good rental agencies ask lots of questions.

The following organizations have a wealth of information on rental abroad. This is a partial list of the many agencies working in this area; other companies may be suggested by the National Tourist Offices listed on pp. 18–26. After the name of each company is a list of islands on which it has properties for rent. BVI and USVI stand for British Virgin Islands and the United States Virgin Islands. In parentheses is the approximate number of properties available through the agency. This number fluctuates constantly since a good company will cull and add properties each year. It may seem odd, but the same property is often handled by more than one agency. These companies are not all of the same calibre. Some are extremely demanding in the properties they list; others less so. However, the goal of any of these companies should be to make a good match between you and the property you choose and to protect you as best they can from potential hassles. And, certainly to handle any complaints in a reasonable manner.

Abaco Vacation Reservations
40 Stone Hill Road
Westminster, MA 01473
Tel: (800) 633–9197
  (508) 874–5995
All of the following are in the Abacos chain of the Bahamas: Elbow Cay (31), Great Guana Cay (4), Green Turtle (5), Lubber's Quarters Cay (5), Marsh Harbour (6), Man-O-War (2), Treasure Cay (7).

All Destinations
19 Scodon Drive
Ridgefield, CT 06877
Tel: (800) 228–1510
  (203) 744–3100
Barbados (4), Grenada (6), Nevis (2), Saint Croix in the USVI (7), Saint John in the USVI (2), Saint Kitt's (3), Saint Martin/Sint Maarten (10), Saint Thomas in the USVI (14), Tortola in the BVI (2), Virgin Gorda in the BVI (1).

At Home Abroad, Inc.
405 East 56th Street
Suite 6H
New York, NY 10022
Tel: (212) 421–9165
Antigua (10), Barbados (116), Dominican Republic (3), Grenada (4), Jamaica (55), Montserrat (25), Mustique in the Grenadines (45), Nevis (5), Saint Croix in the USVI (6), Saint John in the USVI (52), Saint Lucia (10), Saint Martin/Sint Maarten (32), Saint Thomas in the USVI (30), Tortola in the BVI (6), Virgin Gorda in the BVI (11).

Caribbean Destinations
P.O. Box 9098
Metairie, LA 70055
Tel: (800) 888–0897
  (504) 834–7026
Anguilla (10), Barbados (80), Grenada (2), Saint John in the USVI (4), Saint Kitt's (50), Saint Lucia (1), Saint Martin/Sint Maarten (50), Saint Thomas in the USVI (50), Tortola in the BVI (6), Virgin Gorda in the BVI (11).

Caribbean Escapes, Inc.
P.O. Box 550
New York, NY 10018
Tel: (800) 288–8235
   (718) 855–8737
Anguilla (10), Antigua (12), Bahamas (12), Barbados (100), Grand
   Cayman (78), Grenada (15), Jamaica (225), Middle Caicos in the
   Turks & Caicos (3), Montserrat (23), Mustique in the Grenadines
   (42), Necker in the BVI (private island), Nevis (5), Providenciales
   in the Turks & Caicos (28), Saint Croix in the USVI (35), Saint
   John in the USVI (40), Saint Kitt's (4), Saint Lucia (13), Saint Mar-
   tin/Sint Maarten (38), Saint Thomas in the USVI (65), Tortola in
   the BVI (6), Virgin Gorda in the BVI (15).

Caribbean Villas & Condos
P.O. Box 546168
Bay Harbor Islands, FL 33154
Tel: (800) 321–3134
   (305) 861–0411
Anguilla (12), Barbados (49), Grenada (2), Grand Cayman (1),
   Jamaica (1), Montserrat (18), Saint Croix in the USVI (6), Saint John
   in the USVI (6), Saint Martin/Sint Maarten (57), Saint Thomas in the
   USVI (33), Tortola in the BVI (6), Virgin Gorda in the BVI (11).

Condo Club, Inc.
P.O. Box 8280
Red Bank, NJ 07701
Tel: (800) 272–6636
   (908) 872–0788
Anguilla (8), Antigua (5), Barbados (40), Bermuda (15), Cayman
   Islands (40), Saint Bart (10), Saint John in the USVI (40), Saint
   Lucia (4), Saint Martin/Sint Maarten (30), Saint Thomas in the
   USVI (70), Saint Vincent and the Grenadines (45), Tortola in the
   BVI (30), Virgin Gorda in the BVI (30).

Condominium Travel Associates, Inc.
2001 West Main Street
Suite 140
Stamford, CT 06902
Tel: (800) 492–6636
   (203) 975–7714
Antigua (1), Aruba (6), Bahamas (4), Barbados (2), Bonaire (1),
   Cayman Brac (1), Grand Cayman (4), Jamaica (3), Nevis (1),
   Saint Croix in the USVI (6), Saint John in the USVI (3), Sint

Maarten (3), Saint Thomas in the USVI (10), Tortola in the BVI (2), Virgin Gorda in the BVI (2).

Condo Villa Hotel World, Inc.
4230 Orchard Lake Road
Suite 3
Orchard Lake, MI 48323
Tel: (800) 521–2980
  (810) 683–0202
Bahamas (15), Grand Cayman (5), Grenada (20), Jamaica (75), Montserrat (35), Puerto Rico (19), Saint Croix in the USVI (35), Saint John in the USVI (35), Saint Martin/Sint Maarten (45), Saint Thomas in the USVI (65), Tortola in the BVI (35).

Creative Leisure
951 Transport Way
Petaluma, CA 94954
Tel: (800) 426–6367
  (707) 778–1800
Little Saint James in the USVI (private island), Saint Croix in the USVI (6), Saint John in the USVI (5), Saint Thomas in the USVI (37), Tortola in the BVI (6), Virgin Gorda in the BVI (11).

Europa Let/Tropical Inn-Let
92 North Main Street
Ashland, OR 97520
Tel: (800) 462–4486
  (503) 482–5806
Abaco in the Bahamas (4), Anguilla (3), Aruba (1), Barbados (43), Bonaire (3), Caymans (18), Eleuthera in the Bahamas (2), Jamaica (24), Mustique in the Grenadines (26), New Providence in the Bahamas (8), Saint Croix in the USVI (3), Saint John in the USVI (4), Saint Martin/Sint Maarten (18), Saint Thomas in the USVI (36), Tortola in the BVI (8), Virgin Gorda in the BVI (6).

Four Seasons Villas
P.O. Box 848
Marblehead, MA 01945
Tel: (800) 338–0474
  (617) 639–1055
Anguilla (3), Antigua (8), Aruba (6), Bahamas (37), Barbados (60), Bonaire (1), Cayman Brac (1), Jamaica (39), Grand Cayman (4), Grenada (6), Puerto Rico (13), Saint Croix in the USVI (23), Saint John in the USVI (12), Saint Lucia (14), Saint Kitt's (1), Saint Mar-

tin/Sint Maarten (58), Saint Thomas in the USVI (49), Tortola in the BVI (21), Virgin Gorda in the BVI (20).

French Caribbean International
5662 Calle Real
Suite 333
Santa Barbara, CA 93117
Tel: (800) 322–2223
    (805) 967–9850
Guadeloupe (17), Saint Bart (80).

French Home Rentals
P.O. Box 82386
Portland, OR 97282
Tel: (503) 774–8977
Guadeloupe (a few), Saint Bart (a few).

Heart of the Caribbean Ltd.
17485 Penbrook Drive
Brookfield, WI 53045
Tel: (800) 231–5303
    (414) 783–5303
Barbados (81), Saint Lucia (23), Saint Martin/Sint Maarten (115).

Hideaways International
767 Islington Street
Portsmouth, NH 03801
Tel: (800) 843–4433
    (603) 430–4433
Abaco in the Bahamas (6), Anguilla (18), Antigua (20), Aruba (1), Barbados (48), Beef Island in the BVI (1), Cat Island in the Bahamas (1), Cayman Islands (16), Compass Cay in the Bahamas (1), Dominican Republic (2), Eleuthera in the Bahamas (1), Exumas in the Bahamas (2), Grand Bahama (1), Great Camanoe in the BVI (1), Grenada (1), Guana Island in the BVI (private island), Harbour Island in the Bahamas (1), Jamaica (110), Margarita (1), Montserrat (26), Mustique in the Grenadines (46), Necker in the BVI (private island), Nevis (6), Peters Island in the BVI (4), Puerto Rico (3), Saba (1), Saint Bart (35), Saint Croix in the USVI (7), Saint John in the USVI (7), Saint Kitt's (1), Saint Lucia (10), Saint Martin (4), Saint Thomas in the USVI (4), Tobago (1), Tortola in the BVI (5), Trinidad (1), Turks & Caicos (3), Virgin Gorda in the BVI (26).

Island Hideaways, Inc.
4773 Leyden Way
Ellicott City, MD 21042
Tel: (800) 832–2302
 (410) 884–0400
Anguilla (25), Barbados (105), Cayman Islands (25), Grenada (5),
 Jamaica (40), Mustique in the Grenadines (40), Saint Bart (90),
 Saint Croix in the USVI (40), Saint John in the USVI (50), Saint
 Lucia (25), Saint Martin/Sint Maarten (70), Saint Thomas in the
 USVI (50), Tortola in the BVI (15), Virgin Gorda in the BVI (25).

Island Villas
6 Company Street
Christiansted
Saint Croix, USVI 00820
Tel: (800) 626–4512
 (809) 773–8821
Saint Croix in the USVI (70).

Jamaica Association of Villas and Apartments (JAVA)
1370 Washington Avenue,
Suite 301
Miami Beach, FL 33139
Tel: (800) 845–5276
 (305) 673–6688
Jamaica (350).

Jamaica Villa Vacations
31–33 South Prospect Avenue
Park Ridge, IL 60068
Tel: (800) 323–5115
 (847) 698–9303
Jamaica (over 400)

La Cure
11661 San Vicente Boulevard
Suite 1010
Los Angeles, CA 90049
Tel: (800) 387–2726
 (416) 968–2374
Barbados (100), Dominican Republic (20), Grand Cayman (20),
 Jamaica (75), Little Saint James off Saint Thomas in the USVI (pri-
 vate island), Mustique in the Grenadines (40), Necker in the BVI

(private island), Saint Croix in the USVI (10), Saint John in the USVI (20), Saint Lucia (15), Saint Martin (40), Saint Thomas in the USVI (25), Tortola in the BVI (10), Virgin Gorda in the BVI (10).

McLaughlin Anderson Vacations
100 Blackbeard's Hill
Suite 3
Saint Thomas, USVI 00802
Tel: (800) 537–6246
  (809) 776–0635
Grenada (2), Saint Croix in the USVI (6), Saint John in the USVI (6), Saint Thomas in the USVI (35), Tortola in the BVI (7), Virgin Gorda in the BVI (11).

Mustique Company Ltd.
P.O. Box 349
Kingston
Saint Vincent and the Grenadines
West Indies
Tel: (809) 458–4621/456–4565
Owns and operates the entire island of Mustique. Many companies in this list represent houses on the island.

Ocean Property Management
P.O. Box 8529
St. Thomas, USVI 00801
Tel: (800) 874–7897
  (809) 775–2600
Saint Thomas in the USVI (75).

Passport, Ltd.
Dunwoody Creek Circle
Suite 230
Atlanta, GA 30350
Tel: (800) 331–8681
  (770) 998–1725
Barbados (40), Jamaica (38), Saint John in the USVI (6), Saint Thomas in the USVI (43).

Prestige Villas
P.O. Box 1046
Southport, CT 06490
Tel: (800) 336–0080
  (203) 254–1302

Anguilla (2), Antigua (10), Barbados (82), Jamaica (99), Saint Croix in the USVI (10), Saint John in the USVI (42), Saint Martin/Sint Maarten (65), Saint Thomas in the USVI (49), Tortola in the BVI (15), Virgin Gorda in the BVI (18).

Property Rentals International
1 Park West Circle
Suite 108
Midlothian, VA 23113
Tel: (800) 220–3332
   (804) 378–6054
Abaco in the Bahamas (9), Anguilla (18), Antigua (12), Barbados (37), Bermuda (17), Carriacou off Grenada (4), Cooper in the BVI (1), Culebra off Puerto Rico (7), Dominican Republic (16), Eleuthera in the Bahamas (6), Grenada (7), Jamaica (35), New Providence in the Bahamas (5), Providenciales in the Turks & Caicos (14), Puerto Rico (11), Saint Bart (23), Saint Croix in the USVI (41), Saint John in the USVI (25), Saint Kitt's (6), Saint Lucia (17), Saint Martin/Sint Maarten (29), Saint Thomas in the USVI (33), Tobago (3), Tortola in the BVI (17), Virgin Gorda in the BVI (14).

Ralph Locke Islands
806 Broom Way
P.O. Box 492477
Los Angeles, CA 90049
Tel: (800) 223–1108
   (310) 440–4225
Anguilla (1), Aruba (3), Barbados (2), Saint Croix in the USVI (1), Saint Lucia (1), Saint Vincent and the Grenadines (4), Virgin Gorda in the BVI (1).

Rent A Home International
7200 34th Avenue Northwest
Seattle, WA 98117
Tel: (800) 488–7368
   (206) 789–9377
Anguilla (21), Antigua (12), Aruba (18), Bahamas (52), Barbados (39), Bermuda (15), Bonaire (9), Cayman Islands (78), Cooper in the BVI (3), Dominican Republic (15), Grenada (19), Jamaica (52), Montserrat (11), Mustique in the Grenadines (6), Nevis (5), Puerto Rico (30), Saba (6), Saint Bart (22), Saint Croix in the USVI (29), Saint John in the USVI (32), Saint Kitt's (8), Saint Lucia (30), Saint Martin/Sint Maarten (36), Saint Thomas in the USVI

(34), Tobago (8), Tortola in the BVI (18), Turks & Caicos (15), Virgin Gorda in the BVI (10).

Rent A Vacation Everywhere, Inc. (R.A.V.E.)
135 Meigs Street
Rochester, NY 14607
Tel: (716) 256–0760
Anguilla (4), Antigua (5), Bahamas (4), Barbados (10), Bermuda (10), Grand Cayman (12), Jamaica (20), Montserrat (22), New Providence in the Bahamas (1), Saint Bart (3), Saint Croix in the USVI (7), Saint John in the USVI (6), Saint Martin (20), Saint Thomas in the USVI (10), Sint Maarten (15), Tortola in the BVI (4), Virgin Gorda in the BVI (4).

Resorts Management, Inc.
The Carriage House
201½ East 29th Street
New York, NY 10016
Tel: (800) 225–4225
    (212) 696–4566
Guana Island in the BVI (private island), Mustique in the Grenadines (46), Necker Island in the BVI (private island), Pine Cay in the Turks & Caicos (private island), Saint John in the USVI (3).

Saint Barth Properties
2 Master Drive
Franklin, MA 02038
Tel: (800) 421–3396
    (508) 528–7727
Saint Bart or Saint Barth (104).

Tour Host International
141 East 44th Street
Suite 506
New York, NY 10017
Tel: (800) 843–4678
    (212) 953–7910
Barbados (100), Bermuda (25), Grand Cayman (50), Jamaica (200), New Providence in the Bahamas (20), Saint Bart (6), Saint Lucia (10), Saint Martin/Sint Maarten (40), Tobago (10), Trinidad (12), Young Island off Saint Vincent (private island).

Vacation Network
1370 Washington Avenue,
Suite 301
Miami Beach, FL 33139
Tel: (800) 423–4095
   (305) 845–5276
Jamaica (350 through JAVA listed earlier), Grand Cayman (28),
   Saint Lucia (8).

VHR, WORLDWIDE
Vacation Home Rentals
235 Kensington Avenue
Norwood, NJ 07648
Tel: (800) 633–3284
   (201) 767–9393
Anguilla (5), Antigua (9), Aruba (5), Barbados (100), Bonaire (2),
   Cat Island in the Bahamas (1), Darby in the Bahamas (private
   island), Eleuthera in the Bahamas (12), Exuma in the Bahamas
   (5), Grand Bahama (2), Grenada (5), Green Turtle Cay in the
   Abacos of the Bahamas (10), Jamaica (200), Long Island in the
   Bahamas (6), Marsh Harbour in the Abacos of the Bahamas (3),
   Guadeloupe (1), Mustique in the Grenadines (20), Montserrat
   (60), Necker in the BVI (private island), New Providence in the
   Bahamas (4), Peter Island in the BVI (private island), Puerto Rico
   (2), Saint Bart (15), Saint Lucia (15), Saint Martin/Sint Maarten
   (85), Scotland Cay in the Bahamas (private island) Tobago (3),
   Treasure Cay in the Abacos of the Bahamas (60), Providenciales
   in the Turks & Caicos (3), Tortola in the BVI (20), Virgin Gorda
   in the BVI (5), Windermere in the Bahamas (15).

Villa Leisure
P.O. Box 30188
Palm Beach, FL 33420
Tel: (800) 526–4244
   (407) 624–9000
Anguilla (30), Barbados (95), Dominican Republic (100), Grand
   Cayman (30), Jamaica (115), Little Saint James off Saint Thomas
   in the USVI (private island), Mustique in the Grenadines (45),
   Necker in the BVI (private island), Saint John in the USVI (15),
   Saint Lucia (25), Saint Martin/Sint Maarten (49), Saint Thomas in
   the USVI (35), Tortola in the BVI (25), Treasure Cay in the Aba-
   cos of the Bahamas (30), Virgin Gorda in the BVI (15).

Villas & Apartments Abroad
420 Madison Avenue
Suite 1003
New York, NY 10017
Tel: (800) 433–3020
  (212) 759–1025
Anguilla (20), Antigua (15), Barbados (125), Grand Cayman (6), Jamaica (100), Little Saint James in the USVI (private island), Montserrat (20), Mustique in the Grenadines (45), Necker in the BVI (private island), Nevis (8), Saint Croix in the USVI (30), Saint John in the USVI (20), Saint Kitt's (8), Saint Lucia (30), Saint Martin/Sint Maarten (75), Saint Thomas in the USVI (70), Tortola in the BVI (20), Virgin Gorda in the BVI (15).

Villas Carib
6271 South Jamaica Ct.
Englewood, CO 80111
Tel: (800) 645–7498
  (303) 741–2219
Barbados (115), Dominican Republic (6), Grand Cayman (35), Grenada (2), Jamaica (122), Montserrat (32), Saint Croix in the USVI (6), Saint John in the USVI (39), Saint Lucia (16), Saint Martin/Sint Maarten (68), Saint Thomas in the USVI (42), Tortola in the BVI (14), Virgin Gorda in the BVI (19).

Villas International
605 Market Street,
Suite 510
San Francisco, CA 94105
Tel: (800) 221–2260
  (415) 281–0910
Abacos in the Bahamas (15), Antigua (15), Aruba (10), Barbados (100), Bequia in the Grenadines (3), Bermuda (20), Bonaire (5), Dominican Republic (12), Eleuthera in the Bahamas (10), Grand Cayman (15), Guadeloupe (8), Jamaica (175), Martinique (12), Montserrat (5), Mustique in the Grenadines (7), Nevis (8), New Providence in the Bahamas (25), Puerto Rico (8), Saint Bart (25), Saint Croix in the USVI (20), Saint John in the USVI (15), Saint Kitt's (5), Saint Lucia (18), Saint Martin/Sint Maarten (45), Saint Thomas in the USVI (35), Saint Vincent (12), Statia (3), Tortola in the BVI (20), Tobago (3), Trinidad (5), Turks & Caicos (9), Virgin Gorda in the BVI (10).

Villas of Distinction
P.O. Box 55
Armonk, NY 10504
Tel: (800) 289–0900
   (914) 273–3331
Anguilla (20), Antigua (20), Barbados (150), Grand Cayman (40),
   Jamaica (150), Saint Bart (75), Saint John in the USVI (50), Saint
   Thomas in the USVI (50), Tortola in the BVI (15), Virgin Gorda
   in the BVI (30), Saint Martin/Sint Maarten (150), Mustique in the
   Grenadines (30), Saint Lucia (20).

Villa Vacations
52 Burpee Road
Swampscott, MA 01907
Tel: (800) 800–5576
   (617) 593–8885
Anguilla (15), Antigua (15), Barbados (75), Dominican Republic
   (1), Bequia in the Grenadines (1), Grand Cayman (25),
   Grenada (5), Jamaica (25), Montserrat (20), Nevis (5), Saint
   Bart (5), Saint Croix in the USVI (30), Saint John in the USVI
   (35), Saint Kitt's (5), Saint Lucia (10), Saint Martin/Sint Maarten
   (75), Saint Thomas in the USVI (35), Tortola in the BVI (15),
   Virgin Gorda in the BVI (20).

WIMCO
P.O. Box 1461
Newport, RI 02840
Tel: (800) 932–3222
   (401) 849–8012
Anguilla (28), Barbados (110), Jost Van Dyke in the BVI (8), Mus-
   tique in the Grenadines (40), Saba (1), Saint Bart (180), Saint
   Croix in the USVI (37), Saint John in the USVI (35), Saint Mar-
   tin/Sint Maarten (69), Saint Thomas in the USVI (68), Tortola in
   the BVI (25), Virgin Gorda in the BVI (22).

Bed & Breakfasts (B&Bs)

The concept of bed and breakfasts is not as well established in the
Caribbean as in Europe and other areas, but it is growing. These
places are often simple but reasonably comfortable and reasonably
priced. You can get information from the National Tourist Offices
(pp. 18–26) and at local tourist offices once on an island.

Boarding Houses (*casas de huéspedes,* guest houses, *hospedaje, pensión,* pension)

Boarding houses or guest houses go by a variety of names in the region. The definition of these is rather vague, but it generally means someone's home has been converted into a place to stay. There may be a few to a dozen or so rooms, a few more in rare instances. Meals may or may not be included. Most guest houses are quite simple. You'll probably be sharing a bath. Air conditioning is unlikely. What is most attractive about these places are the relatively low price and their true reflection of island life. Some are charming gems, others sparse, and a few grim. Generally, they offer good value and are favorites of budget travelers. Ask about these locally. They're often overlooked in travel guides. Most local tourist offices will give up these secrets if pressed. For example, there are nearly two dozen guest houses in Puerto Rico with 16 right in the main city.

Camping

Not everyone can afford or even wants to stay in hotels. In the Caribbean, there are few organized campgrounds, and some of these are really more like screened-in modest motels. Tent or free-lance camping on bare sites is relatively rare with many disadvantages. There will be those who disagree, ardent campers and budget travelers, but the problems with immigration, finding sites, insects, robbery, safety, and so on, make camping a poor choice in general. Following are some tips.

- On some islands, camping is not allowed at all (as on Anguilla, Antigua, Barbuda, in the Bahamas, on Bonaire, and others). On some it is not advised (as on Montserrat and Saint Lucia). Free-lance camping is allowed during the peak season with police permission or in organized campgrounds on some islands, while it may be allowed without any permission during the off-season. When in doubt, contact the tourist offices (pp. 18–26).
- Areas where camping (either in tents or in enclosures) is most highly recommended: the British Virgin Islands (Anegada, Jost Van Dyke at Tula's, and Tortola at Brewers Bay—the latter is extremely popular); Carriacou (off Grenada); Guadeloupe (Grande Anse Beach); Jamaica (many places); Martinique (many places, including Anse Mitan and Sainte Anne), Puerto Rico (and its offshore islands), and the United States Virgin Islands (Saint John at Cinnamon and Maho Bays). It's also fine on many of the smaller islands with few hotels and fewer visitors. Jamaica and Martinique are the two islands on which camping is particularly popular. Contact the

appropriate tourist boards (see pp. 18–26) for information.
Another good source of camping information on Jamaica:

Jamaica Alternative Tourism, Camping,
    and Hiking Association
P.O. Box 216
Kingston 7, Jamaica
Tel: (809) 927–2097

- Never camp by yourself or in a small group in remote areas.
- Be wary about camping in beach areas, unless you're with a large group.
- In short, you're much better off in recognized campgrounds, which offer protection in numbers. However, such campgrounds are limited.
- Never camp or sleep under a coconut palm. The coconuts drop with an alarming thud—one that can cause a great deal of damage to cars, tents, and unprotected heads. These kill people each year.
- Don't eat any strange fruits. The manzanillo tree has both poisonous sap and poisonous fruit. Don't even camp under it, since the sap can cause a serious rash.
- Always have a place that you can get to when the mosquitoes hit at night. In short, set up your tent well before evening.
- Know your gear before traveling to the islands, which means trying it out at home. Nothing's worse than a so-called waterproof tent that leaks or a mosquito net that's worn through.
- Bring the minimum gear for your brand of camping—for some, that can be quite elaborate.
- Never leave camping gear unattended unless camping in an organized and guarded campground. It will evaporate like water in the tropical sun. Someone should always be close to the camping area. If you stow gear in a truck or car, thieves will smash in the windows to get to it. It's a major headache for campers. This is one of the main problems with free-lance camping.
- If you intend to stay in an organized campground during the peak season, make your reservation as much as a year in advance. The most popular campgrounds are Anegada Beach, (809) 495–9466, on Anegada; Brewer's, (809) 494–3463, on Tortola; and Cinnamon Bay and Mayo Bay on Saint John, (800) 392–9004.

Here are a few items that you will find essential for free-lance camping. Note, however, that some of the campgrounds are already set up with tents or motel-like enclosures, making some of the following gear unnecessary for that particular place.

Air mattress Get the best one available, and bring a patching kit.

Alcohol burner This will be your stove. Alcohol is cheap in the Caribbean.

Canteen The best canvas canteens breathe and cool the water even in the hottest weather.

Flashlight Absolutely essential. Bring a few extra batteries.

Grill This should be tiny, just large enough to cook something on. Carry it in a plastic or canvas bag.

Insect repellent The little stick kind is the most convenient. Get a really strong one (no less than 35 percent DEET).

Knife Don't get anything too fancy or shiny. It will be confiscated by the police. A decent Swiss Army knife with a bottle opener is best.

Lantern Not essential, but really nice.

Matches One container of waterproof matches.

Mosquito netting The single most important item to carry.

Plastic containers Enough for a variety of solid and liquid foods.

Pots For cooking.

Sleeping bag Can be replaced with a blanket or hammock.

Tent Featherlight.

Toilet paper Needed everywhere.

Tools To match your brand of camping.

Water containers Need a gallon of water per day per person.

Cabins (*cabañas*)

In the Dominican Republic you may find little cabins for rent. These are often located in isolated or scenic areas and aimed at people who really want to get off the beaten path. Most are very inexpensive.

Club Med

There are Club Meds throughout the Caribbean. Varying clubs appeal to singles, couples, and families or a combination. Here are the locations and orientation: the Dominican Republic (family); Eleuthera in the Bahamas (family); Guadeloupe (couples and families—mostly European); Martinique (singles); Paradise Island connected to New Providence in the Bahamas (couples); Saint Lucia (family); San Salvador in the Bahamas (couples); and the Turks and Caicos (singles and couples). These vacation resorts combine elegance and casual living with good food and good times. Costs tend to be on the high side but are a good value. For information on all of these villages, call the toll-free number and ask for the lovely, full-color magazine titled *Club Med Vacations*. Most of these are all-inclusive resorts, but ask what is not included in the price to avoid any misunderstandings.

Club Med
40 West 57th Street
New York, NY 10019
Tel: (800) 258–2633
   (212) 977–2100

Clubs

On a few islands you'll find private clubs. You'll hear about these through word of mouth. These are often quite lovely, but reserved for members only. Some may allow guests during off-periods at the invitation of members. The Mill Reef Club on Antigua is just an example.

Condominiums

These are a variation of apartments. They may be inexpensive to ultra-expensive, depending upon the individual condo, the location, or the island on which they are located. Information on these is available from the National Tourist Offices and from companies mentioned under apartments. They have the same advantages and disadvantages mentioned under that category.

Cottage Colonies

Bermuda is the island best known for cottage colonies. These are similar to a club. Often small cottages surround a central clubhouse. You may be served delicious breakfasts in either the cottages or the central clubhouse. Most cottage colonies offer safe swimming in a pool, tennis, and quite formal dining at night. They are usually sophisticated and relatively expensive, but still a good value in the upper bracket. They are excellent for families, particularly ones with older children.

Fishing Hotels

There are certain people who go to the Caribbean to fish—and that's it. Fishing hotels are unique. They're friendly, club-like, and very original. In some hotels you won't find telephones and TVs, because no one wants them. Such hotels attract a special breed of traveler—sophisticated and fun. Many of these hotels can be reached by private plane or charter flights. See Fishing (pp. 277–279).

Gîtes

This is really the French equivalent of a B&B or a home stay. You can get information on these on any of the French-speaking islands. It helps if you speak French well, but it certainly isn't essential. On Martinique alone there are over 200 of these.

Guest Houses (see **Boarding Houses**)

A guest house usually means either a private home with rooms or a small hotel. Some guest houses also serve other purposes, with rooms rented by the hour.

Home Exchange

Home exchange is one way of keeping travel costs down. It is not as practical in the Caribbean as in other areas because the number of properties is limited; most are homes of fellow Canadians and Americans. Here are a few tips on home exchange.

- If you want to exchange your home, get it listed at least a year in advance. People make plans far ahead for this type of arrangement.
- The more flexible you are in regard to dates, the better your chance for an exchange.
- Clean out areas so that people will have plenty of closet space.
- Clean out the refrigerator.
- Discuss exactly how payment will be made for utilities. It's best to have these paid for in advance.
- Leave numbers for possible repair problems, such as for air conditioners, appliances, electrical items, pools or spas, water softeners, and so on. It should be clearly stated that if someone breaks anything they will replace or fix it.
- Maid service and temporary yard care could be included in the exchange. Or, at the very least a thorough cleaning by a professional at the end of the stay should be. No one wants to spend part of their vacation cleaning house.
- A deposit for long-distance phone calls is certainly appropriate. Or there should be an agreement that no long-distance calls that could be charged to the home phone will be made at all.
- Some people allow guests to use cars. I strongly advise against this. In fact, non-use of any motorized vehicle should be specified in the agreement. However, it is helpful to have bikes available at no cost. Again, it should be clear that you're not liable for their use and that they should be left in the same condition as when first used. If you disregard the advice on motorized vehicles, leave a permission letter for their use. Discuss this at length with your insurance agent.
- Discuss too the concept of home exchange with your insurance agent so that the belongings and home itself will be fully insured. You may have to take out a special policy for full coverage or even switch companies.
- Treat all belongings and the home itself as if it were your own. If

you break something, replace or pay for it. Tell anyone if you
have caused damage. It's very irritating for someone to discover
damage after the fact. Goodwill is the basis for home exchange.

- Discuss pets in advance. Many people do not want pets of any
  kind in their homes. Traveling with pets is a hassle and to be
  avoided if at all possible.

- Never leave irreplaceable items in the home. Place these in a
  safety deposit box or with a friend.

- Discuss the use of available food and liquor in advance. Often, the
  easiest policy is simple replacement of whatever is used. Or no
  use at all.

- Home exchange requires a great deal of trust, and you have every
  right to get as much information on the other person as possible.
  Ask agencies to help you in this regard.

- The following organizations specialize in home exchange for a set
  fee.

Intervac US
P.O. Box 590504
San Francisco, CA 94159
Tel: (800) 756–4663
   (415) 435–3497
(Offers a limited number
   of homes)

Vacation Exchange Club
P.O. Box 650
Key West, FL 33041
Tel: (800) 638–3841
   (305) 294–1448
(Offers approximately 150
homes throughout the
region)

Homes (Rooms in Private Homes)

The wages on many islands are extremely low. To gain additional
income, residents often open their homes to guests. Accommodations
are usually basic. You probably won't have a private bathroom. Meals
may or may not be offered. The cost is usually much lower than that
of a budget hotel. If you get along well with your hosts, it can be an
extremely enjoyable experience. You'll also be staying with people
who really know the island and can lead you to places that could easily be overlooked by the average tourist. These places are ideal for
travelers on a strict budget who really enjoy mingling with people.

Hotels (see Inns)

The variety in hotels is staggering. Some are truly first-class, comparable to deluxe hotels anywhere. Others are small and unpretentious.
Price ranges from inexpensive to exorbitant (even outrageous).
Travel agents and travel guides are your best resources in comparing
these, but many places are omitted because they do not fall into the
higher price category. Get information on smaller and less expensive
hotels from the appropriate tourist agencies, pp. 18–26.

Inns (*auberges, paradores, posadas*)

What separates an inn from an intimate hotel is debatable. Perhaps in many cases they are really the same, but most inns are family operated or owned. The ones most sought after are those that really reflect island life. The food is local, often including fresh seafood and tropical fruits. The number of rooms may be limited to under 50 and not be as spacious as those in larger resorts, but they are often decorated in local style. These are places where you'll get to know the owners, who often serve as managers or chefs. They are involved with the community and really care about their guests. Many inns have no air conditioning, no television, no telephones in the rooms; but they are special. So too may be their surroundings: Gardens with tropical flowers, courtyards for moonlight dining or casual breakfasts, views to red sunsets or shimmering seas—very special. Prices tend to be moderately expensive to ultra-expensive on most islands.

Jungle Lodges

The Caribbean isn't like Central America, where you'll find numerous jungle lodges that have been carved out of rain forests and offer spectacular settings for birding and viewing wildlife. However, see the section on birding in the chapter on Doing Things for a lodge which fits this description and must be booked months in advance.

Motels

While there are some motels in the Caribbean, the word *motel* generally refers to a bordello, especially in Spanish-speaking areas. Renting rooms by the hour is not exactly what this section is all about. So if someone smirks when you ask for a motel, now you know why.

Paradores

On Puerto Rico, there is a network of 18 inns sponsored by the government. These are located throughout the island in scenic settings near popular tourist attractions. Prices for all of them during the peak season are under $100 for two, including service and tax. All are relatively clean and comfortable, but don't expect most to be charming or romantic as are those of Spain. For a free pamphlet describing each inn and its nearest attractions contact:

Paradores Puertorriqueños
P.O. Box 4435
301 Calle San Justo
Viejo San Juan, Puerto Rico 00902
Tel: (800) 443–0266 (in the U.S.)
  (800) 981–7575 (in Puerto Rico)
  (809) 721–2884

Private Islands

There are really several types of private islands in the Caribbean. One is called "private" because it is owned by one person or a single company, but, in reality, you may find many villas and hotel rooms available. These islands are often lovely, not terribly crowded, but not truly private as they are advertised. Mustique with its Cotton House Hotel and myriad villas is a prime example. The second type of private island is just that—controlled totally by you or a group of people including you. No one else is allowed on the island. Several of these are available and offer extravagant and appropriately expensive hideaways. Necker immediately comes to mind. Others are resort islands, lovely and expensive, such as Jumby Bay on Long Island or the Meridian Club on Pine Cay. Following are islands which fall into these broad categories. Most are represented by companies listed in the apartment, condo, home, and villa section earlier in the chapter. They will send you detailed and lovely brochures on the islands or properties. Most travel agents are familiar with the majority of these islands as well. A few not mentioned are geared primarily to fishermen and scuba divers. These are more or less "controlled" by companies catering to these sports (see pp. 271–308). And a couple are handled by local agents only. Following are some of the private islands with at least one contact number listed after the island (additional representatives have been listed earlier): **Cooper** 5 miles off Tortola in the BVI (800) 220–3332 or (800) 488–7368; **Guana Island** in the BVI (800) 225–4225; **Ilet Oscar** and **Ilet Thierry** (known locally as Les Ilets de L'Impératrice) off Martinique (596) 65 82 30; **Little Saint James** off Saint Thomas in the USVI (800) 426–6367; **Long Island** with the Jumby Bay resort off Antigua (800) 437–0049; **Marina Cay** just north of Beef Island in the BVI (809) 494–2174; **Mosquito Island** off Gun Creek on Virgin Gorda in the BVI (800) 624–6651; **Mustique** in the Grenadines (800) 225–4225; **Necker Island** just north of Virgin Gorda in the BVI (800) 225–4225 or (800) 624–6651; **Palm Island** in the Grenadines (800) 776–7256; **Parrot Cay** in the Turks & Caicos (800) 777–2022; **Peter Island** off Tortola in the BVI (800) 346–4451 or (800) 223–6800; **Petit Saint Vincent** 4 miles off Union Island in the Grenadines (800) 654–9326, (800) 525–3833, or (800) 223–6800; **Pine Cay** 5 miles northeast of Providenciales in the Turks & Caicos (800) 225–2225 or (800) 331–9154; **Windermere Island** connected to Eleuthera in the Bahamas (800) 633–3284; **Young Island** barely off Saint Vincent (800) 223–1108.

Plantations

Either a former or currently operating plantation, which generally refers to a great house surrounded by extensive fields or groves of trees under cultivation. Many on Nevis and Saint Kitt's.

Relais Créoles

Some of the French islands, particularly Martinique, offer an island equivalent to the mother country's famous Relais de campagne. You can get a free booklet from the National Tourist Office (see p. 23) that lists these inns. Some are terrific, others just okay. Naturally, the tourist office would be reluctant to tell you which ones are outstanding. Take the booklet to a travel agent who knows Martinique well and ask which are the better inns. Things to keep in mind are location on the island, the inn's reputation for good food, and the overall atmosphere of the inn itself. Also, these inns tend to be quite expensive overall, but a good value if you choose the property wisely. Remember that agents have excellent books describing many of these places. Again, a little reading between the lines can lead you to a gem. Many of these are truly romantic hideaways, some with terrific views in lush settings.

Resorts

Travel agents are a good resource in helping you choose a resort and make reservations. Normally, there is no charge involved for reservations, but ask to be sure. However, since you'll probably be staying in a resort for a week or more, this is one time you should ask lots of questions. Below is a resort question checklist to help you get exactly what you want. The checklist is meant only to point out that glossy brochures are just that—paper with some words written on them. Photographers can do marvelous things with next-to-nothing. The questions you ask can help you get what you want. Requesting what you want is smart because it increases your odds of getting it. But in the Caribbean you should have a somewhat relaxed attitude. Things do go wrong. Keep expectations realistic. So what if you don't have hot water for a day or for your whole stay?

Resort Checklist

Working with an Agent
☐ Has the agent been to the resort? When? For how long?
☐ Save the agent a lot of time by telling them your price range. You may have to modify it or the island you want to go to if you're demanding.

Cost Considerations for a Typical Resort
☐ What is the charge for a room?
☐ Are all local taxes included in the price quoted?

☐ Are all service charges included in the price quoted? Most hotels add a service charge automatically, supposedly to cover tips to servants.

☐ Is there an energy charge or any other charge not included in the price?

☐ What is the charge for any and all extras, from food to fishing?

☐ Is the transfer from the airport to the hotel included in the price? What happens if there is no one there to meet you? Will you get reimbursed if you take a taxi to the hotel?

☐ In short, if a resort is not all-inclusive, then you should expect to pay for everything separately as if you were dining à la carte.

Cost Considerations for an All-inclusive Resort

Cruise lines in the Caribbean have had an impact on local hotels. One of the great advantages of cruises is that you know what your overall trip expense is going to be from the start. All-inclusive resorts offer the same advantage to guests. You pay a flat fee to get everything at a set price. The term everything is the red flag. Some places really do mean everything: room, meals, drinks, sports equipment rental, fees for tennis and golf, transfers to and from the airport, local tours—everything. Others mean, well, almost everything. You have to ask for a complete list of what is included in the overall price. A few examples to show how specific you must be:

☐ Can drinks be made from any brand of alcohol?

☐ Is a minimum stay required?

☐ Is there a cut-off time for room service?

☐ Are babysitters available at no cost?

☐ Are dining privileges extended to other resorts?

☐ The most important question: Is there anything at all not included in this price?

☐ Two islands noted for their all-inclusives are Jamaica and Saint Lucia.

Refunds

☐ If the place doesn't match your expectations, can you cancel and get a refund?

Location of Hotel on the Island

☐ How far is the resort from the airport?

☐ Is the resort in the thick of things or off the beaten path?

☐ How isolated is the resort?

☐ What are the surroundings like? Is it lush or arid? Low or high up? Get specifics.

☐ Is it near your favorite activity or something you really want to see? How near?

☐ Can you get a map showing the exact location of the hotel on the island? You certainly better be able to.

Management

☐ Who's running the show?
☐ Is it owner-operated, and is the owner on the premises?
☐ If there's a problem, who handles it?

Clientele

☐ What kind of people go to the hotel? Does it take tours? Is it family-oriented? Do many singles go there? Does it allow cruise-ship passengers for meals?
☐ How old are most of the people who go to the resort?
☐ Is the clientele mostly North American or European?

Ambiance

☐ Is this a glitzy or low-key place?
☐ Are there any dress codes?
☐ Is it personal, or does it tend to be discreet, meaning you'll be left alone unless you ask for something specifically? Both have their advantages.

Overall Layout of the Place

☐ Is it a large or small hotel? Would you call it intimate? Or is it a large commercial complex?
☐ Is a map showing the exact location of buildings and rooms available?
☐ Is there a road between the hotel and beach (very noisy and disagreeable)? How close are other hotels to this hotel? How far from a main road is the hotel?

Age

☐ When was the hotel built?
☐ When was it last remodeled?
☐ Has it been harmed by any recent storms?

Location of Room on Premises

☐ Will the hotel specify the room you'll be getting?
☐ Is it where you want it to be? Some people want to be close to the beach, the pool, or some other area. Others might prefer to be isolated and away from the action. You should know where your room is.
☐ What floor is the room on? Many places don't have elevators. Also, rooms higher up often have better views and better air circulation.

Type of Room

- [ ] What kind of rooms are available? Any special rooms? Any special suites? Any villas?
- [ ] What is the exact size of your room or rooms?
- [ ] What kind of beds do they have? Many have twins with doubles being scarce.
- [ ] How many bathrooms does it have?
- [ ] Is there a tub or just a shower?
- [ ] Are beach towels provided?
- [ ] Does the room have a kitchen?
- [ ] Does it have a refrigerator? Is it stocked?
- [ ] Does the room have air conditioning or a fan or neither? At certain times of year you'd pay anything to have air conditioning (trust me).
- [ ] Will your room face the ocean directly? Or will your room have an ocean view (a euphemism for seeing the water out of the corner of your eye while leaning over the balcony).
- [ ] The room has a balcony? Great! What size is it? Can it be used? Does it have a table and chairs? Can breakfast be served there? Is there any extra cost for such service?

Food

- [ ] Is the resort known for its food?
- [ ] What kind of food does it serve?
- [ ] Is there a wide range of choices on the menu at each meal?
- [ ] What items are included in the price of a meal or excluded?

Transportation

- [ ] Is there free transportation to and from the airport?
- [ ] Will the hotel provide free bikes to its guests (very nice touch)?
- [ ] Does the hotel have rental cars?
- [ ] Is there a parking lot? Is it free to guests?
- [ ] Does the hotel have a free shuttle for sightseeing or getting to special places on the island?
- [ ] Is it near a stop for public transportation?

Activities

- [ ] Is the hotel on or near the beach? Does the beach come right up to the hotel?
- [ ] What's the beach like? How wide is it? What's the sand like? Are there beach chairs?
- [ ] Is the water good for swimming? Is it clear enough for snorkeling? Can you swim in the area? Is there an undertow, riptides, or any problem swimming in the area?

☐ Are there any rooms with access directly to the beach?

☐ What kind of activities are available—both land and water related?

☐ Is the equipment operating?

☐ If you're into a specific sport, get full details. Example: How many windsurfing boards are there? What kind? What condition? Who pays for equipment if it breaks? All of this sounds silly, but I know one person who ended up spending a fortune to replace broken parts on rundown equipment because he didn't ask these kinds of questions in advance.

☐ What does the resort specialize in? Some resorts are geared to golf, tennis, or riding, while others offer pools with swim-up bars and hibiscus flowers floating in pineapples filled with potent drinks.

☐ Does the hotel have a pool? If so, is it used or just a token pool? Does it have water in it (no joke—some don't!)? Is it kept up? Does it have a lifeguard (very few do)? Are there chaise longues or hammocks for the guests? Is it in a good, open location or blocked off from the sun much of the day?

☐ Does the hotel have tennis courts? How many? Do you have to pay extra to use them? What surface do they have? Are they maintained? Is there a pro? What about equipment for sale? Are courts lit for night play? How far in advance do you have to make reservations? Do guests have priority?

☐ Is there a golf course? How far in advance do reservations have to be made? What are the greens fees? Are there carts, and do they work? What's the best time of year to play? Is there a pro? Any equipment for rent or sale? What's the cost? Who has priority?

☐ What kind of water sports are there? Are masks and fins available? What about boats? Windsurfing? Water skiing? Parasailing? Fishing? How much do they cost? Is the equipment in good shape?

Weather

☐ What's the weather like at this time of year? Is it humid? Is it windy? Okay, no one can tell you what the weather is going to be like for sure, but they can tell you what it is likely to be like, so ask!

Restaurants

As strange as it may sound, some very fine restaurants offer a few rooms to discriminating guests. You'll find out about these through newsletters and word of mouth.

Spas

There are a number of spas in the Caribbean, primarily on Jamaica and Puerto Rico. The following company specializes in spa vacations.

Custom Spa Vacations
1318 Beacon Street
Suite 5
Brookline, MA 02146
Tel: (800) 443–7727
   (617) 566–5144
Aruba (2), Jamaica (2), Martinique (1), Puerto Rico (4), Saint Lucia (1).

Townhalls (*préfets, municipalidades*)

You don't actually sleep in townhalls, but they are often a source of information for places to stay. This is especially true when traveling in more remote areas on French- or Spanish-speaking islands.

Villas

(see **Apartments**)

Yachts

Yachts are covered under inter-island transportation, a separate chapter. In areas such as the British Virgin Islands nearly 50 percent of the people are living on yachts.

Overall Cost

How much a place will cost is a major consideration. Costs vary from as little as twenty dollars a night to over two thousand for two people sharing a room. *Whenever you get a rate quoted, ask whether this includes all charges, including those for taxes and service.*

General Guidelines on Cost

- The cost of travel to the Bahamas, Bermuda, and the Caribbean is directly related to the weather. The season when people prefer to travel is referred to as the peak or in-season, while the remaining months are referred to as the slow or off-season. Rates in most hotels drop by as much as 50 percent in the off-season. However, some hotels shut down in October and November.
- The larger the population of an island, the greater the variety in

accommodations. Barbados, the Dominican Republic, and Jamaica are good examples of heavily populated islands with everything from simple, inexpensive lodgings to ultra-deluxe resorts.

- Isolated islands can either have inexpensive places to stay (Dominica) or be overpriced in catering to a sophisticated clientele seeking isolation (Barbuda). You must study the section on itineraries to know what you're in for.
- Places that can afford to advertise or pay travel agents a commission are likely to be more expensive than places listed in local hotel association handouts. The latter are usually just one-color brochures that list hotels with prices. Generally there are no comments about the hotels. Later in the chapter you'll find a list of island-by-island hotel associations. Call or fax them for information if you are really more interested in low-cost rooms than in comfort.

Types of Rates

All-inclusive or ALL means that all of the costs in a resort are included in the price (read the section on All-Inclusive Resorts in this chapter for additional tips). The term (Full) American Plan or (F)AP (full room and board) means that you're staying in a hotel and eating all three meals there. Modified American Plan or MAP (half room and board) indicates that you're skipping either lunch or dinner at the hotel. In most hotels it usually means lunch is left out. European Plan or EP means you're paying for a room only. Continental Plan or CP means you get breakfast with your room. Breakfast may be continental (rolls and something to drink) or American (a full breakfast). The latter may be listed as FB (full breakfast) in some guides.

Keeping Costs Down

There is a general feeling among many travelers that the Caribbean is extremely expensive. It can be. However, there are many ways of keeping costs down.

General Tips on Reducing Lodging Costs

- Don't travel alone. The cost of single rooms is almost always close to that of a double.
- If you travel in the off-season, your costs generally plummet. The off-season varies a little from island to island, but it's generally

from mid-April to mid-December in the Caribbean and the reverse on Bermuda far to the north. Discounts are often 50 percent or more unless some special event is taking place (always ask about festivals and special events when deciding when to travel). Free calendars are available from the tourist offices (see pp. 18–26). And good travel agents know when these special events or festivities are taking place. The price of rooms may double or even triple during these events, whether in the peak season or off-season.

- If you are willing to stay in a B&B, a guest house, or similar lodging you will reduce your costs dramatically.
- If you would enjoy traveling with a group or another couple, you can share the cost of an apartment, condo, house, or villa. Some of these are reasonably priced. The cost per person ends up being more than reasonable.
- Never rule out tour packages or special incentives for honeymooners. So you get married 15 times. If it saves you money and gets you into a special place at a reduced rate, play the game. Find out about these packages from the tourist offices (pp. 18–26), island hotel associations (p. 144), and from magazines catering to honeymooners, such as *Bride's* and *Modern Bride*.
- Reserve far in advance and ask agents to get you preferred rates for early bookings. Avoid paying the rack or advertised rate by working with a skilled agent who knows the ropes.
- Read *Caribbean Travel & Life* and *Islands* magazines. These often offer special incentives to readers who study their ads carefully.

Discounts Through Travel Clubs

A number of fee-based clubs offer both hotel and restaurant discounts for members. These offer cards or coupons to reduce hotel costs by as much as 50 percent. Most properties are in the expensive to very expensive category, so that savings can be substantial. Fees vary by club. If you want to stay in upper-bracket hotels, these cards make sense. Find out the number and location of hotels offered in making your choice of club or clubs. Once a member, make reservations as far in advance as possible. If purchasing a package, get specifics on the point of embarkation. Buy trip cancellation insurance. In peak holiday periods these clubs may be of little value. In the off-season you don't need a club to get a large discount. You just ask for it. *So whether joining a club makes sense depends on whether they can get you discounts at all times of the year*. The islands and number of properties on each follow the organization names.

Carte Royale
1 Premier Plaza
5605 Glen Ridge Drive
Atlanta, GA 30342
Tel: (800) 847–7002
    (404) 250–9950
Bermuda (1), Grand Bahama (1), and New Providence (2).

Encore
4501 Forbes Boulevard
Lanham, MD 20706
Tel: (800) 638–0930
Anguilla (6), Antigua (4), Aruba (3), Bahamas (5), Barbados (1),
    Bermuda (2), Curaçao (1), Dominican Republic (9), Guadeloupe
    (2), Jamaica (3), Martinique (2), Nevis (1), Puerto Rico (5), Saint
    Barthélémy or Saint Barts (1), Saint Croix (4), Saint John (2),
    Saint Kitt's (3), Saint Lucia (1), Saint Martin (2), Saint Thomas (5),
    Sint Maarten (2), Tortola (1), and Trinidad (2).

Entertainment Publications
P.O. Box 1068
Trumbull, CT 06611
Tel: (800) 285–5525
Represents hotels on these islands but number of hotels varies
    yearly and was not available: Antigua, Aruba, the Bahamas,
    Bermuda, Curaçao, Dominican Republic, Grenada, Jamaica,
    Puerto Rico, Saint Kitt's, Saint Martin/Sint Maarten, Saint Lucia,
    Saint Thomas, and Turks & Caicos.

Hotel Express
4405 Beltwood Parkway North
Dallas, TX 75244
Tel: (800) 866–2015
    (214) 991–5482
Bahamas (3), Bermuda (2), British Virgin Islands (1), Dominican
    Republic (15), Jamaica (1), Puerto Rico (16), Saint Croix (1),
    Saint Kitt's (1), Saint Lucia (1), and Saint Thomas (1).

IGT
1111 Lincoln Road
Miami Beach, FL 33139
Tel: (800) 444–8872
    (305) 534–6300
Bahamas (2), Jamaica (11), Saint Barthélémy or Saint Barts (1), and
    Saint Lucia (1).

INFINET Travel Club
P.O. Box 1033
186 Alewife Brook Parkway
Cambridge, MA 02140
Tel: (800) 883–4482
    (617) 553–4300
Anguilla (1), Antigua (1), Aruba (7), Barbados (1), Bermuda (1),
    Bonaire (1), Curaçao (1), Jamaica (2), Nevis (2), Saint
    Barthélémy or Saint Barts (1), Puerto Rico (11), Saint Croix (1),
    Saint Kitt's (5), Saint Martin (2), Sint Eustatius or Statia (1), and
    Trinidad (1).

International Travel Card (ITC–50)
6001 North Clark Street
Chicago, IL 60660
Tel: (800) 342–0558
    (312) 465–8891
Anguilla (1), Aruba (7), Barbados (1), Bermuda (1), Bonaire (1),
    Curaçao (1), Jamaica (2), Nevis (2), Puerto Rico (11), Saint
    Barthélémy or Saint Barts (1), Saint Croix (1), Saint Kitt's (5),
    Saint Martin (1), Sint Eustatius or Statia (1), Sint Maarten (1), and
    Trinidad (1).

Last Minute Travel
1249 Boylston Street
Boston, MA 02215
Tel: (800) 527–8646
    (617) 267–9800
Sells packages to these islands, including air and hotels: Antigua;
    Aruba; the Bahamas—Grand Bahama, New Providence;
    Bermuda; Saint Martin/ Sint Maarten; Turks & Caicos—Providen-
    ciales. Packages to other destinations open up regularly, so call
    ahead to see what's available at the moment.

Privilege Card
3391 Peachtree Road Northeast
Suite 110
Atlanta, GA 30326
Tel: (800) 236–9732
    (404) 262–0222
Barbados (3), Curaçao (2), Dominican Republic (5), Grand Bahama
    (4), Grand Cayman (6), Jamaica (10), New Providence (3),
    Puerto Rico (2), Saint Croix (3), Saint Kitt's (3), Saint Thomas (1),
    Saint Vincent (1), and Sint Maarten (2).

Quest International
402 East Yakima Avenue,
Suite 1200
Yakima, WA 98901
Tel: (800) 325–2400
   (509) 248–7512
New Providence (1), Puerto Rico (4), Saint Croix (2), and Saint
   Kitt's (1).

Discounts Through Consolidators

As with planes, some agencies specialize in buying blocks of rooms at a
set rate to sell at a discount to the public. Many of the companies specializing in discount airfare do the same with rooms (see p. 111–115).

Room Reservations

Reservations are not necessarily essential for enjoyable travel, but
they certainly can help, especially for brief and highly organized
trips. A poorly made reservation may be worse than none at all, however. Here are some tips on doing it right.

When Reserving a Room Makes Sense

- Have a reservation for the first night in the Caribbean. Since you'll
  be exhausted when you arrive, you don't want to look for a room.
- Make reservations if you want rooms of great charm or value,
  especially during the peak season.
- Always have room reservations if you're traveling in holiday periods, such as Christmas or Easter.
- Throughout the Caribbean it is almost impossible to get a room
  during some of the major festivals. If you want to see Carnival in
  Trinidad, you'd better reserve a room a year in advance.
- If you're on a short trip with little time to waste, have reservations
  for every night. You can't afford the hassle or the time involved in
  looking for rooms on your own.
- Have rooms reserved for resort vacations if you want to stay in
  fancy and famous hotels—these fill up months in advance during
  the peak season.
- Have room reservations for special-interest lodges months in
  advance for peak season travel.
- On islands with extremely limited accommodations have reservations for any time of year. A few islands have no more than a
  hotel or two.

Disadvantages of Reservations

- You may have to pay a fee for room reservations and also foot the cost of faxes or telephone calls.
- You're usually renting sight unseen. Unless you have great confidence in your source, you may end up disappointed.
- You'll end up paying for higher-priced rooms or paying the highest price a room will rent for. Reservations take away your bargaining power, and make it very difficult for you to shift from one room to another.
- Reservations tie you down. If you're on a short trip, this will make no difference, but when a trip stretches to 3 weeks or longer, a reservation schedule can begin to feel like an ill-fitting shoe on a 10-mile hike.
- If you cancel a reservation, you may not be able to get your deposit back. More about this later.

Avoiding Getting Bumped by Hotels

You want to make sure to make your reservation correctly to avoid getting bumped.

- Make reservations as far in advance as possible. For hotels in resort areas during the peak season, this could mean booking a room a year in advance.
- Get your reservations confirmed in writing. Most hotels are now doing this by fax. This written confirmation is critical. Bring it with you.
- If you'll be arriving at a hotel after 6:00 P.M., have this late arrival time noted on your room confirmation slip.
- Pay a substantial deposit on the room. With money in the bank, hotels are less likely to bump you. Deposits are commonly required by better hotels.
- If you make reservations through a travel agent, choose one with clout—you will have someone to lean on if things go wrong.
- If you get delayed unexpectedly (very common), notify the hotel. Few hotels will rent out a room if you have contacted them. Get the name of the person you talk to.

Canceling a Room

The refund policy of hotels varies with each hotel. In some instances, you may lose your entire deposit for canceling a room too late. Or you may lose your payment if you leave early after discovering that the place doesn't meet your expectations.

- Before making a reservation requiring a deposit, ask for a copy of the cancellation policy—in writing.
- Working with an agent doing a lot of business with a property greatly increases your odds of a refund.
- Getting money refunded can be difficult. Pay as little down as possible.
- Consider using a credit card. The charge will be billed months in advance, but if they refuse reimbursement unreasonably, the credit card company may help you get a refund. I say *may help you* because, in many instances, they really don't. That's why I recommend using an agent familiar with the property.
- If you are dissatisfied with your room, talk to the general manager before leaving. Make sure that you will get a refund. It's best to get the refund immediately. At worst, get a promise for a refund in writing.

Travel Agents' Reservations

- Most agents charge nothing at all for making room reservations, unless doing so involves a special service, such as faxing or telephoning (their commission is paid by the hotel).
- Ask the agent whether you'll be charged for faxes or telephone calls—or for anything else, for that matter.
- If the agent insists that there is no charge at all, ask whether a surcharge could be added to your hotel bill on the other end.
- If the agent says that no such commission need be paid, ask for a letter typed on the agency stationery stating this in straightforward terms. If a hotel then tries to stick you with a surcharge, produce the letter and refuse to pay.

Making Your Own Reservations

- Larger hotel chains with many establishments have toll-free 800 numbers listed in the phone book or available from information calling (800) 555–1212. All you have to do is to dial the number and make a reservation. Repeat dates, and ask them to send you some sort of confirmation in writing. Also ask for a reservation or confirmation number. You'll usually be asked for a credit card number to make such a reservation.
- When using toll-free numbers, call more than once before making a reservation. Ask for the lowest price possible. This is similar to the tip of calling airlines more than once. You don't want to pay the advertised or rack rate, but the "preferred" rate. After getting a price quote from an 800 number, you might ask a travel agent to beat the price (they often can).

- Some of the larger chains, such as Best Western, have free hotel guides describing their properties in the Caribbean. These can be quite helpful in knowing rates by island and property. Request one of these in advance of making a firm reservation. They normally take about 3 weeks to be delivered to your home or office. The Best Western guide is in the form of an atlas with maps.
- Most hotels, even small ones, use faxes. Request a room by fax, giving all pertinent information and ask for a confirmation in writing by fax. If you have a choice, use faxes rather than phones. Phone reservations are frequently bungled.
- Where there is a language barrier, especially with small hotels, it is especially important to use a fax. Also make it clear that you want the price quoted for a specific number of people occupying the room. In non-English-speaking countries the owners may state that the price quoted was per person. Iron this out in advance.
- Whenever getting a price quote, ask that it include all taxes and possible service charges. For example, on the Dominican Republic there's a 23 percent room tax and a 10 to 15 percent service fee (tip). Imagine the difference between your final bill and the quoted price if you didn't have these included in the initial quote.

Packing

Pack as light as you possibly can, especially if you'll be island hopping. Planes are small and restrictions tight on luggage. You'll often be carrying your own bags, and it's usually hot and humid. Really hot at times. Never forget to pack patience. You'll need it for clearing immigration and customs, long lines to exchange money, delayed flights, and so on. Patience is the number one requirement for travel in the Caribbean.

Dress in the Caribbean

- Dress is extremely casual in most areas. Rarely is a man expected to wear a coat and tie or comparable dress for a woman.
- Formal dress is only necessary for business meetings, when dining out in elegant restaurants, and in a few resorts or clubs. Formal dress may or may not mean wearing a tie. Simply wearing a jacket is often enough.
- The average tourist can get by with simple, casual clothes—nothing stylish at all. In fact, smart travelers keep a low profile while traveling in a region that is quite poor.
- Casual clothing is fine. Dirty or patched clothing is considered offensive—as are clothes with holes in them. You're inviting hassles with immigration if you dress inappropriately.
- Also, skimpy clothing is offensive anywhere but on the beach. Cover up modestly and within reason everywhere else.

Dress Comfortably

- Read the section on when to travel so that you'll match your clothes to the prevailing weather. In general, you do not need warm clothing except for Bermuda during the winter and for hiking into higher regions on mountainous islands during the winter season.
- Bring something warm even though 90 percent of the time you won't need it. Occasionally, a restaurant or hotel will go overboard with air conditioning.
- Bring layers of clothes rather than bulky items. As the temperature drops, add layer upon layer.
- Most of your clothes should be cotton or cotton-blend. Cotton

breathes in hot climates, which makes it the most comfortable fabric to wear.

- Wear light-colored clothes. Local residents wear a lot of white for obvious reasons. The color reflects light. White is hard to keep clean, however, and tan makes a good substitute.
- Keep your clothes loose. Tight-fitting clothing is uncomfortable in hot weather. On women it is sexually provocative and can cause serious problems (see pp. 227–229).
- Have a hat. If you forget, buy one in the islands. Caps, visors, tennis hats, floppy fishing hats—any of these are fine to protect you from the sun. Ideally, a hat will have a 4-inch brim to protect your nose and ears from serious burns.
- Keep your shoes comfortable. Forget style. Shoes can be very casual. Many young and old travelers wear nothing but canvas tennis shoes for the whole trip. Visiting ruins, climbing steep stairs, walking on rough streets, strolling along a beach—these are activities that require comfortable, casual shoes. No one cares in the least whether you're fashionable or not (except in discos and elegant restaurants or resorts). More expensive walking shoes are another good option with a spare pair of cheap, canvas tennis shoes for getting into the water. Inexpensive sandals are ideal for beaches and walking into the water. They dry out faster than canvas tennis shoes.
- If you'll be hiking, bring comfortable boots that give firm support but are well broken in. They should tie tightly around your ankle.
- Coats, pants, shirts—all should have lots of pockets. Add pockets if necessary. Each pocket should close tightly with a button, Velcro lining, or zipper.
- Use each of these pockets for a specific item or purpose. When traveling, you often get tired and disoriented. Always have specific places for specific items to avoid confusion.

Tips for Women

- Keep makeup extremely simple while traveling. You do not want to attract attention; you want to fade into the crowd to avoid robbery and sexual harassment. In a fine resort or secluded enclave, makeup is fine, but elsewhere a totally natural look is preferred.
- Leave your valuable jewelry at home, including your engagement ring and wedding band. Don't even wear inexpensive silver and gold imitation jewelry. Robbers can't tell the difference between it and the real thing. Exception: If you're having trouble with male harassment, wear a fake wedding band made from a cheap material. If it gets stolen, it won't matter. Wearing a band indicates that

you're another man's "property." That comment may make your blood boil, but the band can cut down on unwanted attention.

- Remember that strong perfumes and cosmetics can make you sun-sensitive. So can some antibiotics.
- Samples of beauty products are light, small, and easy to carry. Collect them for short trips.
- A loose skirt is more comfortable than jeans. It has all the advantages and more—it doesn't stain easily, it doesn't show wrinkles, and it breathes. It's also very plain, conservative, and feminine.
- Mimic the way locals dress in town. Avoid any clothes that reveal your breasts. The bra-less look is not advised with the obvious exception of resort areas, unless the locals are doing the same.
- Carry a flat, large purse for all your odds and ends—a folding umbrella, a camera (best kept out of sight), a snack—you name it. Keep your makeup in a makeup case (if you simply cannot do without it) and a little money in a wallet or change purse. These fit nicely into the larger purse.
- One of the most versatile items to pack is a long, cotton beach robe. Not only can it be used on the beach as a cover-up or beach blanket, but it can pass as either casual or elegant dress. It's extremely easy to keep clean, weighs very little, and packs tight with little wrinkling.

Packing Light

Travel like the pros—stewardesses, travel writers, experienced business people, correspondents—**travel light**. Get by with one piece of carry-on luggage. If you can't carry it on a plane, it's too large. If you can't carry it for a mile without setting it down, it's too heavy. There's a wonderful motto: "Take half as much clothing, twice as much money." Backpacks without frames or with minimal support, small suitcases with rollers, or small bags with shoulder straps are excellent for this purpose. My favorite is a canvas backpack with an ultra light frame, both a top and a front, and two side compartments. It weighs next to nothing but carries an amazing amount of clothes (and extra odds and ends). If you need a little more space, carry a second (much smaller) backpack.

- It's natural for you to feel somewhat skeptical about traveling with only one piece of carry-on luggage. Questions will pop into your mind: Can I really get by with only a few clothes? Won't I be embarrassed by wearing the same outfits over and over? Can I get by in more formal places with less-than-formal clothes? What do I do about climate changes? What happens if something gets stained? And so on.

- If you choose your clothes wisely, you'll have no problem at all. The reaction to this style of travel is always the same: Are you ever smart! As long as you're clean and comfortably dressed, you'll exude an aura of contentment and confidence. Islanders judge you more by this attitude than by your clothes.

How to Pack Light

- Leave electrical items at home. They're heavy and bulky and can be damaged by varying voltage. Power outages and surges are common throughout the Caribbean. Varying current is also a problem that may require adapters on specific islands.
- Pack only items you need to survive—the essentials. I met one person who considered a toothbrush as the only item essential for travel.
- Make each item serve as many purposes as possible. A bathing suit or bikini can pass as underwear. Shampoo can wash not only hair but the body as well—think versatility.
- Go for comfort first, style last. But the two need not be mutually exclusive. As mentioned, style is less important than attitude.
- All clothes must be light, easy to wash, and quick-drying. Test them before you leave. Pick up heavier items for special needs in the islands.
- Clothing made of natural fibers and light in color is the norm in most of the islands. Natural fibers are comfortable, breathe, and are not harmed by insect sprays. Light colors reflect light. White is nice, but hard to keep clean. Light tan is often preferable.
- If you'll be involved in activities that might harm clothes, take old ones with you and discard them at the end of the trip or give them away.
- Spray water repellent on any materials that are suited to such treatment. This will help keep them stain-free.
- Take only the amount of anything you'll need for the trip (a tiny tube of toothpaste for a week, as an example). Transfer small amounts of lotions, shampoo, and similar items into minuscule plastic containers. Just enough for your trip.
- Use every bit of space in your pack or bag. Stuff socks into shoes, and so on.
- If anything could leak or spill, place it in a locking plastic bag.
- Pack things that you need often where they're easiest to reach.
- Pack each item in the same place every time so that you know exactly where it will be throughout the entire trip. This one little procedure has a calming effect.

- Here's a typical wardrobe for a light-packing woman: bathing suit or two (easy to dry); blouse or two (light and long-sleeved); windbreaker (best if waterproof—GoreTex is great); dress (light, supple, easy-to-scrunch-up material); handbag (as outlined above); pants (two—both cotton with lots of pockets); skirt (airy and light); shoes (comfortable, walking type—nothing fancy); socks; canvas tennis shoes (for walking, beach strolls, and getting into water); T-shirt or two (one thigh-length); sweater (only if appropriate to weather); underwear (cotton panties and a couple of bras). Add or delete a few things as fits your personality and you'll be carrying one small bag.
- Proof that this trend is finally catching on is the number of articles in women's magazines emphasizing the number of outfits you can create from as few as 7 or 8 items of clothing. The key to the concept is to make the wardrobe revolve around a central color. You look fabulous, but carry next to nothing.
- A light packing man follows the same basic principles, replacing the dress with a sports coat and tie, only if absolutely necessary.

If You Can't Pack Light

Naturally, not everyone can travel light. Some people who are going to a particularly fancy resort may need to have a wider variety of clothes than outlined earlier. Or someone planning to do some sort of sporting activity, such as scuba diving, may need to bring extra gear. Here are a few tips.

Use More Than One Bag

- Divide all of your clothes and accessories into more than one bag. Carrying two smaller bags is easier than carrying one larger one. They balance well in each hand.
- Pack each bag with the idea that one of the bags may get lost. Split essential clothes and accessories up. That way if you end up with only one bag, your trip won't be ruined.
- If you're traveling with another person, split your belongings up so that each of you is carrying some of the other person's essential clothing or gear. If one bag gets lost, you both still have something to wear.
- Consider bags with rollers to help you pull these heavier bags over long distances. Often, porters or carts just aren't available. These bags are only good on hard surfaces, which is why I prefer backpacks no matter how strange they may look.

- Carry-on baggage should contain anything that if lost would ruin your trip. That would include anything valuable and medications. Never pack these in checked bags.
- Theft from bags is rampant. Special straps with locks are highly recommended. Thieves can cut or snap these, but this takes time, and they don't have a lot of it.
- Finally, bags may be deliberately "lost." If you do put anything valuable in checked bags, insure it.
- I cannot emphasize enough how common it is for baggage to be lost, misplaced, or delayed in the islands.

Protecting and Carrying Valuables

The best way to protect and carry valuables such as a passport, plane tickets, traveler's checks, and money is to make or buy a secret pocket (or pockets) that slides under your clothes against your hip or other parts of your body. It is attached by loops directly to your belt (see p. 222). Another good thing to have with you is one of the little tubes sold in dive shops. These have screw-off tops. You can slide money, traveler's checks, and small items inside. You can go right into the water with these. They do have a tendency to leak. The secret is to wrap the threads with electric tape, pulling it taut as you do so. This tape is durable and does not wear through as you screw the top on and off, as long as you apply new tape before each trip. If you want to carry more items than this into the water, get one of the new waterproof pouches. These are available from:

Cascade Designs
4000 1st Avenue South
Seattle, WA 98123
Tel: (800) 531–9531
Tel: (206) 583–0583

Travelers' Checklist

A trip should start off relaxed. Make up a checklist and pack days ahead of time. If you do, you will have a chance to check and recheck what's packed and to remember things you've overlooked. Take only those things essential to your brand of travel. Some things commonly overlooked are calculators (the thin, lightweight ones), cards, clothes-line (rubber, for hanging things out to dry), cup (collapsible ones are great), day pack (or net shopping bag), dictionary (not a book, but the electronic variety), earplugs (Flents), flashlight (tiny, pocket type), insect repellant (high in DEET, but no more than 10 percent for children), tire gauge (if you'll be driving alot), and a water bottle (large and with a flip top that locks when you push it down). Of course, if you're into special interest activities, you'll be adding special equipment to your list. But think light. And travel that way.

Final Steps

Taking the few steps discussed below will ensure a smooth departure and will bring you peace of mind while away from your home or apartment.

The Last Few Days

Sensible handling of last-minute details can help avert all sorts of problems.

Three Days Before Your Flight

- Reconfirm your flight reservation, according to the procedure outlined on your ticket.
- Get the name of the person you are speaking to and note the day and time you call.
- This procedure drastically lowers the odds of your being bumped; but if you should get bumped from your flight, you will have grounds for legal action.
- Reconfirm your order for a special meal if already requested.

The Day Before Your Flight

- Take pets to the place where they'll be staying.
- Check through the things you'll be taking.
- If you plan on checking baggage, place a label with your name and address on the inside of each bag. Make a list of what's in each bag. If a bag gets lost, you'll be able to identify its contents exactly. When the bag is opened after 3 days (airlines wait this long before opening any misdirected baggage), you and it will be reunited quickly.

The Day of Your Flight

- Call the airport to ask whether your flight will be leaving on time. If you are a member of a tour, you'll usually be informed about any delays, but if you are an individual traveler, this would be rare indeed.
- To save money in cold weather, turn down thermostats and close fireplace flues.
- Water the plants for the last time.

- Disconnect any electric appliances other than lights which you want to go on and off at varying times. This is especially important for hair dryers, irons, electric blankets, etc., which can cause fires.
- If gone for more than a week, turn off your hot water heater. Otherwise, simply turn it down to its lowest setting.
- Close the shut-off valves to all toilets. This stops them from accidentally running forever while you're gone. Consider doing the same with all valves to all faucets.

Getting to the Airport

- Get to the airport at the time indicated on your ticket. Charters often request passengers to show up 2 hours ahead of time.
- Figure out how long it takes you to get to the airport. Then allow an extra 45 minutes for delays and traffic jams.
- Add another 30 minutes for Friday and Sunday nights or for either Los Angeles International or New York's JFK.
- Now add another hour if you intend to register items with customs (see p. 190).

At the Airport

All you want to do is get to the airport, get boarding passes (if this can't be done ahead of time), check your luggage (if you're not traveling light), walk through the security check, and board the plane with a minimum of delay and hassle. Today, that's asking quite a lot.

Parking

- At many international airports there are distant parking places owned by the airport that cost less than those right by the airport. Check on these in advance.
- Many private parking companies have gotten into the business and often undercut the prices of the airport-owned lots. These have free shuttles but may be several to many minutes away from the airport itself.
- When parking in a private lot, ask how far away it is from the airport and how often shuttles run (allow yourself enough time for delays).
- Whenever you buy a plane ticket through a travel agency, ask whether they have coupons to reduce the price of parking at special lots. Many of them do but will not tell you about this unless you ask.

Checking Bags

Over a million bags are lost per year. The best way not to lose luggage is to travel so lightly that you never have to check anything. Furthermore, theft from checked baggage is rampant both in the United States and abroad. However, many people need to check baggage. Here are some important tips.

- Check in with time to spare. Most luggage that's lost is checked in less than 30 minutes before flight time. Never use curbside baggage-check service if you're running late.
- Special tip: Con men are now posing as curbside baggage-check service people. Be careful if you use this service.
- Remove tags and stickers from past trips. They make handling difficult and may send bags in the wrong direction.
- At check-in, watch to make sure that each bag is tagged and placed on the conveyor belt. Never assume that either step has happened.
- Keep your claim check in a safe place—or have it stapled to your ticket folder. You'll need to show it to claim your baggage.
- If you're making a connecting flight in the Caribbean, insist on picking up your baggage at each stop and then rechecking it. This requires scheduling flights with much longer stopovers than you might like but avoids lost baggage. The chances of losing bags if you check them through to your final destination is extremely high in the Caribbean. Another point: Long layovers look long only on paper. Often you'll arrive late to begin with, cutting the time you're actually sitting around twiddling your thumbs. I strongly urge long layovers throughout the region.

Protecting Your Belongings

- Lock and strap every bag. Straps keep bags from popping open even under grueling conditions, and they discourage pilfering, an increasing problem.
- Never pack cash, documents, fragile items, furs, jewelry, medicine—anything valuable or hard to replace—in your checked baggage. These should always be carried onto the plane. Baggage containing expensive items is sometimes "lost" on purpose. Furthermore, the airline will not reimburse you for such things.
- Baggage insurance, available at a set price per $100 of declared value, can be purchased to cover more expensive items. Note that it rarely pays off at full face value. Leave expensive things at home!
- Never leave bags unattended anywhere for any reason. Ask someone you trust to watch them or take them with you—even into the bathroom stall.

- Airport security is increasingly stringent. If you accidentally leave a bag unattended, it may be removed and immediately destroyed.

Registering Valuables

It's best to register valuable items before you get to the airport, but if you forget, do it there. Otherwise, when you come back to the United States or Canada, you may have to pay duty on items that you did not actually purchase abroad.

- You'll find registration booths in international airports as a part of the Customs Department.
- You'll be asked to fill out a small white form with pertinent information, including a description of the article and serial numbers when applicable. *You must have the items with you in order to register them.* The official will check over the information, verify it, stamp the form, and give it to you as proof that you had these items before going abroad. The slip is valid for all future trips, so don't throw it away.
- If you have items to register, allow yourself an extra hour for the process. Occasionally, the booths are closed—inexcusable, but true. ***This is one reason why I recommend registration well before a trip.***
- Never carry gifts to and from any foreign country for another person. The unwary sometimes end up transporting narcotics in this way. If you are caught, you will have a nearly impossible time proving your innocence.

Boarding a Plane

It all used to be so simple. All you had to do was tie a string on your finger and point yourself toward the plane. It's not quite so easy nowadays. To get on a plane, you need a ticket, a boarding pass, and in most cases a seat-selection card.

- If you don't have your ticket yet, you'll wait in a line.
- If you have to check baggage, you'll wait in a line.
- However, with a ticket in hand and bags either with you or checked, you can usually proceed straight to the boarding gate. If you arrive too late, you may lose your seat.

Security and Customs

To get to the gate, you'll have to pass through a security check. In a crowded airport, this can take 45 minutes or longer.

- If it's obvious that you're in danger of missing your plane, go right to the front of the line and calmly explain your predicament to security personnel.

- Under no circumstances should you make joking remarks about hijackings, bombs, or drugs.
- If you get hassled for carrying a Swiss Army knife, have them put it in a package to be given to a flight attendant on your flight. If they refuse this courtesy, have them put it in an envelope to be sent to your home. You'll have to pay the postage. Or you can ask for it to be held in the security office until your return.
- If you're carrying film, remove it from the cardboard packages. Place the unwrapped containers in a plastic bag. Hand it to the inspector before going through the metal detector. You'll be told that this is unnecessary. Do it anyway (see pp. 288–289). Place your ATM cards in the bag as well to prevent the back strip from being demagnetized.
- On some international flights, you'll pass through a customs inspection, which may add another 30-minute delay. Start for the gate as soon as possible.

At the Boarding Area

- Unless you already have a seat assignment and boarding pass, you'll wait in line at the boarding area counter. You'll be given both at this time.
- Until you have a boarding pass in your hand, you essentially have nothing—except a contract that gives you specific legal rights. In short, you can still be bumped.
- When the plane is ready for boarding, the flight will be announced. If you don't board the plane when you're supposed to, your seat can be given to a standby.
- Occasionally, intercom systems do not work. Pay attention at the appropriate time to see whether boarding has started without any outward mention of the fact. Believe me, this happens!

Problems with Flights

This section gives you information about problems that you may run into when flying and strategies to help cope with them.

Getting Bumped by Airlines

Your plane ticket is a legal contract with an airline. It guarantees your right to the flight, under specific conditions.

- An international ticket is valid only if you reconfirm your flight within 72 hours of departure. Always get the agent's name when you reconfirm your flight. Follow the instructions on the ticket to the letter.

- You must arrive at the airport within the time limit specified on your ticket. If you do not reconfirm your flight or if you arrive late, the airline can sell your seat to another person (bump you from the flight)—legally! If you do reconfirm your flight and arrive on time, the airline cannot legally sell your seat. However, airlines do so—about 150,000 times a year.

Voluntary and Involuntary Bumping

Nowadays, airlines ask for volunteers to be bumped for a free round-trip ticket or a sum of money that varies with each airline and situation. If there are not enough volunteers, then some people will be bumped involuntarily. This could include you.

- If this happens to you, ask for a written statement outlining compensation for being denied boarding. Depending on the value of your ticket, you'll be paid a minimum to a maximum amount as denied boarding compensation (DBC). This money is yours for the inconvenience caused you by having been bumped.
- Note that DBC is only paid to passengers bumped from flights that actually take place (not canceled or delayed flights). It's meant only to discourage overbooking, which airlines do to survive.
- If an airline cannot get you to your original destination within 2 hours of the original scheduled arrival time for a domestic flight, or within 4 hours for an international flight, the DBC must be doubled, and the airline still must get you to your destination.
- Naturally, it's to your advantage to work out all problems with the airline on a fair, even-handed basis.
- *Important:* These regulations apply in the United States but not necessarily in the islands. Yes, you can get stranded, and some people do for days in more remote areas. Keep this in mind if you're buying highly restricted tickets to and from Canada or the United States and intend to do some island hopping while in the Caribbean. What happens if you don't make it back on time to the original island?

Flight Cancellation

If your flight is canceled, the airline should get you on the next available flight. It will do little good to complain about the cancellation.

- Each airline has its own way of dealing with this situation. As long as you're being treated the same as other passengers, don't make a scene. You can certainly request free meals, a free room, and so on, but the airlines may or may not go along with your demands.

Change of Fares

Once you have paid for and received a ticket, you cannot be charged more money to board a plane within the United States. However, in other countries you may have to pay whatever fare is applicable on that day.

- When buying a ticket, ask the airline about its policy in this regard. The key point to remember is that fares can change if you haven't already paid for the ticket. Reserving a ticket at a set price is no guarantee you'll get it at that price. You've got to pay for it!

Flight Delays in the U.S.

Flight delays have become quite common. Here are a few tips on avoiding and dealing with them when they do occur.

- Flights originating from your city are less likely to be delayed than flights coming from another city and continuing on.
- Flights beginning early in the day are less likely to be delayed. This rule has many exceptions in the Caribbean, but it is a good rule overall in the United States.
- When a flight is delayed after initial boarding has started in the United States, the airline is obligated to provide meals, lodging, transportation, and a free phone call to each passenger. This rule does not apply once in the islands.
- If you have not started to board a plane and a delay is announced, you have no legal right to demand compensation of any kind. Nevertheless, many airlines will provide necessary amenities to stranded passengers.
- You will usually be given a voucher for a set-price meal and, in extreme cases, even a free hotel room.
- If the airline does not volunteer such things, don't hesitate to ask—and be polite, firm, and fair in your request.

Changing Travel Dates

Most discounted tickets require passengers to fly within specific time periods, with no changes allowed. If you try to make a change, the airline may ask you to pay full fare. Or they may have a set amount added to the fare for each change. Always ask about this when buying a ticket. Fare increases are often not enforced for humanitarian reasons, such as death or severe illness of a close relative. Each airline makes its own decisions in this regard. All will require some sort of proof that your request is based on fact.

- You can take out insurance to cover changes in travel plans caused by illness or death in the family (see p. 5). Because this insurance exists, a number of airlines are enforcing penalties on all ticket changes, no matter what the reason.

In-flight Precautions

- If you're prone to earaches, use decongestants before getting on a plane. Use them again when descending.
- Never leave money, valuable papers, or your passport unattended at any moment on a plane. They should be carried on your person at all times—even when you go to the bathroom. This advice is doubly important if you are asked to get off a plane during a stopover.
- Get up and stretch regularly. This keeps your body relaxed and your blood circulating.
- Use pillows if you want to go to sleep. These stop your head from arching to one side, which often results in neck pain.
- Take off your shoes. Move your feet around, and flex different parts of your body to keep yourself loose.
- The carbon dioxide build-up in planes is not good for your system. Use the overhead blowers to get as much fresh air as possible.
- Drink lots of liquids. Dehydration is a problem at high altitudes. The more you drink, the better.
- Avoid alcohol, coffee, colas containing caffeine, and tea. These lead to dehydration.
- Fruit juices, soft drinks, and water are all recommended. Ask for the entire can when attendants offer you something to drink. Most, but not all, attendants will give you the can instead of a wimpy glass filled mostly with ice.
- Dehydration is such a problem on longer flights that you are smart to carry a bottle of water with you. This is true at all times in the Caribbean as well.
- Dehydration is responsible for many ill effects including cramps (also caused by not moving around in cramped quarters).
- If you do bring a flask of alcohol on board, do not let flight attendants know you're serving yourself a drink. It is against FAA regulations for passengers to do this, but this beats relying on overworked attendants to get drinks or come up with correct change. It's also a lot cheaper.

Disinfecting Aircraft

Hopefully, by the time you read this guide the practice of disinfecting aircraft with a pyrethrin-like spray will have stopped. Flight attendants walk along the aisle and spray the insecticide in hopes of killing stowaway insects on board. It's an absurd, archaic practice that has been proven totally ineffective.

- If you're allergic to ragweed, you can get very sick from the spray.
- If spraying is announced, warn the flight attendant of your allergy. Ask for a wet cloth to cover your nose. Breathe through this while the spraying takes place and for as long after as possible.

Special Safety Warning

The use of computers and electronic equipment on board planes may have resulted in crashes. Most airlines ask you to inquire about the use of such equipment. Some passengers seem to ignore this advice and continue to use laptops even when a plane is landing and even after they have been asked not to over the intercom. This is potentially lethal, just as smoking in bathrooms can be. The new smoke detectors in lavatories have made the latter a rare occurrence. Inform attendants if someone continues to use laptops after being asked not to.

Part II
The Trip

Clearing Customs

Clearing customs at an airport may mean a few minutes' delay or a potential hassle.

The Basics

Here are a few of the main tips to keep in mind to avoid problems with officials when entering the islands.

Entry Documents

Each country has its own entry requirements. Some simply stamp your passport; others require you to carry a stamped paper. Always carry your stamped passport (or a photocopy) and any stamped document (or a photocopy) with you at all times. If you do not have the right documents, you can be arrested. If you intend to stay for long periods of time or plan on frequently traveling to and from a specific country, contact their tourist office for up-to-date regulations regarding such visits. Some may require visas. The National Tourist Offices are listed on pp. 18–26. Unfortunately, a few of these are next to worthless, and ones which rarely reply to inquiries will be pointed out in that section.

Immigration

- The immigration official will check the document you've been requested to fill out and match it to your passport.
- If you're a minor, you need a notarized letter signed by both parents allowing you to travel on your own.
- If a parent is traveling with a minor child, then a notarized letter from the other parent granting permission for such travel may be required. It's possible that you would not be allowed onto an island without this letter.
- The immigration official may ask what hotel you're staying in. Be ready with the name of any hotel on the island. Even if you don't have reservations, it's best to give a name immediately. They hardly ever verify this.
- You may be asked to show a return ticket home. This can pose a real problem for anyone who is island hopping with no set itiner-

ary. Have an island in mind from which you will return home. Have the ticket from that island in hand. This is one of the most absurd regulations in the Caribbean. Oddly enough, it may be enforced. You can try to get by with an on-going ticket to another island. This may be enough. Most of the time they don't even ask.

Customs

- Every tourist must pass through a customs inspection, which varies from a few quick questions about your baggage to a thorough and meticulous search, which can legally include a body inspection.
- Most inspections are routine. However, on some islands there are too few inspectors for the number of people getting off a plane. And this can be time-consuming and tiring.

Tips on Going Through Customs

- Never volunteer information while going through customs. You'll seem suspicious if you do.
- Impatience and anger are the two things that really irritate officials—any impatient or sour comment, look, or attitude can only cause trouble.
- If you don't think your profession will look respectable on the entry form, change it. Become a secretary or a teacher for a day. It isn't what you are but what they think you are that counts.
- Never tell an official that you're coming in on business or to study unless you've got the appropriate visas. Just say you're a tourist— no one cares. Also, wear casual clothes, and pack your briefcase.
- Always be positive with officials. If you're nervous or uneasy, the official may pick up on this. If you treat them with respect, that's probably what you're going to get.
- Customs officials can ask you to tell them the exact amount of money you're bringing into the country and in what form you've got it.
- Say that all belongings are for personal use, unless it's obvious that you're bringing in a gift. Anything still in its original package will qualify as a potential gift. If an item hasn't already been used, watch out—it can only lead to suspicion. Officials are constantly thinking gift and resale.
- If you're bringing an unusual item into the country, such as a type-writer, expensive tape recorder, or special film equipment, tell the official that you're a professional. This word seems magical. Still, it won't stop them from noting the items on your entry form. But it often stops all the fuss about bringing the item into the country in the first place.

- The notation of the item on your entry document means that you must leave the country with it or pay a stiff fee. These notations are meant to discourage the sale of items on the island. If the item is stolen, you'll still probably pay the fee.
- Certain items may require special permits to get through customs. This may include movie cameras.
- If you have more than 12 rolls of film, take the canisters out of the cardboard boxes. This will show the official that the film is for personal use. Most of the time they'll let extra film pass without any hesitation.
- It is very useful to have a Swiss Army knife. However, officials will sometimes confiscate these, especially if they're bright, shiny, and new.
- Sexy magazines such as *Playboy* and *Penthouse* will be confiscated as pornographic material. Every official should have the right to read through such magazines as a censor, but you may cause a more thorough search, wasting valuable time. Leave the magazines at home.
- If you're carrying prescription drugs, leave them in the original containers. Officials can get very sticky these days about pills outside the labeled bottles. Telling whether a pill is a controlled substance can be difficult. They assume the pills are illegal.
- On some islands, especially Bermuda, you are supposed to declare the importation of all controlled medications even when they are in prescription bottles. This is what you're supposed to do. This may invite an unending round of questioning. It's a tough choice.
- Countries with strong agriculture are very worried about plant diseases—leave at home anything that grows or has been grown, including fruits for a snack. Eat them on the plane. Coffee must be ground to be imported into many countries, including our own.

A Special Tip on Documents

Keep your documents handy but in a safe place. Try to keep them in the same spot so that you don't lose track of where they are. The idea of having a special place for each item you carry is one of the best ways to prevent its loss.

Getting to Your Hotel

Getting from the airport or ferry into town or to your hotel is one area where many travelers get burned. The islands discourage public transportation from these areas. Following are some helpful tips.

Ways of Getting into Town

There are several options on getting from the airport or port into town. Cost and convenience are usually the trade-offs.

Free Transportation to Your Hotel

Some hotel packages include free transportation from the airport or ferry to your hotel. In some instances the hotel will have someone at the airport to pick you up. Other hotels issue vouchers. These are supposed to be honored by specified companies. Unfortunately, they are not always accepted the way you might expect. Ask in advance exactly how to take advantage of free "shuttles" when a part of any package. Always ask for a refund if vouchers or promised transportation is not provided. But call the hotel first before jumping into a taxi. Do not expect everything to happen instantaneously. If you're exhausted or in a hurry, pick up a taxi and the tab if promised services are not provided.

Bus Travel from Airports

Buses are available only in major cities. Ask about local bus service at the information office. If it is closed (and it often is or doesn't exist), ask anyone who speaks English about departure times, cost, and location of the bus stop for the bus taking people into town. It may be a slight walk to get to it. Buses are always the least expensive way to get into a city's center. Buses are often slow, belch diesel, and can be packed. But they are a real bargain because the local people use them. Also, check on how to get back to the airport using a bus if you will be flying out of the same airport at a later date. Getting back is often far more difficult than getting into town.

Communal Cabs or Minibuses

- Slightly more expensive than buses are communal cabs (*colectivos*) or minibuses. These may or may not be available. Ask.
- Often tourists are delayed by immigration procedures. The locals slide onto the minibuses or communal cabs and disappear before

you've even stepped out into the sunlight. All that will be left are smiling cab drivers, looking for individual fares.

Where There Are Only Taxis

- Some airports do not have buses or communal cabs. In these you must rely on taxis for transportation. In a few cities prices are government regulated, but for the most part prices depend on your knowledge and bargaining skill.
- Always ask whether a hotel will be sending someone to pick you up. Ask whether this is part of the hotel's fee or must be paid independently. Try to get the name of the driver in advance and his telephone number. On some islands you'll be using Citizen Band radios (CBs). The name of your driver may be posted on the bulletin board in some islands, or the driver may hold up a placard with your name on it.
- If you are not being picked up, ask them to tell you what the taxi fare should be from the airport when making a reservation. Hotels should know to the penny what a reasonable fare will be.
- Verify the quoted fare with a flight attendant. Most have a pretty good idea of what fares are in each area. If the attendants don't know, ask someone at the airline desk when you arrive. The point is to try to find out fares ahead of time, not when you walk out the door to the taxi stand.
- In some areas the local tourist information office will post fares from the airport to specific hotels. Or they'll tell you what the fares should be. There was a time when you could rely on tourist office recommendations. In some areas you still can, but in others the tourist offices are in league with the taxi drivers. You find out later that you could have paid a third of the posted price for the ride.
- A good strategy is to find other travelers heading in the same direction to get a group together to share costs. Local residents share rides all the time. Smart foreigners will follow their lead. The cab takes each person to individual destinations, usually a person's home or a foreigner's hotel.
- Never get into a cab without settling on the fare first. If there is a language barrier, have the driver write the fare down on a piece of paper. Don't be afraid to bargain.
- Local currencies are often known as dollars. When establishing a fare, ask whether it is in local or U.S. dollars. On a few islands the local dollar is set to be exactly the same as the U.S. dollar, but on other islands this is not the case.
- In larger cities ask whether local cabs have a certain letter on their license plate. You want to use licensed, not unlicensed, cabs.
- On remote islands there's usually one or two dilapidated vehicles

waiting to take you to your hotel. Occasionally, there is nothing.
Just dust. You'll figure out a solution. Someone's always willing to
help.

- When planning a trip, expect to pay a lot for taxis if you're not
going to be renting a bike, car, or moped. Upkeep and gas is
expensive on the islands, which chew up cars quickly. High taxi
fares in areas without public transportation reflect this.

Ferries and Boats

In a few places you'll have to combine taxi rides with ferries and
boats. Again, ask your hotel about exact details on costs and schedules to avoid being stranded. Some hotels pick up guests by boat
from a spot close to the airport. This fee is often included in the
room charge.

- It is not unheard of for a hotel to forget about your arrival. Or
more commonly to arrive hours late to pick you up.
- You'll probably be angry, but remember that you're now on island
time. Planes come and go on that same time, which means they're
often early or late.
- Wear a hat, bring a book, and carry something to eat and drink.
You're entering the twilight zone.

Hotel Strategies

Getting the room you want with the amenities you want at the price you want—no mean trick. That's what this section's all about.

Finding a Room Without Advance Reservations

Some travelers prefer to travel without reservations. There are several advantages: If you don't like an island, you can move on. If you don't like a hotel or the room available, you look further. If there are a number of rooms available in an area, you can bargain and cut your costs significantly. However, all of these advantages can evaporate during the peak season and during special events in the off-season when virtually every room on an island is prebooked at high rates. The peak season runs from mid-December to early April in the Bahamas and most of the Caribbean. In Bermuda the peak season runs from mid-April to mid-September. Here are a few tips on finding rooms if you don't have reservations.

Tourist Offices

- If you arrive on an island during a peak travel period, during a holiday or fiesta, you may need help locating a room. Ask for the nearest tourist office for help.
- Many airports on major islands have tourist offices. In larger towns you'll find tourist offices in the city centers, usually around the main square.
- Tourist offices close at weird times and often take a break for a siesta. But they can help you locate a room where few are to be found. You may end up in a private home, but that in itself could be a great experience.

Local Travel Agencies

- Local agents often know of boarding houses, homes, or small hotels looking for guests. You may pay a small fee for this service, but it can be worth it in the peak season.
- Travel agents are often your best resource for long-term stays. Agents may find you rooms in homes with meals at a fraction of the price of hotels. Never rule agents out.

- If you're on a budget, the key words are good and cheap! There's only one way to come up with these places: Ask! Many remain totally undiscovered by U.S. and Canadian travelers and even companies producing budget guides.

The Grapevine

- Sometimes simple is best. One of the simplest ways to find out about great little hotels is to ask people where they've been, where they've stayed, and whether they have any suggestions.
- Hotels are constantly opening up. Some are isolated and relatively unknown, so just keep asking. The best hotels I've stayed in have often been "gifts" from other travelers. In return, I tell them about my finds.
- This informal grapevine is often more accurate and up-to-date than any travel guide.
- Once you find a hotel that matches your personality and budget, ask the hotel personnel to make recommendations for other islands. Some owners may never have traveled off their islands; others may know spots that have never been written about.
- As strange as it may sound, some of the most charming hotels have no signs, no indication of being a hotel, no advertising, no nothing to lead you to them except word of mouth. On Trinidad I had been told about a charming hotel on the north coast, but finding it took nearly an hour. The owner simply said that she wanted people staying there who already knew where she was—fair enough.
- Keep a log of all the places that offered good value and would interest others. It's easy to forget names, addresses, and telephone numbers. These can prove invaluable in the future.
- If you feel confident in your source, call ahead to make reservations. Better yet, use a fax and get confirmation in writing.

Using a Travel Guide to Find Lodging

- Each travel guide is aimed at a specific market, usually according to budget. If you're on a tight budget, use a student or shoestring travel type guide. Not so tight? Try any of the more popular guides with varied listings.
- These guides are all out-of-date before they're printed. Many have given up listing prices—for good reason. But they all list a batch of hotels that fall into certain price categories. Although prices may have risen, the listed hotels will fall into the "budget" or "moderate" or "luxury" categories—that, in itself, is the value of the guide.

- The tip: Go to *any* of these hotels that most accurately matches your idea of what you want. The hotel may or may not have a room available, but that really doesn't matter. What you need is help. And almost all hotels will suggest other hotels nearby, and many hotel owners will call those hotels for you. This strategy works 99.9 percent of the time in the off-season and fairly often in the peak season, because hotels often cooperate with each other to book rooms of no-shows.

Finding Hotels by Area

- If you're interested in a specific area, if you want to be near or on the beach, if you want to be near the market or shopping, or whatever—check out the area nearest whatever interests you.
- Hotels that fall into similar price categories often cluster together. If you're looking for budget hotels, you'll usually find a bunch of them in the not-so-prime tourist areas.
- The secret of this strategy is to be traveling light. You want to be able to walk and use public transportation (if available) easily. If you're traveling with another person, it's often best to have one person guard the baggage, as in a restaurant, while the other does the scouting for a hotel.

Judging Hotels

- Never judge a hotel by its exterior or lobby. Some very bleak exteriors hide sumptuous interiors. And some charming lobbies with flower-filled gardens cannot make up for bug-infested and dirty rooms. Ask to see the room.
- Never judge a hotel by its official rating; it's just jargon that's misleading. A first-class hotel can have an empty swimming pool and surly staff, while a budget inn with no stars may provide friendly service and rooms looking over lush hills or onto a beach—you just never know. Ask to see the room.

Checking Out a Room

- Make sure the room is clean. Don't worry about the glasses; half the time they haven't been washed. Just see whether you can live with the colony of bugs or the dust on the tables.
- Does the room smell fresh and clean or, at least, okay?
- Are the faucets dripping? Is the toilet churning? Turn on the hot water to see if there is any. Many hotels in the Caribbean don't have hot water, which, considering the weather, is rarely a problem.
- Check the bathroom. Are you willing to stand in the shower or bathe in the tub? Does it seem clean enough?

- Check the bedding. If it's cool outside, ask whether there are extra blankets. You'll need these only at higher altitudes on a few islands.

Keeping Room Costs Down

Just as travelers pay different prices for plane tickets on identical flights, so do they pay different prices for identical rooms. Here are some tips to get the most for your money.

Bargaining on Room Rates

Once you find a room you like, you'll want to come up with the best price possible. Although it may go against your grain, bargaining in various ways is acceptable. Naturally, it's only effective in an area with many open rooms, and for that reason it's done more successfully in the off-season.

- Ask whether there is an off-season discount if you're traveling in a non-peak period. Off-season discounts range from 30 to 50 percent.
- You'll often increase the discount by being subtle. Tell the clerk that the room is great, but that it's too expensive for you. Ask whether there are any other rooms available at a lower price. This will often bring the price down. Or you'll be taken to a nearly identical room at a lower price.
- Or be blunt: Tell the clerk that you like the room and will pay such and such an amount—a lower, but still fair, price. This works frequently, but you have to have the right temperament to try it.
- Always ask about discounts for prolonged stays, usually three days or longer. If none exist, the hotel will tell you so. You can then either accept the standard rate or shop around.
- Ask whether the hotel offers weekend discounts. This tactic works best in large cities.
- Some hotels will give discounts for people in different professions. Ask to see whether such an opportunity exists.
- Occasionally a hotel will offer a business discount. Carry business cards to use this ploy.

Hotel Costs and Services

Check-in is the time to get everything straight on costs and services. Avoid any potential conflicts by asking questions right away.

- You'll find that all rooms have a base price. Ask to have this written down. Make sure that the price is not quoted on a per person basis—a common trick in a few areas.

- In almost all hotels you'll pay an additional tax on the base rate. The tax varies by island but can be quite stiff. Ask whether the tax is included in the base price.
- Almost all hotels tack on a service charge of 10 to 15 percent. Again, ask whether the service charge has been included in the base rate.
- Single rooms are almost the same price as doubles (just a little less, actually), so you can't get much of a benefit by traveling alone.
- Ask whether there are any additional charges for telephones and television. Many hotels do make a small charge per day for these two items. Find out what it is in advance.
- Air-conditioning can add a substantial price increase to a room. If you're willing to settle for a ceiling fan, the cost drops dramatically.
- If you don't have a bath in your room, ask whether there is an additional charge to take a bath in the communal area. Find out if towels cost extra as well.
- Just keep asking and asking until all of the potential price traps have been worked out.

Types of Rates (see also p. 172)

- Some hotels will force you into an American Plan before they will rent you a room. In short, your room rental must include the often inflated cost of all meals. In the peak season you may have to submit to this racket if you want to get into a particular hotel.
- Ideally, you want to be able to choose whether to eat in any hotel, no matter what plans are available. This gives you the option of eating out or deciding whether the hotel food warrants a full or half room-and-board plan.
- If you do stay on a room-and-board basis, find out whether there is an extra charge for anything, such as wine, dessert, or coffee.
- Most hotels offering half or full room and board post specific meal times. If you miss the meal, you still pay for it.
- Most hotels offer a choice of two or more entrées with each meal, so that you have the feeling of some control—not much, really.

Payment

- Fancy hotels will ask you to produce a major credit card at the time of check-in. They will imprint the information on a charge slip as collateral. When you check out, you can either fill in the total or pay in cash and have the credit card slip destroyed.
- Budget hotels will ask for a cash payment upfront for the first

night's rental. Some places are very trusting and don't ask for any money until you leave.

- You do not want to use a traveler's check to pay a hotel bill in most instances because very few hotels give a fair rate of exchange. Always carry enough local currency to pay your hotel bills. Or ask what the bill would be in dollars. Paying in dollars is quite common.
- When you pay the bill, ask for a receipt. If you pay with a credit card, check the total before signing. Keep all receipts until the charges have come in. Surcharges are commonly added for the use of credit cards throughout the Caribbean. Always ask about this when checking in.

The Front Desk

- Get the name of the person at the front desk. Use it. This is appreciated in the Caribbean, as it is everywhere. Surprisingly, few people make this effort. Those who do often end up with special favors and reduced rates.
- Always have room prices written down for you when checking in. This avoids any discussion of a language barrier at a later date. Consider paying for the first night to see whether the price being quoted is truly what you'll end up paying.
- Don't assume that your name is easy to spell or read. Write it down for the clerk.
- If you have any valuables, ask the front desk about safe-deposit boxes. Normally, there is either no fee or just a small daily charge for these. Better hotels have them in individual rooms; many budget hotels don't. But you won't know for sure until you've asked. If you lose the key or card that opens your box, you may end up paying as much as a hundred dollars to replace it.
- Front desks often have electrical items such as irons and hair dryers. The latter are more common. The fancier the hotel, the more likely they'll have extras like this.
- If you don't have a map, ask for one at the front desk. They usually have tourist-oriented information.

Porters

- Porters expect a reasonable tip for carrying baggage, even if it's featherlight.
- If you're traveling light and don't want to pay for porters, be firm. Simply ask for the room key and the location of the room. Say you'll carry your own bags. This is accepted in all but the upper-bracket hotels. And even there, what can they do if you insist.

Idiosyncrasies of Caribbean Hotels

Half the pleasure of travel comes from discovering the differences between them and us. However, some differences come as a shock. Here are some bridges for cultural gaps in hotels.

Air Conditioning

Air conditioning is really nice in some hotels where winds have died or are blocked from cooling your room.

- Air conditioning is common in more luxurious hotels. In some of the smaller hotels it is an option for which there is a surcharge. Ask.
- While it can be extremely hot and even humid on many islands, air conditioning is often unnecessary if the room is exposed to prevailing winds. Winds die down somewhat in the summer.
- Rooms higher up in the tropics often get cooling breezes. Consider this when choosing a room. The cross-ventilation serves as natural air conditioning.
- Air conditioning units are often extremely noisy. In a quiet area, this is an irritant, but if there is lots of noise outside, the drawback becomes a plus.
- Air conditioning helps keep mosquitoes out of your room. They like it warm and moist, not cool and breezy.
- Air conditioning can make you sick if you're vulnerable to fluctuating temperatures (coming in from the heat and humidity into a cold room).
- However, most people who have an illness, such as a heart condition, are better off with air conditioning. It lowers humidity dramatically.
- Controlling the temperature on some units is virtually impossible. Ask whether units have individual controls or are controlled centrally.
- Most honeymooners see air conditioning as a plus.

Children

Some hotels in the Caribbean discourage family travel or simply do not allow children. Some welcome families and even have special facilities for children. Since policies vary considerably from one hotel to the next, ask about this when making reservations.

Electricity (*la luz, la lumière*)

- The only way to get electricity (light) in some hotels is with a generator (*planta*). These usually run for a set time each day. They are quite noisy. They are most common on remote islands. If you are going to a hotel using a generator, request being as far from the generator as possible if you're sensitive to noise.

- On a few islands, power is provided by solar-charged batteries. In these areas you'll be asked to conserve power by using lights infrequently and flushing toilets only when absolutely necessary.
- In some areas, lights go off at the oddest times. In others, electricity just stops being produced at certain times. If you see candles in your room, it's a good indication that this is a common problem. Get matches.
- Also, carry a pocket flashlight. It will help you get into the room when all lights go off outside, and it will help you from tripping over odds and ends on your way to the bathroom at night.
- Electric shocks are also common in older hotels or in ones using electric apparatus above the shower to heat water. Never stand on a wet bathroom floor when plugging in an electrical item or turning on a light.
- Avoid carrying electrical items. These often short out local systems or are ruined by fluctuating voltage. On a number of islands they require adapters—another nuisance.

Kitchens

A number of inns in the Caribbean open their kitchens to guests to allow them to store beverages and snacks in the refrigerator. A few even encourage cooking, but this is relatively rare.

Noise

- Loud music, roaring mopeds, never-ending fiestas—these are a part of island life in many locations. Loud talking at night and so on is not considered an invasion of your boundaries, although it is certainly annoying and to be avoided by guests at all times.
- If you're sensitive to noise, if you're a light sleeper, or if you prefer to listen to your own brand of music, bring earplugs or a cassette player with soothing tapes.
- These countries are lands of constant crowing, mooing, mating of cats, grinding of gears, unloading of cement blocks—and a dozen other noisy gerunds.
- When checking out a hotel, pay attention to noise: Are you just above the lounge or disco? Are you right next to the reception area? Near the elevator or public toilet? Is your room overlooking a noisy street, right on a busy highway, steps from the town's generator, or near the market?
- By the way, you never really know how noisy a place is going to

be until night. Ask if noise is a problem. You might be within ear range of a discotheque.

- Many local people consider music as a wonderful part of a hotel's ambiance. The louder it is, the better. Either join the party, adapt to the cultural difference, or invest in superfine earplugs. Or change hotels.

Parking

- If you plan to rent a car or moped, make sure your hotel has a safe place to park the vehicle overnight.
- Ask whether there is any charge for this. Most of the time there isn't, except in major cities.
- In urban areas, street parking at night is not advised. Pay to have your car in a secure area.

Refrigerators and Servi-bars

The better hotels often have refrigerators or servi-bars in the room. You open these little boxes with your room key or a specially provided one. Inside, you'll find fruit juices, colas, beer, wine, mini bottles of booze, and an assortment of snacks. Having a small refrigerator in your room can be a delight. The more luxurious hotels are more apt to have these. Some add a surcharge; others include them in their rates, which are often already steep. When in doubt, ask. You pay for each item used, often through the nose. If a price list is not in your room, ask for one.

Telephone

- Most hotels charge a small fee per day for the use of a telephone or a small fee per local call.
- Most, but not all, hotels charge a surcharge for long-distance calls. You should ask ahead of time what the surcharge is, if any. It is possible that surcharges may double, triple, or even quadruple the normal bill. Unfortunately, people at the front desk often lie about the true hidden charges. If saving money is important, make calls from a public phone using a telephone card.
- Hotels may add a charge to your bill for any collect calls as well. The charge can be higher if the collect call was not accepted. Again, ask what the charge will be.

Towels

Most hotels supply towels. The better hotels offer large towels but ask guests to use them several times to avoid the waste of water in washing. Many hotels ask you to pick up a different towel for use at the pool. Ask about any potential charges in advance. Travelers who stay in smaller hotels or outright dives might be smart to bring along a thin beach towel or one of the newly marketed products that are lightweight and absorbent like a towel but take up far less space.

Water (for washing)

- Some hotels have minimal water pressure. Water comes out in a drizzle. Others consider a strong shower a mark of good service.
- Hot water is considered a luxury in the Caribbean. Some hotels do not offer it because they see it as non-essential.
- Ironically, on some islands water pipes from desalinization plants run above ground so that getting cold water out of the spigot is impossible. The water in the pipes bakes in the noonday sun and becomes extremely hot.
- Since water is at a premium, showers are more common than baths. Shower heads often provide a mist rather than a spray.
- You're expected to get wet, then turn off the shower. Lather your body, then turn on the shower to remove the soap. All of this conserves water, which can be more expensive locally than rum.

Water (for drinking)

- The purity of water varies by island and by season. In some areas the water is desalinated and safe; in others, it is collected in cisterns (safe at times, unsafe at others); and in still other areas, the water is collected in ways that are never safe. On a few islands, water must be brought in by boat.
- In general, skip tap water in hotels, and don't brush your teeth in it unless you're convinced by hotel owners that it is completely safe.
- Some of the larger deluxe hotels claim to have pure tap water. They probably do. Some of the smaller hotels make the same claim. They probably don't. The situation is not uniform, varying greatly by island.
- Some hotels provide bottles of pure water by the sink. Or they have carafes filled with what they claim is pure water. Frankly, I'd be suspicious of non-bottled water.
- Why not carry bottles of mineral water (*agua mineral, l'eau mineral*) with you? You can find small to large bottles, with or without carbonation, in local stores. Carbonated mineral water is the safest bet, since tap water could be placed in sealed bottles and sold as mineral water—it does happen.

Money Matters

Getting the most for your money is on every traveler's mind. Following are some straightforward tips.

Money Basics

Even if you've traveled a great deal, there are some oddities included in the following sections. These special tips are worth noting to avoid problems that you would never suspect.

Cashing Traveler's Checks

Usually the easiest and sometimes the only place to cash a traveler's check is in a bank. Fortunately, more and more hotels are now accepting traveler's checks. However, many of them offer a less favorable rate of exchange than a bank.

- Bring your passport to cash checks. Without this identification you will not get them cashed. You may have to write the number on each check. Do this ahead of time if you want to hurry up the process at the bank.
- Avoid getting your checks wet because it is not easy getting mutilated or faded checks cashed. In some cases it's impossible. If no one will take your checks, rip them up and declare them lost.

Personal Checks

Leave your personal checks at home, unless you plan to pay for duty with them on your return home.

Credit Cards

These are as good as gold in much of the region. There is very little suspicion of credit cards, which surprisingly raise fewer eyebrows than traveler's checks.

- If you plan to be in the islands for more than a month, send in a prepayment. If you send in enough money to cover your charges, you will not have to pay interest on the balance.
- Always find out if there is a way to call your credit card company toll-free from abroad before traveling. There often is.

Using Credit Cards to Get Cash

Many credit cards allow you to get cash in a pinch. The regulations and fees for such a service change frequently.

- If you think you'll be using this service, get a list of the places where it's available. Make sure that it's very specific.

Protecting Credit Cards

Protect your cards like cash, and count them from time to time to make sure they're all there. Thieves are smart enough to steal just one, hoping that you won't notice.

Exchanging Currency

One of the realities of travel is the necessity of exchanging U.S. dollars into foreign currency. In many parts of the Caribbean, U.S. dollars are accepted as readily as the local currency. However, on some islands you should exchange your dollars into the local currency. Just ask if you're not sure. It's always a good idea to carry small bills and coins in local currency for tips and small purchases.

Money Basics

- The names of the respective currencies used throughout the region have been listed in the thumbnail island-by-island sketches (see pp. 32–71). These include the Eastern Caribbean dollar (or "Bee Wee") on a number of islands, the French franc (on French islands), the Netherlands Antilles guilder or florin (on Dutch islands), or a specific island's own dollar (Trinidad and Tobago dollar, for example).
- Almost all islands accept U.S. dollars in place of local currency, except on Dominica, in the Dominican Republic, in the Grenadines, and on Guadeloupe, Martinique, Saint Bart, Saint Lucia, Tobago, and Trinidad. And even in many instances they'll accept them there as well.
- Always ask whether you can pay a bill in U.S. dollars, since this is a pleasant way to avoid currency exchange hassles. Even on some of the islands where you "officially" must exchange U.S. dollars into local currency, some of the residents may prefer U.S. dollars. However, they'll want hard currency—actual dollar bills, not traveler's checks.
- In areas where you must exchange currency, you'll need identification for each exchange. A passport is always the most reliable form. On some islands, you may technically have to produce an

on-going airline ticket for exchange, but I have yet to find this enforced.

- Exchange rates fluctuate daily for some currencies and are preset for others. Ask about this on arrival.
- Where currency rates do fluctuate, extremely experienced travelers study rates for several weeks before traveling to see whether the U.S. dollar is getting weaker or stronger in relation to a specific foreign currency. If the dollar is getting stronger, they exchange less money on arrival. If it's getting weaker, they exchange lots of money on arrival. Money is a commodity, and this follows the basic principal of that type of exchange.
- Exchange money in major tourist areas. The more off-the-beaten-path you get, the lower the rate tends to be.
- No matter what the trend, always exchange the most money you can afford to lose. The reason is that you usually get a better rate of exchange for larger amounts of money.
- You almost always get a better rate of exchange for hard currency (dollar bills) than traveler's checks. There are occasional exceptions to brighten your day.
- Never exchange currency in the United States or Canada. The exchange rates are absurdly low.
- On some islands you get a poor rate of exchange at international airports. But from a practical standpoint, it may still be best to exchange enough currency to get by for a couple of days.
- Generally, you get your best rate of exchange from a reputable bank. Rates of exchange do vary from one bank to the next unless the exchange rate is preset by the government. Knowing the rate of exchange is important, but you must also find out what kind of commission is charged. Before you exchange money, ask if there is a commission or service fee for the transaction. Commissions may vary according to the amount of money being exchanged. There may be a set amount or a set overall percentage of the amount exchanged. And if you're exchanging traveler's checks, the commission may be per check. There may also be a tax per check, such as stamps in the British Virgin Islands. Ask. Without knowing how the bank charges a commission, you really don't know what the final exchange rate will be.
- In most instances you'll find the same rates at moneychangers as at reputable banks. Moneychangers are less common in this region than in other parts of the world. The big advantage: An instant transaction with none of the hassles of a bank. Always know the current rate of exchange before dealing with a moneychanger.
- You usually get a poor rate of exchange in hotels. A few give a better rate of exchange than banks as a way of pleasing cus-

tomers, but don't count on this. Ask what their rate is before going to a bank.

- Calculators prove invaluable when exchanging currency.
- Keep all receipts for money exchanges. You may need these to exchange extra local currency back into U.S. dollars when you leave. If you can sell your excess money to incoming tourists, do so. You'll all benefit.
- Definitely do not bring Caribbean currency back home where you'll get next to nothing for it on exchanging it back to U.S. dollars.

The Black Market

Exchanging currency on the black market is not particularly common in the Caribbean. It is done on a few islands, especially on Jamaica and Margarita.

- When you land on the island, ask what the current official and unofficial rates are. Virtually everyone knows this.
- To take advantage of the black market, you must have hard currency—actual dollar bills, not traveler's checks.
- You must also know what the local currency looks and feels like, so buy money in different denominations before going to the black market.
- Many tourists leaving the island are anxious to get rid of excess local currency. Approach them at the airport if you'd like to get more for your money than at the bank.
- If that doesn't work, try to exchange your money in a small hotel, restaurant, or shop first. They may be reluctant to give you the black market rate. If they are, ask which streets are presently centers for black market exchange.
- Make your exchange during the day.
- Go with one other person, preferably a local. You'll make enough on the exchange to pay the person a tip. It could even be a cab driver.
- The people working the black market make enough money so that they don't have to rip you off. And as mentioned, they congregate along specific main streets that all of the locals know. Since there is competition, you should get a good rate, certainly far better than the official rate.
- The savings are substantial. On a $1,000 trip you could be talking from $250 to $400, especially on Margarita.
- You also save lots of time—lots.

Money Confusion with the $ Sign

- The $ sign is used for some local currencies and for money from the United States. Always ask whether an item is marked in the local currency or in U.S. dollars to avoid any misunderstanding.

- Whenever rates for any service or transaction are quoted in dollars, ask whether the person means in local or U.S. dollars. There are many currencies in the Caribbean referred to as dollars.

Taxes and Service Charges

Prices are often quoted without taxes or service charges added, especially in hotels and restaurants. Always ask what a price will be with taxes and with service. Local taxes vary by island. The service charge is usually 10 percent, but in a few places may be higher. The Aggregate Value Tax (IVA) is the common name for the "tourist tax" on goods and varies from country to country and from item to item. Some luxury goods have as much as a 20 percent tax.

- The only way you can avoid taxes is by eating in inexpensive restaurants and staying in inexpensive hotels and by shopping in the open market—these all cater to locals who don't have to pay the tax. In some instances, this doesn't work. As a tourist, you just get stuck with the tax no matter how much a place caters primarily to locals. The only place you'll never get taxed is in open markets, whether for food or goods.
- Since most tourists don't eat, stay, and shop exclusively in such places, they get socked with a tax that can really add up over a period of time.
- This tax should never be confused with a service charge! You're still expected to leave a tip in appropriate situations, for example, in restaurants unless the service charge has already been added (see tipping below).

Tips

Many locals depend almost entirely on tips for their living. Since wages are extremely low, tips take on an added importance to the average worker. It's a good idea to ask about appropriate tipping from a local person when arriving.

Miscellaneous Money Tips

- Carry a small change purse. It's extremely helpful for tiny transactions. This way you don't have to take out your wallet. You can put in a few small bills as well. The less money you show, the better.

- If you're flying out of a country, always save enough money to pay for the departure tax. If you don't know what the tax is, ask. It is usually cheaper to pay this tax in local currency than in U.S. dollars, although the latter are readily accepted.
- Always have the exact change for the departure tax since in many places they will not make change.
- In a few places, such as from Saint Martin/Sint Maarten, you have to pay a departure tax even for a ferry ride to a nearby island (Anguilla). A tiny piece of extortion to boost the local economy. You pay less from the French side.
- Get rid of all change when going from one country to the next. It'll be useless there. Buy something with it—even if it's just a piece of candy. At least, you'll get something for it.
- The importation and exportation of local currency may be illegal on some islands. Ask locally about any such regulation.

Protecting Property

Suspicion and wariness require energy and are not very pleasant sensations, but they do prevent trouble, which can be even more unpleasant. Islands in this region are often poor, and you'd have to be naive or careless not to take protective measures. Please read the chapter on Personal Protection since many of the tips overlap with the following information.

Protecting Your Belongings

Protecting your belongings requires a bit of preparation, lots of common sense, and enough street sense to stay out of trouble. Follow the strategies outlined below, and you'll cut to almost zero the odds of losing things or being robbed.

Basic Protection

- Never count or flash money in public. Local residents consider this cruel, stupid, and dangerous. You're asking for trouble if you do.
- Leave all expensive jewelry at home. It's out of place in poorer areas. In fact, don't even wear imitation jewelry. Thieves have a hard time telling it from the real thing. It's not worth getting hurt for an item worth pennies.
- Never wear an expensive watch. Get an extremely cheap one. If it's lost or stolen, consider it dispensable. If you have a special watch for scuba diving, keep it hidden until you need to use it.
- Never carry all of your valuables in one place. Split up your documents and money. If you put your passport, tickets, money, traveler's checks, and credit cards in one place, they're all gone in one shot. *This is basic street sense*, and absolutely essential in developing countries.
- Keep anything valuable out of sight and in inconspicuous containers. If you have to leave something valuable in a car (not a good idea), put it in the trunk. Stow your cameras in an inexpensive bag—one that looks like it could just as easily be carrying groceries.
- After cashing a large amount of money at a bank, get most of it into your hotel safe as quickly as possible. Carry just what you need for the day.
- ***Just what you need for the day (or for the next few hours)*** is the key phrase. You don't need to carry a passport, three credit cards, all your traveler's checks, most of your money, and your air-

line tickets—leave them in the hotel safe. Take just enough to get you by for the day—one credit card will often do the trick.

- Dress casually. Ninety-nine percent of the time you do not have to dress up.
- Never, ever set your luggage down and leave it unattended, not even for a second.
- Put your original passport in a safe, and carry a reduced photocopy with you for identification.

How to Carry Valuables When You Must: Pickpocket Proofing

There are times when everything you own is either on your body or in your bags. Violent crime is relatively uncommon in the Caribbean, but rip-offs of bags and pickpocketing are. Tens of thousands of cases are reported yearly. Here are some tips.

- A small, durable traveler's pouch that can be attached to a belt and worn under your pants or skirt is the *best* place to carry valuable documents and money. These can be improvised by anyone with a basic knowledge of sewing and should have a good zipper. Hidden pockets can also hang from your neck, be strapped to your leg, or placed anywhere else on the body. Having several pockets is a good idea. These hidden pockets or pouches are now commonly sold in catalogs and stores catering to travelers.
- Second best but good is the inside pocket of a coat or jacket that has been modified with a zipper. You can alter these pockets so that they're twice as deep, and twice as hard to pick. The zipper is crucial. No zipper? Use a safety pin as a deterrent to nimble fingers. However, you won't be wearing coats or jackets very often, so this tip is of limited value.
- Never carry your wallet in a rear pocket! A pickpocket can rip it off in a second. A side pants pocket is only a little better. If that's all you've got, buy a nappy-surfaced wallet or put a rubber band around it—this can give pickpockets a fit.
- If you're carrying a purse, put it in front of you with your arms crossed over it. Your wallet should be at the bottom. If your purse is to your side or behind you, a thief will slash it open with a razor blade and be gone in seconds.
- Many travelers are now wearing fanny pouches for their valuables. They generally reverse them so that they are facing forward. Getting to passports and money is extremely easy with one of these pouches. So is stealing them. Despite their incredible popularity, avoid these at all costs. Your money and documents must be *under* your clothing.

- In the Caribbean you'll often be in the water. See p. 185 for information on tubes and waterproof packs in which to carry valuables directly into the sea.

Protecting Valuables in a Hotel

- In some hotels you'll find security boxes in each room. Get a key and instructions on how to use these. Occasionally, there is a small fee, but it is usually reasonable. Often, there is no charge at all. If you lose the key, the charge for a replacement runs from $50–$100.
- A few hotels have larger safe-deposit boxes at the front desk. You put your valuables in a sealed envelope. This is placed into the box until you ask for its return.
- When getting valuables out of a safe, be attentive. This is one time when thieves will try to distract you.
- If you're in a budget hotel, don't leave valuables unattended. Carry them into the shower or bathroom if you have to.
- If you end up inviting a local into your room for the night, there is an implicit agreement that the person has a right to take a little something for the favor. Trying to get that little something back through the police is next to impossible, since favors exchanged for sex are often implicit.

Protecting Valuables at the Beach

- Leave as much as you can at your hotel, preferably in a safe-deposit box.
- Pin your money to a beach robe or piece of clothing that no one would suspect as a hiding place. Leave nothing of great value in your purse or bag, which will be the first thing stolen. The purse becomes a dummy.
- Use a waterproof tube for valuables as mentioned earlier.

Losing Things

It is very easy to lose things while traveling because you're constantly disoriented, frequently tired and fuzzy, and often moving at such a quick pace that it's hard to keep track of where you are or what you've got.

- Consider a special bag for things that are really important to you. Carry everything in that one bag (I'm not talking about money and valuables, which should be in a hidden pouch). You'll be less likely to forget the bag than an individual item—such as a pair of sunglasses or a small camera or a favorite pen or a lighter.
- The quickest way to lose something is to set it down. You put a camera on the seat next to you and the next minute you're four

blocks away and realize that the camera didn't come with you. What a sinking feeling and a mad dash to claim it—if it's still there!

- Try to establish a place for everything. This routine helps you know at all times where things are. This has a calming effect and really helps cut down on the loss of items through carelessness, fatigue, or simple oversight.

Personal Safety

Personal safety is a major travel concern. By using common sense and doing what the local residents do, you should have few problems. Note that 50 percent of life-threatening situations involve accidents, and 60 percent of these are road related.

What the Locals Advise

The local inhabitants follow certain precautions as if they were second nature. They've learned not to put themselves in situations that could turn nasty.

Air Travel

As pointed out in the chapter on inter-island travel, many planes in this region are not as safe as they could be. Ask locals about airlines. Certain of them have built up an extremely poor safety record.

Boating

- Locals often make a living by taking tourists out on boats. If you're going out into the ocean, the boat should have two motors, plenty of gas, and a good anchor. A boat with one motor is fine if you're staying close to shore or just doing an excursion around an island.
- When boating in the tropics, carry lots of food and water with you—just in case the boat breaks down.
- If fishing, don't go out in rough water. Definitely come in if a storm seems to be brewing. The storms here can be extremely violent.

Camping Out

If you're into camping, do it in legal campsites. Or at the very least, do it with a group of people. Campers routinely disregard this advice and tell others that there's no problem camping out—and they're right, most of the time. But they're wrong enough times to be scary. Ask the people who have had problems—not the ones who haven't. On many islands camping is illegal.

Dogs

Dogs are probably more of a threat in the islands than wildlife.

- If you'll be doing a lot of walking, consider taking a stout walking stick or long, pointed umbrella. These are helpful in warding off attacks.

Driving

Driving can be quite dangerous. Following are critical safety steps.

- Don't drive at night. Not only could you have an accident, but you could expose yourself to the risk of robbery, rape, and murder. This is not the time of day to be traveling anywhere in the Caribbean.
- Know where not to drive. The local people will give you advice on potentially dangerous areas. Certainly, you will want to stay out of poor areas in some of the region's major cities.
- Avoid off-road travel in areas where marijuana is likely to be cultivated, especially in Jamaica.
- Never stop if flagged down. Let locals handle local problems.
- Do not pick up hitchhikers.
- Reports of locals deliberately running into tourists have been reported. Their intention is to rob you. If you suspect this, don't stop, but drive to the nearest police station.

Drowning

- You're not allowed to swim on many beaches in the Caribbean. When in doubt about which beaches are safe, ask.
- Many people drown each year, most from carelessness. Always ask whether an area is safe for swimming. Many of the most beautiful beaches have dangerous riptides, even at waist level. Ask several people, not just one, about local conditions.
- A riptide is a fast moving river of water within the ocean itself. It does not pull you down, but moves you along the shore very rapidly, then out to sea. Most people struggle against the water and drown from exhaustion. Riptides may move out several hundred yards or more from shore but always go back in. Don't fight the water. Relax. Stay calm. Go with the flow. When you come back in toward shore with the tide, slowly swim across the current at a 45-degree angle. Eventually, you get to the edge of the current and can make your way into shore.
- If you get caught in a riptide, throw your hand up into the air and yell a few times—possibly someone will see you're in trouble and come to your aid. Otherwise, relax and follow the preceding advice. It is difficult not to panic. If you can control yourself and stay calm, you will survive.
- If you see that someone is in trouble, get a surfboard, boat, or float and get to the person as quickly as possible. Ask the person whether they need help. Do not get close to them until they answer "yes." A drowning person is extremely dangerous until coherent. When they answer "yes," then help them.

- If a person is unconscious, act quickly. Begin artificial respiration from the moment you make contact, that usually means in the water. Get air into the person's lungs as *quickly* as possible. Don't wait for the perfect moment or ideal conditions.
- Fifty percent of people who drown have a high blood alcohol level. It's not just drinking and driving that don't mix.
- *Special note:* Never dive into water. Always slide in gently. It is often difficult to detect submerged structures.

Rape

The basic rule for women is to not travel alone. Yes, many women do, but overall this is not a good idea. Single women are breaking a cultural taboo in many areas, and their behavior suggests sexual promiscuity. You're an easy catch (*conquista*). Following are tips from women who have traveled extensively in the Caribbean.

- Travel light. Remember that the weight of your luggage will affect both your attitude and your vulnerability.
- Get by with a single piece of luggage, one no larger than a carry-on bag for a plane. This gives you freedom and mobility in every situation, from public transportation to checking in at a hotel. Keep the bag with you at all times, even on buses.
- Two women traveling together are much better off than a single woman, but they should still be wary and avoid provocative situations.
- Whenever possible, travel with a group. If sightseeing, just blend in with a group if you think you might be hassled.
- Schedule most of your long-distance travel for the day. Try to avoid travel at night when you're more vulnerable.
- Women do not go out at night alone in some areas. Ask locally about any safety considerations.
- Never tell a stranger your room number. Always meet strangers in the lobby at a pre-fixed time.
- Be unattractive. This is totally contrary to what most women have been taught. Watch your hair—cover it up, keep it in a tight bun. Skip makeup, any kind of nail polish, and all perfume.
- Don't carry or wear any jewelry. This includes even cheap imitation jewelry. Thieves can't tell the difference. Is it worth getting hurt over a piece of jewelry?
- If you're hassled by men, wear a cheap wedding band even if you're not married. If you are, replace your real band with a fake one.
- Watch your dress. Avoid tight-fitting clothes that show off your figure. Don't wear high heels. And don't expose much of your body, especially your breasts and legs. Always wear a bra. If possible,

wear a light, loose-fitting blouse or shirt that covers your arms completely. If possible, wear cotton pants or a skirt that goes over your knees. Wear shorts only at the beach. Many women ignore this advice without serious consequences. However, their behavior is considered offensive by local residents.

- As silly as it sounds, wear glasses, even if you don't need them.
- Don't get into a cab by yourself, and make sure that you're not the last person to be left off. You can almost always share a ride (see p. 202).
- Don't get into an elevator, an alley, or any enclosed area with a man alone. Don't be anywhere alone with a stranger—period. And that includes a beach or jungle path.
- In a hotel, have your key in your hand as you make your way to the room. You'll avoid fumbling through your purse outside the door.
- Almost all hotel rooms have bolt locks in addition to the regular lock. If the lock seems flimsy, jam a chair underneath the knob to make it difficult to open. Tiny, portable alarms can be attached to doors to go off with a forced entry.
- It is not unknown for a proprietor of a hotel to take advantage of a passkey to make a pass. Bear this in mind when bolting or blocking a door.
- Do not leave windows open unless you've asked about safety first. Open windows may be a near necessity in some hotels without air-conditioning, so this becomes a sticky decision. Opt for a room as high up as possible.
- Do not accept gifts from anyone, unless you want a sexual relationship. The meaning of the gift outweighs its value and may force you into a compromising position.
- Simply ignore hissing and staring in the street—don't respond to any comments. If someone starts to hassle you, turn and say, "¡Deja me!" or "Laissez-moi!" which roughly means "Leave me alone!"
- Whenever possible, don't say anything at all. Responses often bring on more harassment.
- Topless and nude bathing is absolutely taboo on some islands. There are many exceptions. Follow the local lead. Never bathe topless or nude in an inland or isolated area.
- Beach boys who try to pick up foreign women are extremely common. It is understood (at least by them) that you will be paying for any future costs, such as dinner or evening entertainment. Beach boy, then, is a euphemism for gigolo. Some can become hostile if the unwritten rules are not followed.
- Find out where you're going before leaving a hotel in a major city.

Have directions figured out so that you don't have to stop in the
street.

- Walk confidently and rapidly. Look straight ahead. Don't look at
  men. Watch how the local women act and walk.
- Consider walking against the flow. This is a good way to see
  whether anyone is following you.
- Always carry the amount of money you'll need for the next few
  hours in small bills and change. You never want to ask someone
  to exchange large bills. And you don't want to carry lots of money
  with you unless necessary—and then it should be hidden.
- If it's possible, always let someone know where you're going and
  when you intend to be back. This could be a friend or just someone at the front desk of a hotel.

Robberies

Most robberies do not involve personal injury. However, a few
may. Particularly dangerous areas are found in Kingston on
Jamaica, Nassau on New Providence in the Bahamas, and Port-of-
Spain in Trinidad. Saint Thomas in the U.S. Virgin Islands is rough
in parts of the port area. Curaçao and Sint Maarten have been having problems recently. To avoid being harmed or killed, follow
these tips.

- Ask locally about dangerous areas. Stay out of ports, rowdy bars,
  and red-light districts. These are particularly dangerous at night.
- Finally, if you do get robbed, don't resist. Give them the money or
  the car. Say absolutely nothing. If you don't move, resist, or talk,
  your chance of bodily injury is minimal. As in the United States,
  some victims are shot for no reason. But this is not a reason to
  stop traveling. It can and does happen everywhere in the world
  today.
- Car robberies are on the rise. Deliberate bumping into rental cars
  does occur. If you feel that someone has deliberately run into you,
  drive away from the scene immediately and head to a populated
  area or the nearest police station or police officer. This kind of
  robbery involves a higher risk of personal danger and should be
  treated as a personal assault.
- Men should avoid all dealings with prostitutes, not only because
  of the threat of venereal disease, including AIDS (SIDA), but also
  because robbery with violence and drugging is common.
- Avoid the use of ATM machines.

Sharks

The danger of sharks should not be underestimated or exaggerated. I
was on an island when two men were killed by sharks, yet I have

never seen one in countless snorkeling and diving trips. The two men who died ignored critical advice given in the following tips.

- Ask locally about bays or areas known to have problems with sharks. Avoid these.
- If you are allowed to spearfish in an area, spear only one fish. Then get out of the water immediately. Go to another area miles away to get the next fish. When a fish is speared, it gives off vibrations that can be picked up easily by sharks. Spiny lobsters do not give off these distress signals.
- Never swim at night unless accompanied by professionals.
- If you see sharks, get out of the water—quickly but calmly. Certainly do not try to follow or get a closer look at a shark. Yes, there are shark encounters run by professionals. But then you would be with experts, told exactly what to do, how and when.

Snakes

Poisonous snakes are found on a few islands, especially on Martinique, Saint Lucia, and Trinidad. They are most prevalent at night, although you occasionally see one during the day. If you intend to hike in tropical forests, it's best to go with a knowledgeable local guide. Boa constrictors are also found on a few islands, but generally pose little danger.

Tropical Storms

There's an old saying that "tropical storms have no rudders." They are hard to predict. However, most storms occur in late summer through fall in the Caribbean. Whenever a storm approaches, get out. Don't take chances. Some are extremely deadly. The period after a storm is also painful for everyone involved with food and water shortages. Getting to the airport and out from an island can be difficult and, in some instances, dangerous. Looting is common.

Volcanic Eruptions

There are a number of volcanoes throughout the region. Volcanoes can be extremely dangerous. Both lava and poisonous gases emitted from the cone kill people. If one shows any signs of activity, get off the island. For example, the island of Guadeloupe was evacuated in 1976 when La Soufrière volcano showed signs of coming back to life. Most tourists fled Montserrat in 1995 when its volcano blew. Get off any island that has an active volcano as soon as you can.

Walking at Night

- In some cities tourists have been warned not to go anywhere at night except in a taxi. This is certainly true in Kingston on Jamaica, in St. Thomas, and in Port-of-Spain in Trinidad. Some areas are even dangerous in the day. Listen to local advice.
- Don't go out on beaches at night. This is a sad comment and *not* universally true throughout the region, but in many areas beaches are no longer safe. Ask if you're in doubt. The exception: Turtle watchers go out at night. It's best to be accompanied by a local guide. In fact, it may be required.

Yachting

Following are some basic safety tips for yachters. Others will be covered by any company from which you rent a boat (such as watching out for plastic fish traps). Follow their directions to the letter.

- Get to a mooring by late afternoon at the latest. Seeing reefs is extremely difficult in low light.
- Never sail at night—never! The waters are dangerous, and many local boats run without lights.
- Storms can be serious. Swells can be a problem along the northern coasts of many islands from November through April.
- You should have a life raft properly equipped with food, water, flares, and other safety items.
- Your boat should have enough water for at least one week and enough fuel to travel 700 to 800 miles in a pinch. This may require additional plastic fuel containers.
- Your anchor should be one that will hold. You should have a spare.
- Don't respond to distress signals without a full discussion of this with the company from which you are renting the boat. They'll give you several detailed tips in this regard.
- Whether to carry a gun or not depends on the area in which you'll be sailing. Personally, I'd avoid any areas where local companies indicate recent or even past troubles. Ask about this. Guns will have to be surrendered in most ports. Whether to carry a gun or not is highly controversial, but if you do, you should know exactly how and when to use it (which requires extensive training) and have the willingness to use it if should a crisis occurs (that's not necessarily in everyone's makeup).

Travel Between Islands

How you decide to travel between islands will depend on how much time, money, and energy you have. The possibilities are outlined below.

Plane Travel

Plane travel is the fastest and most convenient way to get to most islands. People behind the desk at most airports speak excellent English with some exceptions, such as Isla Margarita (Venezuela).

Flying Throughout the Caribbean

Much of the advice given on flying to the Caribbean (pp. 107–110) applies to flights within the region as well. But there are a few things to keep in mind that are quite different.

Regional Airlines and Reservations

Regional airlines vary in size, from serving just a few islands to a couple of dozen at most. Here are some important tips.

- Whenever possible make your reservations before traveling abroad through an agent specializing in Caribbean travel. You will often pay lower fares and taxes if you plan ahead and use a competent agent. You also don't go through an artificial currency exchange process, which often inflates the price of tickets bought abroad.
- Good agents know the difference between the carriers. One may have spacious seating and a good flight record; another flying the same route can be dismal. Good agents ask for feedback from their clients and sort out the bad lines.
- Regional airlines come and go. But, generally there is one or more line serving any destination with an airport. Most (not all) inhabited islands have an airport. The term airport might mean a shanty next to a dusty road with a taxi or two waiting for incoming passengers.

Reserving Flights Once Abroad

- Make onward flight arrangements when you arrive on an island. The longer you wait, the more difficult it may be to get a seat. It's generally easiest to reserve a seat right when you get off the plane if the counter is open. Do the same for reconfirmations of onward flights.
- Unfortunately, you may arrive at an airport with the intention of making onward reservations only to find no one behind the appropriate booth.
- Follow up the next day in any of the following ways.
- Call the airline directly. If there is a language barrier, ask someone at the front desk to help you. Tip accordingly. Get a confirmation number and the name of the person you (or your helper) spoke to. And, most importantly, go back to the airport and get your tickets.
- Or work through a local travel agent. If the agent tells you that a plane is fully booked, don't assume that this is true. Try another agent. If you're told the same thing, go to the airport.
- Call before going to the airport to see that someone will be at the booth. Get the name of the person you intend to talk to. At the airport ask for that person. Try to establish a bond and let the person know how important it is for you to get on a specific flight. A plane listed as full rarely is. Kind and persuasive people often will get an agent to issue a ticket on so-called full flights. Having done this on numerous occasions, I cannot stress enough the importance of persistence combined with courtesy and patience.
- In some instances, planes are indeed full. Ask about alternatives and waiting lists.
- Alternatives include other scheduled airlines or charters.
- Getting on a waiting list (*lista de espera*) as early as possible is the key to success. Have the agent explain how the local system works.
- The waiting list may be quite informal. For instance, on Isla Margarita you write your name on a paper on the day of departure. The person who gets their name on first will get the first available seat—you may have to show up hours in advance. As the time for departure arrives, a salesperson behind the counter begins reading off names. You have to hear and respond to your name to get on the plane—it's chaotic.
- There is yet another strategy. Ask the person behind the counter for the name of someone who might help you in regard to reservations. They may steer you to a separate booth or office. Now, ask for help in such a way that you are asking for a favor. Where

there is a language barrier, ask for someone who speaks English, even if you speak the local language. Explain the importance of getting on a certain flight and that you will really "appreciate" any assistance. The way you say this is clearly meant to disclose an intended gratuity. I don't like to use bribes, but occasionally they're necessary. Generally, the person who helps you does not want any exchange of money to be seen. Therefore, you might be led towards the gate as a cover for discreet tipping.

Regional Airline Idiosyncrasies

- Price may vary by airline. Prices on short hops often seem extremely high when compared to longer ones.
- Since convenient access to a number of islands is available primarily by air, you have no choice—you have to fly in at the inflated rates.
- Ask whether the price can be changed once you've paid for the ticket. Fares often go up at a moment's notice. You may be stuck with a surcharge if local law allows the raising of prices on tickets already paid for.
- When you buy a full-fare ticket in the United States, you can make last minute changes at no cost. However, foreign countries have different regulations. When you buy a ticket, ask whether there is any additional charge for cancellations or changes in flights.
- The regulations in regards to no-shows are also quite different. Ask about this when purchasing tickets.
- Always reconfirm your ticket as indicated. The easiest time to do this may be on your arrival.
- The term "confirmed" is almost meaningless on some islands. However, follow through with the appropriate motions and get the person's name.
- In all instances, show up when told to. If you are told to come an hour and a half early or even earlier, do it.
- Do not be surprised if there is no one behind the counter. Just stand in front of the counter and wait until someone shows up.
- If you arrive late, you may have a ticket but not get on the plane unless you're aggressive. In some areas the locals crowd around the counter trying to pressure the agent into selling tickets of "no-shows." Don't be timid. Just shove your way to the front and hold up your ticket indicating that you have the right to a seat you've already paid for.
- Seat assignments, if they exist, are often disregarded. Don't bother to get in a huff. Anger is considered poor form. Worrying about specific seats is simply not considered worth the effort. So if someone is sitting in your assigned seat, just find one that is open.

Actually, on most inter-island flights you just get on the plane and find a seat.

- Delayed or canceled flights are so common that they are a nonoccurrence. Experienced travelers carry a paperback to pass the time.

- In remote areas planes often show up two or three hours late or not at all. In some of these outback airports there is no shelter from sun or rain. Bring an umbrella, a good book, snacks, and something to drink.

- As mentioned earlier, flights are frequently canceled because they are not full or not full enough to make money. Of course, there is always a different excuse. Getting angry and frustrated does nothing except get you angry and frustrated. You are not going to change the system.

- Write off every day of your trip that includes a plane flight. Getting to the airport, waiting for the plane to come or take off, the flight itself, the trip into town or your resort from the airport—these all burn up time. Accept the fact in advance.

- There is practically no compensation for lost luggage, which is a good reason to travel with carry-on bags only. However, on small charter and commuter planes even the smallest bag is placed in the baggage compartment. If you absolutely cannot afford to lose something (such as medications), carry them with you onto the plane in a lightweight daypack. No one makes a fuss about these.

- Lock and label all your luggage.

- Again, keep your carry-on baggage light and simple. Local planes have little room for luggage, and walks to planes can be long, hot, and humid. You can also end up in a downpour when you least expect it.

- *Important:* From the above tips you've gathered a critical point. Planes are often not on time. This leads to an ultra-important strategy when traveling through the Caribbean. Leave lots of time between connecting flights. No one likes to do this, because sitting in airports is dreary. But most of the time you will not be sitting, but running to the next gate to catch a flight. Furthermore, if you miss a flight because of an earlier delay, it is amazing how little importance this carries in the Caribbean. One woman I met spent two days waiting to get a seat in just such a situation—not to mention having missed all other connecting flights along her intended route home; apparently, bribery didn't occur to her. This leads to the second point that I make repeatedly throughout the guide. Travel with carry-on bags only. I cannot tell you how many people arrive at a destination with lost or misdirected bags.

Small Private Companies (Scheduled and Charter)

- As mentioned earlier, there are a number of small companies operating in the Caribbean. A few have printed schedules, which they follow somewhat loosely, depending upon demand. You can often charter them to get you to some remote area or to some area at an inconvenient time.
- Flights offered by these companies tend to be more expensive than flights of a comparable distance offered by regional airlines running on a rough schedule. You'll learn about these tiny little outfits through word of mouth.
- Whenever chartering a plane, line up others who are willing to make a flight at the same time. The cost is then divided and becomes more reasonable on a per-person basis.

Airport Departure Taxes

When traveling between islands, ask in advance about departure taxes. The tax is often related to your destination, not to the fact that you're leaving the airport. In some instances, you may not have to pay any tax at all if your destination is within a specific area. But no one will tell you this unless you ask. They'll just hit you with the highest tax possible. Also, taxes may vary by destination: one price for one island, a second price for another island. Get this information from a local travel agent in advance. Ask several people for a consensus. This tip is especially important for someone who plans to fly to many islands during an extended trip.

Boat Travel

Many islands are connected by ferries, by mailboats, and by small motorboats. Following are some tips.

Cargo Ships

Getting on cargo ships is for the long-term traveler spending months in the islands. You can get to a surprising number of destinations if you can work through local companies and adapt to the schedules. The ships have vague schedules; you could be on a specific island for a couple of weeks before a cargo ship would even arrive or leave. But, if you're wily and willing to wait, this is an option.

Ferry Crossings

Ferries are common throughout the Caribbean. In some areas they carry passengers and freight between islands. On some islands they carry passengers to beaches and remote resorts. Some restaurants and resorts are located on their own islands. You'll be taking boats or ferries to get to these hidden treasures. When dealing with such restaurants or resorts, make reservations in advance and get specific instructions on how to get there. And finally, as on Martinique, you may have to take a ferry to cross a port. The ferries are in this way connected by yet another ferry. It's all part of the fun.

General Tips on All Ferries

- Ferries are most useful in the Grenadines, Guadeloupe (to nearby islands), and in the British and United States Virgin Islands.
- Schedules change constantly, and there is no way for a guidebook to keep up with them.
- Local people are often as confused about ferry schedules as you are. You have to go to the ferry office to find out reliable times of departure and current costs. Do not assume hotel clerks have either.
- Ferries may not operate on certain days.
- There is usually an inexpensive way to get to ferries, because locals use them regularly and don't have a lot of money to spare.
- If you keep your luggage to a minimum, you can easily take advantage of public transportation to and from ferries.
- Public transportation and ferry schedules, however, do not always match, so you may have a long wait.
- Bring food and water with you when taking any ferry, not only because you'll get hungry on board but because you may get hungry waiting.
- Ferries are very popular because they're cheap.
- Find out whether you can buy tickets in advance. Do this whenever possible.
- If you plan on carrying a bike or moped on a ferry, make sure this can be done in advance. They are not allowed on all ferries.
- Watch the weather. You don't want to be on a ferry in rough seas.
- There may be more than one port for ferries from one island to another. Prices may vary somewhat by which port you leave from.
- Ferries may vary in size and speed. Some of the smaller ferries may be extremely crowded because they are less expensive. So you're often saving money at the expense of comfort.

Mailboats

- The main center for mailboats in the Bahamas is in Nassau (New Providence). Go to the Dock Master's office on Potter's Cay near the Paradise Island bridge, or call (809) 323–1064.

- Mailboats travel to most islands in the Bahamas. If you have lots of time and patience, you can save a great deal of money by taking one of these.
- Mailboats do not leave every day of the week. Inquire locally about fares and schedules.
- Always arrive earlier than the given departure time. And expect a long wait. Schedules are "flexible."
- Travel light. Bring lots of food and water.
- Bring something to lie down on. A light, foam pad or similar material from a camping store is recommended.
- Expect bathrooms to be foul. Bring some toilet paper.
- Pack lots of patience and a good sense of humor. If you don't like it rough, take a plane.
- You will also find mailboats in other areas with equally ill-defined schedules.

Motorboats

- Motorboats may be hired to get you to remote areas. Or they may be provided by certain lodges to get you to private islands.
- When making a reservation for a hotel or resort on a private island, always ask whether the price of the ride to and from the hotel is included. These trips can be very expensive if not a part of the room rate.
- In many areas it often pays to rent a boat during your vacation. Not only can you get to and from your hotel, but you can explore nearby islands, go snorkeling or fishing, and so on.
- If you do intend to rent a boat in the peak season, make reservations well in advance.
- Also, make sure that you get a boat large enough to handle the potential swells from bad weather. The weather can change in minutes.

Yachts

You can hire yachts with or without crews in many areas of the Caribbean. This is an excellent way to island hop. Yachting is not only a means of transportation but also considered a place to stay and is covered in detail in the introductory chapter covering inter-island transportation, pp. 126–133. Some people are able to hitch rides (see p. 133).

Travel on the Islands

This chapter covers the basic information on getting around islands. A few tips will make this much easier and keep costs to a minimum. By getting around the way the local residents do, you'll save a great deal of money.

Bikes

Biking as a way of getting around is fine on some islands, almost impossible on others. The heat and humidity can be overwhelming unless you're in superb physical shape and used to biking at home. However, on some islands, especially the dry, relatively flat ones, biking is a reasonable option. The main problem is getting a bike. Don't count on this.

Bus Travel

Bus travel can get you just about anywhere on some islands, but it is often slow and extremely crowded since it's the only practical mode of transportation for many local people since cost is low. Buses don't exist at all on some of the most remote and scantily populated islands.

Car Travel

Although car travel is extremely expensive, it's often one of the best ways to see an island. If two or more people are traveling together, it may be cheaper than renting two mopeds or scooters. Reread the section on cars (pp. 134–139) for critical information on rates and insurance. *Make sure you can drive a stick shift.*

Important Note on Car Rental

Following are a few major tips in regard to renting a car in this region.

- Airport car rental agencies are sometimes oblivious to plane schedules. This means that they may close minutes before an incoming flight. This seems absurd to the foreigner, but it is a fact of life.

- The fact that you've reserved a car in advance does not mean that the car rental office will be open or have a car for you. If possible, schedule flights to arrive during the day and during the week rather than on the weekend.
- Car rental agencies are not always at airports. It may be easier to go your hotel, call from there, and have the car brought to you.
- A number of islands require you to buy a local license. You'll need your regular or International Driver's license to do this. Yes, this is a scam. It's also time-consuming and annoying. It does, however, help the local economy. Unfortunately, you may have to get this license even if renting a moped.

Bargaining

If you've made reservations in advance, this is not a consideration. If you're traveling in the peak season, I recommend reservations on most islands. However, when traveling in the off-season, learn to play the game. Be polite. Talk to the people behind the counter for awhile. Tell them what you're doing, how much you're looking forward to being on the island, and so on. Get to know their name. Then ask for a price. Don't get angry when you hear the outrageous figure. Just smile and tell them that you really can't pay that much. Continue negotiating until you arrive at a fair compromise. You may have to do this with several agencies to come up with the best price. Since the agencies in some areas are not located at the airport or ferry terminal, you may have to do this over the phone. You will save a great deal of money if you follow this advice. Again, this applies to off-season travel. On some islands there may be a language barrier, and you might ask someone in a tourist office or local travel agency to help you out (for a tip).

About Deposits

The deposit should be a reasonable amount. You should be able to make a deposit with a credit card. *Never use cash for deposits.* Getting cash back can be difficult. Or U.S. dollars may be converted into local currency. The deposit is returned to you in the island's currency, often difficult or next to impossible to convert back to dollars. When making a deposit, get in writing that the credit slip will be returned to you *immediately* on return of the car. If you are told that the car must be checked out, then have a reasonable time limit for inspection written on the contract.

About Deductibles for Collision

This subject is a sore one. It has already been covered in detail under trip preparation (see pp. 138–139). Do your homework in advance.

Who Can Drive

Generally, you and your spouse can drive the car if you have this in your contract. Some companies charge extra for an additional driver. You should have worked this out in advance. *Never, ever let anyone drive your car unless they've been registered as drivers with the car rental agency—never. This is illegal and will void your insurance in case of an accident.*

About Unlimited Mileage Agreements

- Some companies claim to be offering an unlimited mileage agreement when they are really not. For example, they offer a week's rental for a set price, but then you have to pay an additional charge after the first 600 miles (1000 kilometers). Avoid this trap by asking several times whether there's any mileage restrictions whatsoever. On non-English-speaking islands, write this on your contract: "Accepted with the understanding that this is an unlimited mileage agreement with no charge for kilometers (miles) driven."

- If you ask questions in car rental agencies only once, you'll often be told later that you "misunderstood" because of the language barrier. The language barrier has a way of crumbling under a barrage of questions, all really the same question asked in a lot of different ways. Use the technique of *repeated* questions to get a straight answer. And make notes of your agreements directly on the contract as outlined above.

- If time and mileage come out to be less than the amount of your unlimited mileage agreement, find out whether you can pay that smaller amount.

Checking Out the Car

When you rent a car, pretend that you're actually buying it. The extra time you take will pay off. However, on some islands you will have little choice in cars. The potholes and salt take their toll. Roads may be bad, cars worse. The point: Have any damage or anything that is not working noted on your rental agreement. If it isn't in writing, you may end up paying for it.

Directions

See the section on Communicating, p. 266. Getting good directions is difficult. Often, you will be told the wrong directions anyway. Always confirm directions several times to avoid going in the wrong direction. The lack of good road signs is extremely frustrating at times. Just remember that you're never really lost, just temporarily disoriented and having a good time, right?

Driving in the Caribbean

Driving on the islands is not at all like driving in the United States or Canada. However, using common sense, not drinking, wearing seat belts (if available), and resting when tired are certainly stressed worldwide.

Checkpoints

In some areas you may run into checkpoints. These are set up to check on contraband, guns, and drugs. In some countries the police or military are heavily armed. This can be disturbing, but it's a fact of life. Checkpoints are especially common on Isla Margarita. Locals insist that they are checking for people trying to dodge the draft and for stolen cars. Never drive through these checkpoints without being waved through. And carry all appropriate documents related to you and the car.

Destroying Car Rental Documents

Car rental documents contain valuable information for crooks. Throwing these into a trash bin is a bad idea, even if they have been ripped to shreds. As paranoid as it may sound, it's presently advised to burn these. Or, toss shreds into different garbage cans.

Hitchhiking

Overall, hitchhiking is not recommended. It is difficult to get a ride, and it's also potentially dangerous. Since public transportation is so cheap, why bother with hitchhiking? However, I do agree that on a few isolated islands with little traffic, it's easy, almost necessary, and relatively safe.

General Hitchhiking Tips

- Wherever you see trucks, you may be able to pick up a ride.
- Pick up a ride at a gas station. Offer to pay for part of the gas.
- Always carry all documents, money, and valuables on your person. Other important odds and ends should be in a little daypack that you take with you at all times—even to the bathroom.
- It's more comfortable and more productive getting rides in the early morning.
- Keep your gear light. People don't like to pick up lots of baggage with hitchhikers.
- Stay clean—this will help you get a ride, especially if you're asking tourists for help.

- Go through large cities or towns on the public transportation system. It's incredibly cheap. Start hitching from the edge of town.

Motorbiking or Motorcycling

Many islands have scooters, mopeds, or motorcycles for rent. On Bermuda this is the only way to get around on your own, other than walking, since car rental is not allowed. A few tips:

- If you haven't driven a moped, motorcycle, or scooter before, take it easy. Ask for explicit directions on how to start and drive the "bike." Some are quite simple; others more complicated.
- Mopeds are the easiest to handle. Motorcycles are too heavy for many people. Scooters are quite wobbly compared to mopeds, but they have more power and are recommended over a moped for hilly terrain.
- In hot areas it's natural to wear as little clothing as possible. This is not a good idea on motorized bikes. You should wear a long-sleeved shirt, long pants to protect your legs from super hot mufflers, and solid shoes instead of sandals or tennis shoes. Boots are best, but most people don't travel with them.
- Wear a helmet—not a pretend one, but an approved type that is solid. Yes, it is hot and uncomfortable, but it can save your life.
- Glasses with so-called unbreakable lenses or a bubble are recommended since you'll often be showered with dust and pebbles when a car or truck passes you.
- Consider wearing a bandanna over your mouth in dusty areas.
- Carry something to eat and drink. You never know when or where you might break down. Motorized bikes are often abused and rarely reliable.
- Costs for rental tend to be high on most islands. Bargain hard.

All About Taxis

Although you can use other forms of transportation for a fraction of the cost of taxis, the latter are sometimes the only realistic choice. Few taxis have seat belts, and in some areas meters do not exist.

Minicabs

On many islands there are vans that run along specified routes picking up and leaving off passengers along the way. These replace buses for the local inhabitants. Understanding routes and fares can be a bit complicated for the tourist, but using them can save a lot of money. Ask how to use this service when and where available. Always carry coins and small bills to pay for the fare. Always have a map with you and tell the driver exactly where you want to get off.

Regular Cabs

- Before getting into a taxi, agree on the appropriate fare. Never take a taxi without settling on a price first.
- If a fare is being quoted in dollars, ask whether the driver means U.S. or local dollars.
- In non-English-speaking areas, you need to be able to say only two things: Your destination and *"¿Cuànto cuesta?"* or *"Combien coûte-il?"* The latter mean "How much does it cost?" If you can't understand each other, resort to pen and paper.
- In a few towns you run into a rip-off situation where all the drivers refuse to quote you a fair price. Keep trying different taxis until one caves in.
- Your best strategy for keeping the cost of taxis down is to share a cab with other travelers.
- The more people traveling, the less the individual cost. Be aggressive. Ask other travelers if they'd like to share a ride with you.
- Your success ratio will be about 90 percent or higher. Very rarely should you have to take a cab by yourself. Couples can do this as easily as solo travelers.
- Payment should be exactly what you agreed upon. Most drivers do not try to cheat you once you've agreed upon a price, but a few will. Don't let the driver intimidate you into paying more—a good reason to get all prices in writing. No one can claim that the problem is the language barrier in this instance.
- If you alter your agreement by having the driver stop for an errand or shopping, by having him drive to a new or added location, or by making any change at all, then the driver has every right to charge you more than the negotiated price. So each time you ask for a change, discuss the *new* price.

Tours

On some islands getting around by taxi is extremely expensive. Car rental also may be difficult or overpriced. Tours are often a good option, especially for anyone traveling alone. Many guides put local tours down. Some really are pretty bad, but if you think of them as a way of getting from A to B, getting an overview of an island and perhaps a few insider's tips, and so on, it may be worth it if the price is right.

Walking

Many times the simplest and fastest way to get around a small town or city is by walking or combining walking with public transportation. On some of the smaller islands or ones with extremely limited public transportation, walking or hiking is the only practical choice. Travel light!

Staying Healthy
Once Abroad

This chapter covers the basics on health care in the islands plus detailed information on how to prevent or cure common health problems once there. The incidence of disease is lower in the Caribbean than in Central America and Mexico, but there are common problems, including bacteria and viruses on fresh foods, unsafe tap water, improper food preparation, and temperatures that favor the reproduction of disease-causing organisms.

Basic Health Vocabulary
(French/Spanish)

dentist	*dentiste, dentista*
doctor	*médecin, doctor*
fever	*fièvre, fieble*
hospital	*hôpital, hospital*
I am sick	*Je suis malade, Estoy enfermo*
I need a doctor	*J'ai besoin d'un médecin, Necessito un doctor*
medicine	*médicament, medicamento*
pain	*mal, dolor*
pharmacy	*pharmacie, farmacia*

Health Care in the Islands

Hospitals generally can't provide the same standard of care as you may be used to. Local blood supplies are definitely not safe, because these islands cannot afford the expensive screening process. However, doctors in the region often recognize common health problems and tropical diseases quickly because they have seen so many cases. Health care costs, including the price of drugs, is usually far more reasonable than in the United States.

Symptoms to Watch Out For

Go to a doctor during or after a trip if you have any of the following symptoms: bites that turn color or won't heal, chills, coughing (chronic), diarrhea that lasts over a week or is recurring, diarrhea with blood or mucus, excessive gas, fatigue, fever, headaches, itching, pain, rash, sweats, vomiting, welts or spots on your skin, or undue weight loss. *Important tip:* Tropical diseases may take weeks, months, and even years to appear. Keep a record of all countries you visit in case symptoms occur at a later date. Again, see a doctor specializing in tropical medicine.

General Health Problems

All travel involves some health risks. Following are some tips on the most common problems as well as a few warnings about relatively rare illnesses that may crop up.

Chagas' Disease

High fever is the most common symptom of this disease (also known as American *Trypanosomiasis*). Others include convulsions, swollen lymph nodes, stiff neck, and vomiting. A bite that swells, turns color, and gets hard is another warning sign. Each of these is a good reason to go to a doctor specializing in tropical medicine. Note, however, that the disease may not have any symptoms at all. The disease is caused by vampire-like biting insects called assassin or kissing bugs (*vinchugas*), which infect the blood with a parasitic protozoa (*Trypanosoma cruzi*). Bugs carrying this disease are most commonly found in dilapidated buildings, mud dwellings, thatched huts, and palm fronds. If you protect yourself with netting and use insect repellents, you decrease the odds of insect bites dramatically. Obviously, this is a disease most common with vagabonds and backpackers who sleep out in remote, rural areas. Don't delay getting medical help because the disease is most easily cured in its early stages.

Ciguatera (fish poisoning)

Fish poisoning is caused by a toxin (*ciguatoxin*) in reef plankton. Fish poisoning (*ciguatera*) causes a tingling in the mouth, nausea, and diarrhea. It can also cause persistent neurological problems. Fish that sometimes cause it are barracuda (usually ones over 2 feet), jacks, moray eels, parrot fish, and snappers. Local fishermen say that fish poisoning occurs only at certain times of year and with certain people, which suggests it may be an allergic reaction. However, in Florida the sale of barracuda is illegal. In the Caribbean, barracuda and other reef fish are routinely sold and eaten. It is true that the problem is sporadic, but it does exist and is worth noting. To be safe, eat fish that are caught offshore, such as dorado (dolphin), mackerel, marlin, swordfish, tuna, and wahoo.

Cuts

Any cut or wound in the tropics is dangerous. If you cut yourself seriously, wash out the wound with purified water and a disinfectant. Apply a sterile bandage, and see a doctor immediately. If you're bleeding a great deal, apply pressure to the wound to stop the bleeding. Small puncture wounds often do not bleed. Squeeze the wound until it bleeds. Clean with alcohol, Betadine, or Hibiclens. Apply an antibiotic ointment. See a doctor if the wound throbs or gets hot, painful, or red. Don't go barefoot. Wear sandals or old tennis shoes to avoid cuts and abrasions—even on beaches or in the water. Many beaches are covered with broken shells, and these can be razor sharp.

Dengue Fever

Dengue fever is a flu-like illness. The disease generally causes high fever and aches in your joints as well as headaches and a rash several days later. The virus (actually 4 types) causing the disease is carried by a mosquito (*Aedes aegypti*) that normally comes out at dawn and dusk in tropical areas. Prevent the disease by avoiding mosquito bites. If you do get dengue fever, drink lots of liquids, take acetaminophen (not aspirin), and rest. *Important:* A few people develop hemorrhagic dengue about one year after having dengue fever. Signs of this disease are high fever, rapid pulse, measles-like spots, and blood vomiting. Go immediately to a doctor specializing in tropical medicine, because this can be fatal if not treated immediately. Islands known to have cases of dengue fever: Aruba, the Bahamas, Barbados, Curaçao, Dominican Republic, Grenada, Guadeloupe, Jamaica, Martinique, Puerto Rico, Saint Lucia, Saint Vincent, Tobago, Trinidad, Venezuela, and the Virgin Islands (both British and United States).

Dehydration (also see Diarrhea)

In tropical climates you lose water quickly. The signs of dehydration are not sweating when you should, infrequent urination, a dry tongue, or extremely dark (deep yellow) urine. Dehydration is a common side effect of diarrhea. Dehydration is dangerous for everyone, but especially so with young children. Drink lots of fluids every 5 minutes, even if you aren't thirsty. Add salt to all fluids. Drink so much fluid that you have to urinate. Keep drinking until your urine is pale. No matter where you are, carry water or soft drinks with you as a safety precaution against dehydration.

Diarrhea (also see Dehydration)

This is a common problem for travelers anywhere. It can ruin a vacation. Diarrhea is not a disease, but a symptom of an underlying problem. In some cases, overeating, too much drinking, food allergies (such as to milk), menstruation, stress, dietary changes, loss of sleep, or fatigue may be the cause. Diarrhea is sometimes a side effect of Chloroquine phosphate, an anti-malarial medication. In many instances the problem is a bacterial infection. Occasionally viral infections and parasites cause this problem. Persistent diarrhea can also indicate a more serious underlying illness.

HOW TO TREAT DIARRHEA

- If diarrhea is accompanied by high fever (100°F), chills, severe dehydration, or blood or mucus in the stool, then see a doctor immediately. If you can't get to a doctor quickly, take antibiotics. Get to a doctor as soon as you can.
- Many antibiotics can make you sun sensitive or sun reactive. You get a rash. Ask about this ahead of time.
- If you have none of the above symptoms but have to travel immediately on a bus, ferry, or small plane without a toilet, go ahead and take something such as loperamide, commonly called Imodium (preferred) or Lomotil. Both lock in infections, but you don't have much choice.
- As soon as you can, stop taking these. Never take them for more than 3 days. They basically shut down movement in your digestive tract, and you don't want to do that for long.
- Pepto-Bismol (Bismuth subsalicylate) is milder and good for minor infections. This medication frequently causes stools to be black. This is not a problem. In some people, it causes ringing ears (*tinnitus*). Stop using the medication in this case. Aspirin does the same thing for a few people.
- The main danger of diarrhea is dehydration. So here's a diarrhea potion: In one glass, put 8 ounces of fruit juice (lots of potassium), $1/2$ teaspoon of sugar or honey, and a pinch of salt. Fill another glass with 8 ounces of purified or carbonated water and $1/4$ teaspoon of baking soda. Alternate swallows from each glass until both glasses are empty.
- Or pour salt and baking soda into a bottle of Coke and drink that.
- Also highly recommended is chicken broth with lots of salt.

- Some travelers on longer trips carry powdered electrolyte mixes, which help you recuperate quickly from a bout with diarrhea. Ask your doctor or pharmacist about possible choices, since there are numerous brands.
- If you drink clear liquids and eat bland food for 3 days without improvement, see a doctor.
- If you know ahead of time that getting to a doctor will be difficult, carry something like Cipro with you. This is one of the newer and more effective antibiotics. Unfortunately, it's outrageously expensive. The price is worth it when you're isolated and on a long trip. However, other antibiotics are available and quite effective if the cost seems unreasonable. Cipro cannot be taken with antacids.
- *Warning:* Diarrhea can make anti-malarial drugs, oral contraceptives, and some cardiovascular medications less effective. If you're on the Pill, it's a good idea to back up its use with other contraceptives if you've got diarrhea.

Fish Hooks

If you get hooked, push the barb through and out your skin. Cut the shank under the eye with wire cutters. Pull the hook out. Do not try to pull the hook out until the shank has been cut. Force the cut to bleed profusely. Clean and apply an antibiotic ointment. If the wound gets red or painful, see a doctor immediately.

Fish Poisoning (see **Ciguatera**)

Fish (poisonous)

There are some creatures, many of them fish, you don't want to encounter when snorkeling or diving: bristle worms, eels, fire coral, porcupine fish, scorpionfish, stonefish, and zebrafish. As one local fisherman put it, stepping on a scorpionfish is like seeing your grandmother naked. Avoid such stings by keeping your hands out of holes and your feet off the ocean bottom or coral while snorkeling or diving. Anyone stung while swimming should seek immediate medical attention. People have died from stings.

Heat Prostration/Sunstroke

Tropical sun can cause a lot of damage, especially between 11:00 A.M. to 2:00 P.M. If you're going to be out in the sun for long periods of time, never underestimate its effect.

- Wear light-colored, lightweight, and loose clothing.
- Never travel without a wide-brimmed hat.
- Drink lots of fluids. Carry soft drinks and bottled waters with you.
- Put more salt on your foods than you normally would.

- Avoid hiking, playing tennis, jogging, and other strenuous activities in the middle of the day. Do these in early morning or late evening when it cools off.
- If you know you're getting too hot, get out of the sun into any available shade.
- Lie down and rest.
- Anyone who gets flushed, hot and dry skin, and runs a rapid pulse should get to a doctor immediately. If ice is available, get into an ice bath until your temperature drops to 102°F. Sunstroke can be fatal.

Infections

All infections should be taken seriously, even if they seem minor. Clean them frequently, preferably with alcohol, and treat them with an antibiotic ointment.

Jellyfish

If you find yourself surrounded by jellyfish, dive down and try to swim under them. If you're already in the tentacles, dive down to get out of them. Note that a turtle's favorite food is jellyfish. That should tell you something about swimming in areas where lots of turtles are coming into shore to lay eggs. Leave jellyfish stranded on shore alone. They may still be able to sting you. Jellyfish are most common in summer and early fall. They vary from quite small to giants such as the Portuguese man-of-war with tentacles streaming out as far as 100 feet.

- Here are a few things that might take away the sting: ammonia (mild), antihistamine cream, Benadryl (*jarabe*), cortisone cream, meat tenderizer, Windex, papaya juice, rubbing alcohol, vinegar, or warm saltwater. A fisherman told me that urine, as awful as it sounds, is the most effective and immediately available remedy.
- If you're trying to help someone else, wear gloves if available. Rub the area off with saltwater and sand. Never use freshwater.
- If a person faints or can't breath after a jellyfish sting, get them to a doctor immediately. Some people are highly allergic to the toxin and react to it like a bee sting.

Leishmaniasis (see Sandflies)

Malaria

Prevent malaria by taking Chloroquine phosphate and protecting yourself from mosquito bites. Malaria is primarily a concern on the island of Hispaniola (Haiti and the Dominican Republic).

Manchineel Trees (*Hippomane mancinella*)

Many plants in the tropics are poisonous. The most common problem for tourists is the manchineel tree, which produces poisonous apple-like fruits. On some islands these trees have been destroyed. On others they continue to be a problem. Some are marked with a red stripe as a warning; others may not be marked at all. Ask to see a manchineel tree so that you know what it looks like. Never touch any part of the tree. Never stand under it during a rain. The sap can cause a rash or even blisters. The fruit is highly toxic and should never be eaten. These trees are most common on Barbados, Grenada, Martinique, Montserrat, and St. John. Many are located near beach areas.

Mosquitoes

Mosquitoes are responsible for dengue fever, malaria, and yellow fever, as well as some lesser-known ailments. Protecting yourself from mosquito bites is very important. Use DEET.

Motion Sickness (Sea Sickness)

You're either susceptible to this or you're not. Common symptoms are nausea, dizziness, and vomiting. To prevent this illness, take medication such as Benadryl, Bonine, Dramamine, Marezine, Phenergan, and Scopolamine (Transderm-V). The latter consists of a little patch placed behind your ear. Follow directions exactly because many have to be taken well before travel to be effective.

Rabies

If you're traveling with small children, tell them not to play with stray animals. Rabies is quite common in developing areas. Anyone exploring caves should be extremely cautious about this disease. Besides dogs and bats, the mongoose (introduced to a number of islands) may also be a carrier. Although painful, prevention is well-advised for anyone planning to explore caves. Anyone bitten by any animal while traveling abroad should see a doctor *immediately*. If it's possible to capture the animal without getting bitten yourself, do it. If not, kill the animal, but do as little damage to its brain as possible. Bring the animal to the doctor for testing. Clean any wound immediately with sterile water and disinfectant.

Sandflies

These minuscule insects attack tourists in many beach areas, mainly at dawn and dusk. The Dominican Republic (*Republica Dominicana*) has many beaches infested with no-see-ums (*purrujas*) and sandflies (*jejenes*). They most commonly bite your legs from the ankles up to the knee. Insect repellent works. So does clothing saturated with insect repellent. Wading in the water also stops immediate attacks. Sandflies do carry diseases. If a bite gets larger than a dime, begins to ulcerate, or turns a strange color, see a doctor specializing in tropical medicine. You may have Leishmaniasis (*Papalomoyo*). This disease normally takes several weeks to develop, and, in some cases, much longer. The earlier it's treated, the better.

Schistosomiasis (Bilharziasis)

This is a curable but unpleasant parasitic (blood fluke) disease caused by the larvae (*cercariae*) of freshwater snails. These snails are found only in freshwater (not chlorinated or saltwater) on a number of islands, most commonly on Guadeloupe, Martinique, Puerto Rico, Saint Lucia (especially here), and the Dominican Republic. They are most common in still, rather than rapidly moving, water, although the latter may also be infected. The larvae penetrate your skin and then work their way into your system. The disease may or may not cause symptoms that include coughing, diarrhea, fever, gut pain, headache, joint pain, loss of appetite, nausea, seizures, weakness, and weight loss. The simplest way to avoid this disease is to not swim in freshwater in the tropics. Freshwater used in showers in many remote areas is also not safe, unless heated above 122°F for 5 minutes. Many water heaters do not reach this temperature. It is very difficult to get information about this disease because much of the romance of the Caribbean is summed up in photos of nearly nude tourists bathing under a cascading fall in the middle of the jungle. If you do swim in freshwater, dry yourself off immediately with a towel. This reduces but does not eliminate the risk of being infected by these flukes. Applying rubbing alcohol, no less than 70 percent pure, over all exposed skin areas also helps reduce the chance of infection. If you come in contact with freshwater in the tropics and have any suspicion that you might have become infected, have a stool and urine test 6 to 8 weeks after exposure. Schistosome eggs can be detected. Treatment should begin immediately to avoid long-term damage to your bladder, intestines, liver, and lungs.

Sea Sickness (see Motion Sickness)

Sea Urchin Spines

If you step on a sea urchin or get pushed into one by a wave, you will get pricked by one of the sharp spines, which may lodge in your skin.

- Pull it out with tweezers (almost impossible), or use a needle to get it out. Get the wound to bleed slightly. Or squeeze lime over the spines, drip candle wax over them, and let the wax peel off on its own.

- Anyone stuck by a sea urchin should see a doctor to make sure that all pieces of the spine are removed because they may migrate to other parts of the body.

Stingrays

Stingrays like to rest in the sand along the shoreline. When you walk into the sea, shuffle your feet instead of taking big steps. The rays scurry off, more afraid of you than you are of them. If you get whipped by their tail and poisoned, get to a doctor immediately.

Sunburn

Sunburn and diarrhea are the two most common health problems. Dangerous ultraviolet rays come through even on cloudy days. With hundreds of thousands of cases of skin cancer reported each year, doctors insist that *no* sunbathing is best. Deadly melanoma has doubled in the last 10 years among the young. As you approach the Equator, the power of the sun increases by as much as 25 percent. Damage to the skin by sun is cumulative. Unfortunately, if you're older, most of the damage has already been done. Locals often refer to tourists as *backra*, local trees with stringy bark, in reference to the common look of our skin. So to avoid looking like a local tree, use sunscreen with a sun protective factor (SPF) of no less than 15 and wear protective clothing (especially a wide-brim hat to protect your nose and ears).

Typhus

This is a serious disease with symptoms of high fever, severe headache, delirium, and a red rash. It is caused by being bitten by lice or ticks, which carry tiny, disease-causing microorganisms (*Rickettsia*). Get to a doctor immediately. Avoid sleeping in hotels that are obviously dirty and insect ridden. Use insect repellent to keep lice and ticks off your body.

Yellow Fever

If you plan to travel to Tobago, Trinidad, or Venezuela en route to islands off their coast, you should get vaccinated (see p. 14).

Eating and Drinking

Many Caribbean restaurants and resorts serve rather bland dishes meant to appeal to timid tourists. Others take advantage of local fruits, meats, seafood, and vegetables and create both *haute cuisine* (matching the finest European cooking) or native cuisine, commonly called Créole or West Indian (*cocina criolla, comida criolla, cuisine créole, jibaru cuisine*). This native cuisine is intricate and varied, relying on a wide assortment of spices to give local ingredients a special flair. It blends many traditions from native Amerindian to African to European. On Trinidad you'll find exotic Indian cuisine, which offers vegetable dishes served in every imaginable way. Finally, there are numerous local restaurants and food stands that serve extremely basic foods at a fraction of the price of more trendy or tourist-oriented restaurants.

On some islands you'll be offered certain dishes made from endangered animals. Please do not eat the following: agouti (like a guinea pig), armadillo (manicou, tatoo, or tatou), iguana (even where they claim to raise it domestically), lobster (if out of season or undersize), opossum (manicou), and turtle (not even on Grand Cayman where they raise it commercially—wild turtle is much better and close to extinction).

Special Tips on Spices

The following spices are commonly used throughout the Caribbean. A brief description parenthetically follows each: allspice (dried, pea-size berries of the Pimento tree); bay (leaves from an evergreen tree—should be removed from any dish since spines can be dangerous if eaten); capsicum (the spicy hot flavoring found in hot peppers—technically not a spice, but used in many Creole dishes); cinnamon (bark of an evergreen tree removed and rolled into sticks or "quills"); clove (unopened and dried flower buds of trees); curry (a combination of spices); ginger (tuberous root of reed-like plant); mace (lace-like red membrane around nutmeg seed—dried); nutmeg (dried and processed seed taken from a yellow apricot-like pod of a tree); pepper (dried and ground pea-size berries—peppercorns—from the vining *Piper nigrum* plant); turmeric (aromatic root commonly referred to as "false saffron"); vanilla (distilled liquid made from the beans taken from the pods of a climbing orchid); and vanilla substitute (made from the almond-shaped seeds stripped from Tonka bean pods).

Special Tips on Rum

When sugar is made, the by-products of molasses and juice are fermented into rum. Some of this is so strong that ice sinks in it as with Jackiron made on Barbados and often referred to as "Jack." Most rum is used in mixed drinks. The quality of such rum varies from marginal to quite good. Rums vary in color by how they are aged. Darker rums are usually held in oak barrels, giving them not only their distinctive color but flavor as well. Some rums are extremely dry, while others are sweet. A few are flavored with local herbs and spices. However, there are some very special rums that you drink like a fine cognac or whiskey. These are delicious and reasonably priced, one of the great buys in the Caribbean. Producing the finest rum in the region has become an obsession for certain distilleries. Following are some of the finest rums as rated recently in the *Wine Enthusiast* (ratings are in parentheses with 100 as perfection)

Bermuda
Gosling's Black Seal Rum (96)

Dominican Republic
Brugal Anejo (88)

Jamaica
Appleton Estate Extra 12 Year Old (97)
Appleton Estate Dark (94)
C.J. Wray Light Dry Rum (86)
Myer's Original Dark (84)

Martinique
Rhum Saint James Royal Ambre (91)
J. Bally 1986 (85)
Chauffe Coeur Dark Rhum (85)

Puerto Rico
Captain Morgan Original Spiced Rum (85)
Bacardi Reserve (85)
Bacardi Dark (81)

Virgin Islands (British and United States)
Cruzan Premium Estate Diamond Rum (88)
Cruzan Light Dry Rum (85)
Pusser's British Navy Gold (81)

Finding Places That Serve Local Food

Few residents of the islands can afford the food in fancier restaurants and resorts. Most go to places with prices that may be just a fraction of those oriented to tourists. Some of these are individual places that become famous over time; others are streets with numerous small restaurants, such as Baxter's Road in Bridgetown on Barbados at night, or open stands serving local specialties, as in Port-of-Spain on Trinidad; and still others are just simple spots close to the sea or in town that cater to local tastes. These may just offer service at a communal counter. Places serving rum or beer often have snacks for sale. Take out may be referred to as take away.

- Ask locally about restaurants noted for local foods. Ask about areas with numerous restaurants serving simple, local dishes.
- On some islands there are few restaurants, so you may have to go to small local hotels.
- Some hotels are noted for serving fine local foods, and you may choose to stay in them just for this reason.
- Papers often advertise church or social gatherings. If you go to these, you'll often be treated to dishes that are not normally served in restaurants or hotels. Church bulletin boards often list such gatherings.
- Churches and organizations also have fundraisers, just as in Canada and the United States. These often feature local specialties.
- Many of the islands produce liqueurs and rums. If you want to sample these, ask about distillery or factory tours. You often can sample varying types for free or at a minimal charge.

Fashionable Restaurants

Fashionable restaurants are found in the major cities, in world-class resorts, and occasionally, but rarely, in remote areas. Capital cities often have more upscale restaurants, some in hotels, than the entire rest of the country because they are supported by local businesses and diplomats. Most of these restaurants are very well-known by local residents. Travel guides cannot keep pace with what restaurant is in and what's out. If you really want to know, go to a luxury hotel and ask the concierge. If a restaurant is difficult to get into, tip the concierge and ask him to make reservations. Eat at the same time that locals would for best service and food. Dress appropriately.

Islands Noted for Exceptional Food

Certain islands in the Caribbean are noted for fine cuisine. This means that many, not just a few of the restaurants and resorts, offer excellent cooking. These include Anguilla, Aruba, Barbados, Curaçao, the Dominican Republic in Santo Domingo especially, Grand Bahama, Guadeloupe, Jamaica, Martinique, New Providence in the Bahamas, Saint Bart, Saint Lucia, and Saint Martin/Sint Maarten. Choosing which island is the very best from this list is next to impossible, but many lean toward Guadeloupe.

Hours

Do not assume that finer restaurants will be open every day or for both lunch and dinner. Furthermore, some may shut down for part of the year when tourists are a rarity.

Getting to Restaurants

If you don't have your own transportation, you may have to hire a cab to get to a restaurant. Have an agreement with the cab to pick you up. Get the taxi's telephone number or set a specific time giving yourself plenty of time to eat.

Reservations

Better restaurants usually require reservations. So do many others, preparing only the amount of food for expected customers.

- It's best to call immediately on arrival to make sure that you'll get into a restaurant with a fine reputation, especially during the peak season.
- Reservations are most difficult in the evening, so if you're willing to eat your major meal at noon, you'll have a better chance of getting into a famous place.
- If you're traveling alone, try to make a reservation for an off-peak period. Go early for lunch and early for dinner. Most elegant restaurants frown on diners eating alone because they take up a table that could be used for more people. By avoiding the prime dining time, you'll have better and friendlier service, and you'll still have a chance to enjoy a finer restaurant.
- Still, it's more enjoyable to go to a fine restaurant with another person, because the livelier atmosphere at the peak dining time is part of the fun. Furthermore, if you're a single woman, you'll avoid many hassles by finding a dinner partner for the evening (see p. 227).
- If you have difficulty making a reservation and absolutely must eat

in a certain place, ask your concierge or one in a luxury hotel to make reservations for you. Tip appropriately.

- On more remote islands it is often necessary to make reservations for both lunch and dinner, even in modest places. The restaurant simply may not be prepared to take unexpected guests. If you don't call well in advance, you may not be served.
- Part of the fun of the Caribbean is that some restaurants are on isolated islands. They can only be reached by boat. The island's sole dwelling might be the restaurant itself. These require reservations far in advance and are favorites of yachters.

Dress Requirements

When making a reservation at a fine restaurant, ask about dress requirements. Very few places have stringent dress codes—a small percentage in the Caribbean require coats. Ties are required in only a few. Bermuda, farther north in the Atlantic, tends to be conservative. Coats and often ties are required in many restaurants.

- In expensive resorts go with the tide, which often means zany and outlandish costumes for the "in" places—festive and beachy. Or it might mean the most casual outfits imaginable. Every place sets its own tone. You'll know almost immediately what goes. But it is wise to ask ahead when making reservations, especially if you don't want to dress up for meals.
- Even fancy resorts lean toward casual in *most* instances because people are on vacation. Residents equate a tie with a hangman's noose, even though it is common in some businesses.

Drinking with Meals

- Imported liquor tends to be extremely expensive. You may be stunned by the prices of American-style cocktails.
- Mixers, such as soda or tonic, are part of the reason such drinks are so expensive. These often cost more than local liquors.
- Drinks made with local rum are generally reasonably priced. Still, in fashionable restaurants you're going to pay as much as ten to twenty times what you'd pay in a local restaurant for a local drink.
- Beer goes well with regional dishes. Drinking beer is not considered gauche. Local beers are varied and excellent. They are also less expensive than mixed drinks.
- Wines are served in the finest restaurants, but they may be stored improperly. If you're in doubt about wines, why not try a glass first?

- Wines tend to be outrageously priced. Know the price before you order. This will avoid confrontations at bill time.
- Wines from Chile are often better buys than those from other areas. They are also quite good if properly handled. The following publication rates wines throughout the world and has covered Caribbean rums and Chilean wines in earlier editions.

> Wine Enthusiast
> 8 Saw Mill River Road
> Hawthorne, NY 10532
> Tel: (914) 345–8463

Service

- Slow service is not considered bad service. Fine restaurants allow you to enjoy a meal at a leisurely pace. Truly poor service does exist—sometimes where you would least expect it.

Good but Cheap Restaurants

On most islands it's possible to find good but cheap restaurants.

Finding Budget Restaurants

- If you're staying in a budget hotel, ask someone where a good but cheap restaurant is located. They'll usually be glad to offer a suggestion or two.
- Define the amount of money you're willing to spend so that they know what is meant by cheap.
- Your idea of good is very subjective. You might want to be more specific. Who has the best chicken in town? Where can I get *fresh* fish? Which place has the best local food? Which offers the most food for the best price?
- Ask other travelers about their finds. This is one of the simplest and most effective ways to come up with current information— much better than most books.
- Look around. When you're out sightseeing or shopping, check out the little places available. Start to get a gut feeling about the options.
- Good local places for foods may not be immediately evident. Pubs and rum shops may serve tasty and reasonably priced food. Keep your options open.
- Eventually, you may discover that you're thinking in terms of cheap but good dishes, rather than cheap but good restaurants.

Barbecues, Brunches, Buffets

Special meals are available throughout the week and become island traditions. A barbecue might be right on the beach or on top of a hill with a fabulous view and lots of local music. These are fun because you're often mixing with local people and enjoying local food and entertainment. You have to ask about these. And in some cases a certain brunch or buffet is such an island tradition that you need to make reservations immediately on arrival. The buffet at the Atlantis Hotel in Bathsheba on Barbados or Sunday brunch at the Lookout Restaurant at Shirley Heights in Antigua are examples.

Tea

On a number of islands with a British heritage the custom of tea continues. A number of hotels offer this special treat. Ask locally about hours, usually around 3 or 4 P.M., and the best places to eat. Some offer tea around the pool in '90s style; others are much more traditional, with settings reminiscent of Great Britain with lots of silver and white linen. Cakes, pastries, scones, sandwiches, and, of course, a wide variety of teas are served at these, often on terraces overlooking the sea. *Warning:* Teas on some islands are made from mushrooms, the kind that produce hallucinogenic side effects. Make sure you know what kind of tea is being offered in food shacks, not to be confused with the proper teas outlined above.

Food and Money

Get full value for your money, while being fair in your demands and tips. Here are a few pointers.

Tax

All restaurants catering to tourists charge a stiff government tax on the total bill. This tax is not a tip, it is not a service charge, it is not going to the waiter. And it is rarely included on the prices listed on the menu. In small, informal restaurants catering mainly to locals you may not get charged this tax. But if you are, it's perfectly legal.

Tips

Wages for waiters are very low, and they make most of their income from tips. Tip generously. Tip waiters directly to see that they really get the tip. But read the following sections before tipping at all.

Checking the Bill

- As you're ordering, try to keep a rough idea of the total cost of the meal.
- Check the bill carefully for errors. If the bill seems especially high, ask to see the menu again.
- Locals do not like to make separate checks for customers. They much prefer overall bills for large groups of people. One person should pay the bill.
- Bills may already include local taxes and service charges. Ask to be sure.

Credit Cards

- Credit cards are useful in most restaurants catering to tourists. American Express and Visa cards are the ones most commonly accepted. Surcharges are sometimes added for their use in restaurants. If you don't want to pay a surcharge, simply rip up the receipt and pay in cash.
- Keep the receipts filed until the charges come in—that could be several months later in the case of some charges in more remote or laidback areas.
- *Special tip:* The amount noted on the top line of the charge slip may already include local tax and a service charge (tip). However, the line for the tip may be left blank. If you add an additional amount on that line, you're tipping twice. Ask whether the tax and service has already been added. If it has, strike the tip line and fill in the total on the bottom line. This practice is quite common.

Cutting Costs

- ☐ One of the simplest ways to cut costs is to eat less—a good idea for your health in a hot region.
- ☐ Don't eat breakfasts in hotels, unless the price of your room includes it. Ask when you check in. Most breakfasts at hotels are simple, including coffee and rolls. In a few hotels they are substantial, including cheese, meats, fresh juice, even pancakes. Such a breakfast adds real value to the room price.
- ☐ Don't eat breakfasts in restaurants. They are a poor value in most of this region.
- ☐ Improvise your own breakfast with pastries, fresh breads, tropical fruits, and "home-brewed" tea or coffee.
- ☐ Eat your biggest meal at lunch to take advantage of daily specials, local specialties, or set-price meals, which give you every-

thing from soup to nuts at a reasonable price. In many areas lunch is the main meal for the locals. It's usually filling and reasonably priced.

☐ Eat in truly local restaurants where dishes are a fraction of the price of the more commercial tourist spots. Go to places that are busy. Ask to see a menu. Sometimes there is no menu. Dishes are posted on the wall.

☐ Stick to hearty, simple dishes. With these dishes in mind you can be on a starvation budget and still not starve.

☐ Stew is commonly available in local restaurants and is generally a good buy.

☐ Chicken is also a good value on most islands.

☐ Fresh fruit plates—slices of oranges, moist mangos and papayas, cubes of cantaloupe, slices of fresh pineapple—are not cheap, but usually next to great.

☐ An excellent buy is the fish of the day. If you're trying to keep the bill down, the cost of this kind of fish is very reasonable.

☐ Split inexpensive combination platters. These usually come with oversize portions, easily enough for two. Simply ask for a second plate. Waiters do this with little problem. Occasionally there's a small charge for an additional plate, but not very often. You're in an area where thrift is seen as a virtue.

☐ Some of the budget restaurants serving local dishes don't charge government taxes.

☐ Skip lunch and settle for a picnic. Fresh bread, a few slices of cheese and canned ham, peanuts, a bar of chocolate, some tropical fruit—what more could you ask for if you're on a tight budget?

☐ If you want to save money but eat in a really fine restaurant, prices at lunch are often much lower than they are in the evening, especially for the set-price meal. So if you're mainly interested in an elegant meal at an excellent price, lunch is the best time in fashionable restaurants.

☐ Drink water in better hotels and resorts, if it comes free with the meal and if it's purified.

☐ Soft drinks are more expensive than tap water, but you can't drink the tap water in budget restaurants, so you're stuck. Soft drinks fill a void and are safe and reasonably priced. You won't be able to live without them. Neither can the locals.

☐ Drinks may be served at room temperature. This includes soft drinks and beers, which most tourists would like to be ice cold.

☐ If you're at all anxious about the ice in a bar or restaurant, ask for your drinks without it. Don't worry about ice in fancier places. It's made from purified water.

☐ Try freshly squeezed fruit juices. The huge glasses of fresh orange juice are simply delicious. Many tropical fruits are also available. Pure juice is more expensive than soft drinks but loaded with vitamins. Avoid juices mixed with water, ice, or milk unless you're in a reliable hotel or restaurant. It is very common to find juices mixed in this fashion. They taste great and are safe as long as they are made with purified water and ice or pasteurized milk.

☐ Stick strictly to local beer and rum. All imported liquors have a huge tax added to their cost and rarely are worth the extra charge. Local beers are universally good throughout the entire region, reasonably priced, and safe to drink.

☐ Skip coffee at the end of a meal, if you can, because it's expensive and has little food value. In most hotels or boarding houses serving meals as a part of the overall room price, coffee is considered a part of the meal, but ask to be sure. Coffee is exceptionally good in Jamaica and Puerto Rico.

☐ Always carry food and water with you when traveling, especially from one island to the next. You'll often be stuck waiting. Having something to eat and drink makes these waits bearable.

Communicating

English is spoken throughout most of the Caribbean. On some islands Dutch, French, Papiamento or Papiamentu, and Spanish are the main languages. Dutch is spoken on Saba, Sint Eustatius (Statia), and Sint Maarten. French is spoken on Guadeloupe, Martinique, Saint Bart, and Saint Martin, and on a number of smaller islands off these. Papiamento is the main language of Aruba, Bonaire, and Curaçao. And Spanish is spoken in the Dominican Republic, Puerto Rico, and Venezuela's offshore islands (Isla Margarita).

Communicating on Non-English-speaking Islands

Don't let the language barrier discourage you from visiting non-English-speaking islands. On all Dutch-speaking islands most of the people speak English. You'll have little trouble communicating in areas where there's heavy tourist traffic on French and Spanish islands. You'll usually find someone in most hotels, restaurants, shops, and travel terminals who speaks English. However, when you get off the beaten path, you may run into a language barrier. You'll manage by combining a few key words with sign language. Knowing the local language is most useful in rural areas of the Dominican Republic, on Guadeloupe, on Martinique, in rural areas of Puerto Rico, and on the islands off Venezuela.

The Fundamentals
Although it takes years to learn a foreign language well, take the time to learn a few basic expressions and how to count; it will not only prove helpful but also prove to be the right thing to do. No book can show you how to pronounce foreign words correctly. Have a native speaker pronounce them for you, and don't be afraid to ask. Most people are complimented that you're taking the time to try. A few words that come up frequently in the Caribbean are Anse (a bay), Arawak (one of the original tribes on the islands), Carib (another local tribe, which killed off the Arawaks), Cay (pronounced "key" and meaning a small island), Caye (a reef), and Créole (people or type of cooking native to the region).

Dictionaries

You don't have to carry books with you anymore. There are tiny calculator-like translators that convert English to French and Spanish (and vice versa) available in many office supply stores. They generally contain 40,000 words and expressions. Some of the translators cover up to 5 languages.

Tricks for Communicating

- Don't be complicated. Say "Menu, please," not "I would like a menu, please."
- Repeat statements or questions only once—slowly and without raising your voice. No go? Smile and thank them in the foreign language.
- If your comprehension is limited, try to communicate in writing. Carry paper and pen, and get waiters and clerks to write down prices for you.
- By all means, try. Say something, even if it's in English. Silence is considered rude.
- In short, don't be intimidated by the language barrier. Don't let it stop you from venturing into remote areas that may end up being the highlight of your trip.

Hissing

On some islands the way people get your attention is by hissing. Don't be offended. It's considered more polite than yelling out your name.

Asking Directions

Asking directions is a real art, one that comes with experience and common sense.

- Always greet someone before you ask any questions. This is considered basic good manners.
- Keep your question ultra-simple. Don't get fancy. All you want to do is to get to where you're going.
- The simplest way to do this is to use the word *à* or *a* in French or Spanish. This means "to" and is pronounced "ah" as if you're showing your tonsils to a doctor. Follow *a* by the place you want to get to. For example, "ah" whatever destination. Now say this as a question, and you've found the simplest way to ask a direction.
- If you're not going in the right direction, the person will shake his finger and point you in another direction. If you're going in the right direction, he'll just nod and say "oui" or "sí." You do not need an extensive vocabulary to communicate directions.

Sense the Nature of the Response

- It is considered more polite to give a wrong answer than none at all. You can sometimes tell when someone really doesn't know the right direction.
- Some people may be confused by your accent or your looks. They don't really listen to what you're saying because they're intrigued by how different you are.
- If you don't trust an answer, ask again—but this time ask someone else. If you get a different answer, ask yet another person. You're trying to get a consensus.

Things Not to Do

- Don't take out a fancy multicolored map and ask for directions.
- Don't get angry if someone doesn't understand you. It's not their fault that you're lost and don't speak their language and can't understand their accent.

Other Tips on Directions

- A small compass can be very useful on any trip. If you're traveling in unfamiliar terrain, this can at least get you headed in the general direction. Obviously, in some areas you have to drive away from a point for awhile to get to it in the end.
- Remember that some areas may have more than one name. Or locals may use a local landmark for directions rather than a town. Yes, it can get confusing. "Oh, just go up the hill and down, look for this little red house on the right. You can't miss it." You can.
- Always ask about how far it is from here to there. When someone says it's a long way, it may mean a long way on foot. A short distance might mean ten miles to someone else. Try to have some idea how far they mean when they say close, short, long, nearby, far away, just over the hill, just down the road, and so on.

Faxes

Faxes are now the best way to communicate in writing. Some hotels have no phones. Faxes are sent to a central location, then delivered by the mailman to the appropriate address. If you know where you'll be going, try to get fax numbers. Faxes are much more reliable than mail service.

Telephoning

Telephone systems have improved greatly in the Caribbean. This is an easy way for people to keep in touch.

Calling from Hotels

- Many hotels do not have phones in the room. You may have to call from the front desk.
- The hotel surcharge (as high as 300 percent) is probably the single biggest rip-off in the travel business today. The hotel jacks up your phone bill by whatever amount it can get away with, calling it a service charge. You should always ask what this charge will be *before* making a long-distance call. You pay this charge even on a collect call.
- Another interesting charge: You may pay a fee if no one answers. You may pay a larger fee if someone refuses to accept your collect call. Try to work out an *exact* time to contact someone if you plan to call long distance. Make sure that the other party knows that it may take several hours for you to reach him. For example, tell the person that you'll call Sunday evening between 9 P.M. and midnight.
- Finally, you pay a steep VAT (Value Added Tax) on calls.
- Hotels often lie about surcharges. Make all calls from a pay phone or telephone (post) office if possible when you're trying to keep costs down.

Better Alternatives Than Hotels

- You can make long-distance calls from the telephone (post) offices in many towns and cities, at the airport, at cruise ship terminals, and at booths displaying long-distance signs.
- You will never pay a surcharge when making calls in these places. Places to make long-distance calls are often limited, but they are worth seeking out if you want to save money.

Ways to Make Calls

- You can dial directly to Canada or the United States following directions provided with whatever calling card you have. Your regional calling card may be valid from some islands.
- You can easily call collect or with a telephone calling card. Get information from AT&T at (800) 874–4000, ext. 332; from MCI at (800) 283–9977; or from Sprint at (800) 877–4000.
- Collect is *P.C.V.* (pronounced "Pay-Say-Vay" in French) or *pago*

revertido (in Spanish). Most operators speak English, but the owners of small hotels or inns may not understand what you are doing unless you explain it to them.

- *Warning:* Whenever using a calling card, be wary of anyone watching or listening to your conversation with the operator. They may be after your codes.

Keeping the Costs Down

- Each company has varying times when rates are lowest. There is no uniformity among companies. Ask your company what the best times to call are if you want to save money.
- Finally, if you'll be on the line for a long time, have the other party call you back station-to-station.

Messages

Check with your local company at home about how to use a "voice mailbox" and message services. Each has its own method. This allows you to communicate "indirectly" with someone.

Local Calls Once in the Islands

- Never make local calls using your telephone card from the U.S. Never! Always use the local system, or you will be stunned by the charges.
- The simplest place to make a local call is from your hotel.
- If you have a phone in your room, you may be charged a small daily fee for its use. Or you may be charged on a per-call basis. Ask if you're concerned about the cost of frequent local calls.
- If there's no phone in your room, you can often make local calls at the front desk. There may or may not be a charge for this service depending upon the hotel policy.
- You can also use public pay phones. Many of these are for local calls only. In a few areas, calls are free—what a bargain!
- Many pay phones are broken.
- On some islands, such as Guadeloupe and Martinique, you buy a prepaid calling card (Telecarte) to make calls. These are available from exchange offices, newsstands, post offices, and shops. They are available in varying amounts depending on how many calls or how long you intend to speak.
- Since phone systems vary so much by island, it's best to ask locally about how to use them. On non-English-speaking islands, it's easiest to get clear explanations from hotel personnel even if you do not intend to call from the hotel.

Boat Phones

Cellular service is available in some areas where yachters or others will find it particularly useful. Contact the following company, which has offices on these islands of the Caribbean: Anguilla, Antigua, Barbados, Barbuda, British Virgin Islands, Grenada, Grenadines, Guadeloupe, Jamaica, Martinique, Montserrat, Nevis, St. Kitt's, Saint Martin/Sint Maarten, Saint Lucia, and Saint Vincent.

Boatphone
P.O. Box 1516
St. John's, Antigua
West Indies
Tel: (800) 262–8366 (in U.S.)
   (800) 567–8366 (in Canada)
   (809) 480–2628

Mail

Mail to and from the Caribbean is notoriously unreliable. Communicate by fax or phone—period.

Doing Things

This section is devoted to special-interest activities. Each appeals to different people in different ways and can make any trip to the Caribbean especially memorable.

Adventure Travel

Jamaica seems to be the main island for "adventure" travelers who really want to get into remote areas for that special feeling of isolation and exhilaration. If you have the time on the Dominican Republic or Grenada to check on "adventure" tours, those two islands offer similar experiences to Jamaica. Two companies to consider for Jamaican travel.

Adventure Center
1311 63rd Street
Suite 200
Emeryville, CA 94608
Tel: (800) 227–8747
    (510) 654–1879

Sense Adventures
P.O. Box 216
Kingston 7, Jamaica
Tel: (809) 927–2097

Aquariums

A number of the islands have aquariums. Seaquarium on Curaçao is unique in that you can get into the water to feed sea creatures (for a fee, of course). You feed the sharks through holes in a window and sea turtles through a net, but stingrays and many types of fish swirl about you in a graceful dance as they dart in to snatch small fish from your hands. It's a wonderful experience. And a great and safe initiation to scuba diving under controlled conditions for beginners.

Art and Architecture

Although a number of islands have interesting art and architecture (see historical sites later in the chapter), the islands of Barbados and

Bermuda stand out. The following organization offers study programs to these islands with art and architecture in mind.

National Trust for Historic
   Preservation Study Tour Program
1785 Massachusetts Avenue
Washington, DC 20036
Tel: (800) 944–6847
   (202) 673–4000

Beaches

The beaches in the Caribbean are among the best in the world, with sands varying in hue from pure white to light pink to jet black. Some are isolated and arid; others lined with luxury hotels and elegant palms. The best-known beaches or beach areas in the Caribbean are **Anegada** in the British Virgin Islands (whole island ringed with beaches); **Anguilla** (Shoal Bay and numerous others); **Antigua** (Half Moon Bay); **Aruba** (Palm Beach); **Barbados** (Crane Beach); **Barbuda** (Coco Point); **Bermuda** (Horseshoe Bay, Warwick Long Bay); **Carriacou** (Sandy Cay off the coast); **Culebra** (Playa Flamenco and Playa Soni); **Dominican Republic** (Playa Bavaro); **Grenada** (Grand Anse, L'Anse aux Epines); **Grand Cayman** (Seven Mile Beach and West Bay); **Guadeloupe** (Anse Canot); **Jamaica** (Negril); **Little Cayman** (Owen Island off its coast); **Martinique** (Anse-Trabaud, Les Salines); **Providenciales** in the Turks and Caicos (Grace Bay); **Puerto Rico** (Playa Boqueron); **Saint Barthélémy** (Anse du Gouverneur); **Saint John** (Cinnamon Bay, Trunk Bay); **Saint Martin** (Baie Longue); **Saint Thomas** (Magens Bay and Sapphire Bay); **Tobago** (Great Courtland Bay or Turtle Bay); **Trinidad** (Blanchisseuse, Great Courland Bay, Las Cuevas Bay, Lovers Beach—reached by boat only, Pigeon Point, and the north coast); and **Virgin Gorda** (Tetor Bay or Mahoe Bay). The above list is like trying to name the best French cheeses when in reality the best beach is strictly a matter of personal preference.

Birding

Birding in the Caribbean is excellent. More than 400 species have been spotted on the islands, including a wide range of land, shore, and sea birds. Some of the birds are extremely rare, a few possibly extinct. Trinidad stands out for birding. And on Trinidad one place stands out from all the others:

Asa Wright Nature Centre
P.O. Box 10
Spring Hill Estate
Arima, Trinidad
West Indies
Tel: (800) 426–7781 (Caligo Ventures in U.S.)
   (809) 622–7480 (in Port-of-Spain)

• Following are companies recommended for birding expeditions. They do not cover every island, but you can often find locals who will know less-visited spots well.

Academic Travel Abroad
3210 Grace Street Northwest
Washington, DC 20007
Tel: (800) 556–7896
   (202) 333–3355
(Bermuda, Dominica)

Caligo Ventures
156 Bedford Road
Armonk, NY 10504
Tel: (800) 426–7781
   (914) 273–6333
(Tobago, Trinidad)

Field Guides
P.O. Box 160723
Austin, TX 78716
Tel: (800) 728–4953
   (512) 327–4953
(Grenada, Dominica,
   Guadeloupe, Martinique,
   Montserrat, Saint Lucia, Saint
   Vincent, Tobago, and Trinidad)

Holbrook Travel
3540 Northwest 13th Street
Gainesville, FL 32609
Tel: (800) 451–7111
   (904) 377–7111
(Dominica)

National Audubon Society
Nature Odysseys
700 Broadway
New York, NY 10003
Tel: (212) 979–3000
(Bermuda. Cruises: One
   that includes the British
   and United States Virgin
   Islands; the other
   includes Anguilla,
   Dominica, Grenada, the
   Grenadines, Saba, Saint
   Kitt's, Saint Lucia, and
   Saint Martin. Other tours
   offered vary by year.)

Nature Expeditions International
P.O. Box 11496
474 Willamette
Suite 203
Eugene, OR 97440
Tel: (800) 869–0639
   (541) 484–6529
(Dominica, Tobago, and
   Trinidad)

Victor Emanuel Nature Tours
P.O. Box 33008
Austin, TX 78764
Tel: (800) 328–8368
   (512) 328–5221
(Jamaica, Puerto Rico, Tobago,
   and Trinidad)

Wings
P.O. Box 31930
Tucson, AZ 85751
Tel: (602) 749–1967
(Bahamas, Great Abaco, New
   Providence; Bermuda;
   Dominican Republic; Puerto Rico;
   Tobago; and Trinidad)

Wonder Bird Tours
P.O. Box 2015
New York, NY 10159
Tel: (800) 247–3887
   (212) 727–0780
(Aruba, occasionally;
   Barbados; Tobago;
   and Trinidad)

Butterflies

Just under 300 species of butterflies have been counted on the Caribbean islands. There are no spectacular migrations as can be found in Mexico, but if you watch for these lovely creatures, you may be surprised by the variety seen. Jamaica offers a good chance to see beautiful butterflies during hikes. These include giant swallow-tailed butterflies (*Papilio homerus*) with 6-inch wing spans. These are the largest butterflies in the Western hemisphere. You have the best chance of seeing them in May and June. They are found only in Jamaica.

Dance

In the Caribbean, dancing can go on for days, especially during local festivities. Dancing can be anything, from rhythmic with swaying hips to nearly frenetic, depending upon the music and occasion. A few of the popular dances include béguine (popular on Guadeloupe and Martinique), Junkanoo (Bahamas), jump-up, *la bomba*, *la danza*, limbo, merengue, rushing, *salsa*, skank, tamtam (dancing to drums on Guadeloupe), and zouk or zouc (a variation of béguine). These will seduce you into participation. Popular to watch are the dancers during Junkanoo on the Bahamas in late December; those on Bermuda known as Gombey Dancers (pronounced "gum-bay") during local festivals from mid-November until the end of March; Jamaica's National Dance Theatre and Ward Theatres in Kingston; Martinique's Les Grands Ballets de la Martinique; and Puerto Rico's Areyto Folkloric Dance Company and the Ballet Folklórico Nacional.

Fauna

The Caribbean is known more for its sea life than its land animals, although there are 5,600 animal species on the Dominican Republic alone. A few islands have snakes, but these are often hard to spot and frequently come out at night only. You may spot the following animals if you're lucky: agouti (rabbit-size, tail-less rodent—once abundant on Montserrat but now rare), ant-eater, armadillo (tatoo—mainly on Grenada, Saint Vincent, and Trinidad), caimans (like alligators in the Dominican Republic and Trinidad), deer (Antigua, Barbuda, and Curaçao), geckos (man lizards), iguanas, land turtles, lizards, manicou (relative of kangaroo), manatees or manatés (commonly called sea cows and actually related to elephants—endangered from boating accidents, herbicides, and hunting), mongoose, monkeys (green—Barbados, Nevis, Saint Kitt's; mona—Grenada; red howler—Trinidad), ocelot (tiger cats), opossum (manicou), paca (lappe), raccoon (protected on Guadeloupe), solenodon or solenodonte (probably extinct, but possibly still existing in the Dominican Republic), tayra (wild dog or chien bois), and wild boar (peccary or quenk). Some spots worth visiting are Barbados' Wildlife Preserve (mainly for green monkeys—best seen at feeding time), Curaçao's Christoffel Park (for Curaçao deer—only a few left), Dominica's Papillote Wilderness Retreat (a resort with a few rooms), Grenada's Grand Étang Park (mona monkeys threatened by legal hunting, but relatively common at the National Park Center), Puerto Rico's Mona Island (6 to 8 hours by boat from Cabo Rojo and Parguero respectively; 100 species of birds; 3-foot iguanas—see Turtle and Whale Watching as well), Trinidad's Nariva Swamp (alligators, anacondas, manatees, and red howler monkeys) and ASA Wright Nature Preserve (see birding). Some people truly enjoy trips that involve research or environmental protection. Most organizations accept volunteers. The term volunteer is somewhat misleading since you may be asked to pay for the trip, sometimes a substantial amount. Following are organizations worth contacting if this fits your style of travel.

Earthwatch
680 Mount Auburn Street
P.O. Box 403
Watertown, MA 02272
Tel: (617) 926–8200
(Bahamas, Bimini, San Salvador,
   Tilloo Cay; Saint Croix; Saint John;
   Saint Lucia; Tobago; Trinidad; and
   Turks and Caicos, Grand Turk)

Encantos Ecotours
P.O. Box 619
Guaynabo, Puerto Rico
   00970–0619
Tel: (800) 272–7241
   (809) 272–0005
(Wide range of tours on
   Puerto Rico, including
   trips to Mona Island)

Festivals

You can get a list of local festivals for each of the islands from the tourist offices on pp. 18–26.

- The major festival throughout the entire region is Carnival. The celebration in Port-of-Spain in Trinidad early in the year is considered among the best in the world. The colorful and exotic costumes that take over a year to make, the dancing to exciting music, and the overall atmosphere are considered by many to be better than Rio. You are expected to participate in this festival. It's not for onlookers. This is a lusty and lavish event, a riot of color and noise.
- Crop Over in Barbados takes place in mid-July to early August and is one of the major events in the Caribbean during the summer.
- Junkanoo in the Bahamas is an exuberant and colorful event taking place in the Christmas to New Year's season. Here you'll also see wonderful costumes and hear African-influenced music but not on the same scale as you would in Trinidad.
- Other major events in the Caribbean are special yachting regattas (pronounced "re-GRET-tahs" in the Bahamas). You would think that only sailors would be interested, but, in fact, the entire islands are in a festive mood with lots of parties and local celebrations. The best-known are International Sailing Week in Antigua and the Out Island Regatta in the Exumas of the Bahamas in April. You need to make reservations months in advance for any of these periods.
- Another very special event is the Fête des Cuisinières (Festival of Cooks) in Guadeloupe on the second weekend of August—the best time of year to sample the greatest number of dishes offered by the island's finest chefs.

Fishing

Fishing with line or spear is allowed in many areas of the Caribbean and not allowed at all in others. It is illegal to bring spearfishing gear onto some islands (Martinique). The most popular game fish are amberjack (tough fighters that dive toward bottom), barracuda (fierce fighters and easy to find, but not to be eaten), blue marlin (difficult to find, hook, and land—a true trophy; most common in summer and early fall), bonefish (bony, bolting bullets caught in flats—perfectly edible despite what people say, although best released to preserve stock), bonito (lively on light line and often found in schools—lots of quick action), dolphin (brilliantly colored, leaping, delicious eating, most fun on light tackle), kingfish or king mackerel (fight somewhat like wahoo; delicious eating), permit (large and equally good fighters as bonefish), sailfish (often found in the Bahamas in April), snook (wonderful fighters and perhaps the best eating fish in the world—found primarily in the Dominican Republic), tarpon (prehistoric battlers—wonderful to catch on streamers), tuna (several types, but all put up a fierce struggle and are delicious to eat), wahoo (torpedo-like, often making runs—good to eat despite what some captains tell you), white marlin (smaller than the blue, but still a great catch on light tackle).

Companies Specializing in Fishing

Following are companies specializing in fishing. Here are a few tips about these companies.

- These companies are aimed at anglers looking for trips of several days or longer. If you just want to fish for a day, make arrangements locally.
- Each company does a lot of work in scouting areas to offer you the best fishing possible. They know how to match you to your destination.
- Contact them for their brochures and current offerings to compare accommodations, fishing, and prices. You'll cover just about all of the best possibilities. These companies don't let opportunities slip through their fingers.
- If you're after a specific type of fish, companies know exactly where and when to go after it. So be specific in what you want.
- Companies often reserve space in peak fishing periods. You may need their help to get into a lodge at a specific time (usually the best time to catch a specific type of fish, and naturally often the most expensive time as well).
- Some companies can get you reduced airfare. Compare what they

offer to what you can arrange on your own. It may save you a lot of money.

- Getting confirmations from some lodges can be time-consuming and difficult. By working through the listed companies, there is less chance that your reservation will be bungled or difficult to make.
- Companies insist that you pay no more for your stay by working through them than you would if you contacted the lodge directly.
- These companies will tell you exactly what you need to bring for the type of fishing you'll be doing. Their checklists are detailed and come from years of experience.
- Some of the companies even have catalogs with suggested equipment and prices.

Angler Adventure
P.O. Box 872
Old Lyme, CT 06371
Tel: (800) 628–1447
  (860) 434–9624
(Bahamas—Abaco, Andros, Eleuthera)

Anglers Travel Connection
3100 Mill Street
Suite 206
Reno, Nevada 89502
Tel: (800) 624–8429
  (702) 324–0580
(Bahamas—Andros, Exuma; Venezuela—Los Roques)

Club Peace and Plenty
P. O. Box 29173
Georgetown, Exuma
The Bahamas
Tel: (800) 525–2210
  (809) 345–5555
(The place to learn how to catch bonefish on Exuma)

Fishing International
4775 Sonoma Highway
Santa Rosa, CA 95409
Tel: (800) 950–4242
  (707) 539–3366
(Bahamas—Acklin, Andros, Bimini, Exuma, and Grand Bahama; Jamaica; Venezuela—Los Roques; Puerto Rico; Saint Thomas; and Turks and Caicos)

Frontiers International Travel
(Fish and Game Frontiers, Inc.)
P.O. Box 959
100 Logan Road
Wexford, PA 15090
Tel: (800) 245–1950
    (412) 935–1577
(Bahamas—Abaco, Andros, Grand Bahama, Exuma, and Long
    Island)

John Eustice & Associates
1445 Southwest 84th Avenue
Portland, OR 97225
Tel: (800) 288–0886
    (503) 297–2468
(Bahamas—Andros and Exuma)

PanAngling Travel
180 North Michigan Avenue
Suite 303
Chicago, IL 60601
Tel: (800) 533–4353
(Bahamas—Abaco, Andros, Exuma, and Grand Bahama;
    Venezuela—Los Roques)

World Wide Sportsman, Inc.
P. O. Drawer 787
Islamorada, FL 33036
Tel: (800) 327–2880
    (305) 664–4615
    (305) 238–9252 (Miami)
(Bahamas—Abaco, Andros, Berry Islands, Bimini, Cat Island,
    Exuma, Grand Bahama, Long Island, and Walker's Cay; Cay-
    mans—all 3; Jamaica; Venezuela—Los Roques; Puerto Rico;
    Turks and Caicos—Providenciales; and United States Virgin
    Islands—Saint Thomas)

Flora (also see Gardens)

The Caribbean islands have an enormous diversity of plant life. Particularly popular for those interested in local plants are the more lush
islands of **Dominica** (wonderful rain forests), the **Dominican**

Republic, **Grenada**, **Guadeloupe**, **Jamaica**, **Martinique**, **Puerto Rico** (small areas), **Saint Lucia**, and **Trinidad**.

A Sampling of Interesting Plants

Here are just a few of the thousands of plants appealing to plant lovers and photographers in the Caribbean: **allamanda** (lovely yellow blossoms); **bananas** (thrive in humid, hot plains and valleys; take 8 to 10 months to mature into plants with wide broad leaves, thick stalks [trunks] with stems supporting broad bunches [hands] of bananas [fingers] that are curved upward—these hands are often protected by blue plastic bags on commercial farms, which grow 1400 plants per acre.); **aloe** (known for its sap that is good for burns and sores, but does stain most fabrics); **angel trumpet** (with exquisite, fragrant blossoms); **bamboo** (forests of it on Montserrat); **barrel cactus** or **turk's cap** (produces brilliant red flowers in season); **blue mahoe** (*Lignum vitae* or *guayacan* noted for its lovely wood); **bois pin** (up to 150 feet high); **bougainvillea** (vine with showers of small, brilliant blossoms that come in array of colors; found wild or trained up walls on even the most modest homes; blooms prolifically over months); **century plant** (after its blooms dry, the stem is sometimes used as a Christmas tree in the tropics), **cocoa trees** (mature trees grow to about 30 feet; begin bearing pods in the fifth year and peak by the thirteenth—some live as long as a century; the pods grow randomly from branches and trunks and contain seeds surrounded by a sticky, white substance, which is allowed to ferment and then dry; the seeds are then tumbled until shiny and then sold by the pound); **dildo cactus** (its pink flowers produce sweet, edible fruit); **divi-divi trees** or **watapana** (found on dry islands like Aruba; winds distort them into varied shapes; they produce tannin used in curing hides; named for their pods that look like ears [*divi*]); **ferns** (don't miss Fern Gully on Jamaica, a 4-mile road in a riverbed with over 550 varieties of ferns); **frangipani** (also known as red jasmine or plumeria—so fragrant that it is often used in local perfumes; flower colors include pink, red, white, and yellow; once used in Aztec and Maya religious rites); **ginger thomas** (shrub with yellow clusters of bell-shaped flowers); **gumbo limbo** (also called *gommier rouge*, gum tree, tourist tree, West Indian birch; the *Bursera simaruba* can reach heights of 80 feet; has stringy bark that looks like the back of a peeling tourist—hence the common name; used by locals for numerous purposes, from building boats to enhancing the smell of perfumes; its leaves used in some areas for teas); **heliconia** (looks like a multicolored lobster claw); **hibiscus** (over 200 varieties of this small bush with delicate shaded flowers can be found throughout the Caribbean; now a popular indoor plant in the

North, it can be seen growing abundantly on many islands); **immortelle** (stunning orange blossoms); **mountain fuchsias** (shrubs or small trees, varieties of *Charianthus*, producing vivid cream, red, and yellow flowers that turn into reddish berry-like fruits; flowers attractive to hummingbirds; common on Jamaica); **nutmeg** (the tree takes up to 6 years to sex—only females bear fruit—and 20 years to mature, when it produces 5,000 nuts per tree; after the nuts fall to the ground, their red exterior netting is removed and dried until it turns yellow [this dried netting is known as mace]; the dried, shelled meat of the nuts is made into nutmeg; tree grows only above 1,000 feet in the tropics); **orchids** (hundreds of varieties of orchids are found throughout the Caribbean—many extremely rare, one grown for vanilla; visit Crystal Springs in Port Antonio on Jamaica to see one of the largest collection of orchids in the region); **palms** (the Caribbean boasts numerous palms, from the coconut to the towering royal palm); **passion flowers** (beautiful vining plant known for its unusual blossoms); **poinciana** (originally from Madagascar, this tree goes by many names including *flamboyana*, *flamboyant*, and flame tree; produces brilliant clusters of red blossoms, which bloom at different times depending upon the island and season); ***pompon rouge*** (blooms March to September on Martinique); **poui trees** (known as *kibrahacha* on Dutch islands, where it blooms only for a few days after a heavy rain; blooms several times a year in Tobago and Trinidad; some covered in gold, others in pink blossoms depending upon the variety); **red cordia** (this small tree, *Cordia sebestena,* produces red, trumpet-like flowers that eventually produce spongy, white fruits; found mostly near beaches); **soapberry** (yellow fruit crushed to create soap in water; seeds sometimes used in local jewelry); **tulip tree** (locally known as maho or portia, the *Spathodea campanulata* produces large, bell-shaped flowers that are brilliantly red with contrasting yellow tones; its wood is prized for boats).

Important Tips on Plants

- Never touch tropical plants or eat tropical fruits without consulting locals first. The leaves and sap of some can cause severe allergic reactions. Many fruits and berries are toxic.
- Travelers are tempted to bring exotic plants, especially orchids, back to Canada or the United States. This is illegal without the proper paperwork. You must have permission from foreign governments to remove any plants. This regulation is strictly enforced.
- For information on importation of plants, get in touch with the local branch of the Customs Department. Importing plants must be done within extremely tight controls for numerous reasons—pri-

marily to protect our own plants from disease and endangered plants from extinction.

Gambling

Gambling is very popular on a number of Caribbean islands where casinos flourish. Slot machines are also found in a few hotels where there are no casinos. Many cruises offer gambling as well. Travel agents are familiar with the best areas for gambling. The following club offers discounts on rooms, food and drink, gambling, and floor shows in casinos on the islands listed with it.

Players Club International
3391 Peachtree Road Northeast
Suite 110
Atlanta, GA 30326
Tel: (800) 236–9732
    (404) 262–0222
(Aruba, Dominican Republic, Grand Bahama, Jamaica, New Providence in the Bahamas, Puerto Rico, Saint Kitt's, and Saint Thomas)

Gardens

There are numerous public and private gardens throughout the region. The public gardens are often mentioned in pamphlets appealing to tourists, but some of the finest gardens are private. The following organization specializes in garden tours in many areas of the world. If it is not leading a tour to a specific island, it may guide you to an organization doing so.

Expo Garden Tours
101 Sunrise Hill Road
Norwalk, CT 06851
Tel: (800) 448–2685
    (203) 840–1224

Golf

Golfing is possible on many islands, some with holes along steep, seaside cliffs, others along green ribbons floating on arid, coral islands. Following are islands with golf courses (superb or extremely beautiful golf courses in parentheses): Antigua, Aruba, Barbados

(Sandy Lane), Bermuda (a golfing mecca), Curaçao, Dominican Republic (Casa de Campo—fantastic), Eleuthera in the Bahamas, Grand Bahama (Bahamas Princess Golf Club, Lucaya Country Club), Grand Cayman, Grenada, Guadeloupe, Jamaica (Runaway Bay), Martinique (Country Club de la Martinique), Montserrat, Nevis, New Providence in the Bahamas, Providenciales or Provo in the Turks and Caicos, Puerto Rico (Cerromar, Dorado, and Palmas del Mar), Saint Croix, Saint Kitt's, Saint Lucia, Sint Maarten (Mullet Bay), Saint Thomas (Mahogany Run), Tobago (Mount Irvine), and Trinidad.

- Following is a company specializing in cruises combined with great golfing. Some courses would be difficult to get into on your own. Islands to play on include Antigua, Aruba, Barbados, Bermuda, the Dominican Republic, Grand Bahama, Grand Cayman, Jamaica, Martinique, New Providence in the Bahamas, Puerto Rico, Saint Croix, Saint Kitt's, Sint Maarten, Saint Thomas, and Tobago. Call or write for a brochure with course descriptions.

Cruise Holidays
8170 South University Boulevard
Littleton, CO 80122
Tel: (800) 533–4588
    (303) 7711–7245

- For a company that specializes in setting up land packages with golfers in mind, contact:

Golf Trips International
747 East 86th Street
Suite B
Indianapolis, IN 46240
Tel: (800) 536–3637
    (317) 254–1887

Hiking

Hiking is popular on many Caribbean islands. Hiking is fun on all the islands, but truly memorable on **Barbados** (tame hikes organized by the National Trust), **Bermuda** (along the old railway route), **Curaçao** (Washington-Slagbaai National Park—13,500 acres), **Dominica** (the hike to Boiling Lake is spectacular), the **Dominican Republic** (with guide), **Grenada** (Grand Étang National Park), **Guadeloupe** (Basse-Terre's Parc National—200 miles of well-marked trails, tremendous views from La Soufrière volcano—great drive or 3 to 4 hour hike), **Jamaica** (in the Blue Mountains with guide to avoid marijuana farms), **Martinique** (La Caravalle Peninsula, the Mont Pelée trail from Aileron, and the Trace des Jésuites from Morne Rouge), **Montserrat** (Bamboo forest with 100-foot bamboos; Galway's Soufrière—to active volcano if not too active), **Puerto Rico** (El Yunque or El Faro parks), **Saint Lucia** (Barre de l'Isle trail across the entire island; Maria Islands and Pigeon Island National Park; the Rain Forest Trail—lovely waterfalls and exotic birds; the Gros Piton—with a guide and if in good shape), **Saint Vincent** (to the Soufrière or to the falls of Baleine—guides advisable to avoid marijuana farms), and **Trinidad** (at the ASA Wright Nature Center—see Birding).

Hiking is a part of many trips for birding and other activities. Nature Expeditions International listed under birding considers its trips to Dominica as both hiking and birding adventures. There are many volcanoes and steep hikes in the Caribbean. Ask the locals about trails and terrain. Some walks are easy trails to follow, others are true climbs.

• The following organization offers hiking and snorkeling programs on the United States Virgin Islands.

Sierra Club
Outing Department
730 Polk Street
San Francisco, CA 94109
Tel: (415) 923–5630

Historic Sites (see **Art** and **Architecture**)

Some of the islands have ancient ramparts and forts; some lovely, restored plantations (especially on **Barbados**); ruins of old sugar mills; underwater cities (buried by quakes and volcanoes); underwater wrecks; and so on. Most of the on-land sites are quite modest but provide historical insights, lovely views and interesting hikes. Visiting the old section of **Puerto Rico** is enjoyable. It does have a special feeling, lots of fun places to eat, and some good shops. **Bermuda** has many fascinating old buildings. The restored synagogue in **Curaçao** is not mentioned in the following list, but is lovely. And so are many other landmarks that may not be mentioned but have a haunting appeal to those interested in the past. The only site in the Caribbean recognized as of worldwide importance by UNESCO is the Colonial City of Santo Domingo on the **Dominican Republic**. The city, founded in 1498, is truly worth a special detour. Still, the following have been singled out for recognition over the years.

American Express Historic Preservation Awards

American Express for several years promoted preservation of historical sites through an awards program. Following are sites selected: **Antigua** (Redcliffe Quay in Saint John's), **Bahamas** (Fort Charlotte in Nassau on New Providence, Wyannie Malone Historical Museum in Hope Town in the Abacos), **Barbados** (Barbados Synagogue in Bridgetown), **Bermuda** (Commissioner's House), **Dominica** (Fort Shirley and Harbour Project in Cabrits National Park, Old Mill Cultural Centre), the **Dominican Republic** (Santa Maria de la Encarnacion in Santo Domingo), **Grenada** (Old Roman Catholic Church in Saint Andrews), **Grand Cayman** (Old Courts Building in Georgetown), **Jamaica** (Devon House and Old Half Way Tree House in Kingston), **Montserrat** (Galways Plantation in Plymouth), **Nevis** (renovation of Charlestown), **Puerto Rico** (Casa Roig in Humacao, the Lighthouse in Las Cabezas de San Juan Nature Reserve, Simón de la Torre Cemetery in Ponce), **Sint Eustatius** (Doncher House in Oranjestad), **Saint Kitt's** (Brimstone Hill Fortress National Park), **Saint Thomas** (Old Unity Lodge, Tutu Archaeological Village), and **Trinidad** (Knowsley in Port-of-Spain).

Kayaking (Sea)

Sea kayaking is gaining popularity because it takes you into areas barely touched by other tourists. Outfits will tell you exactly what to bring, but at the very least you'll need a bathing suit, extra clothing in a waterproof bag, food, helmet, kayak, lifejacket, paddles, tennis shoes, and lots of water. Some places offering sea kayaking include the **Bahamas**, **Puerto Rico**, **Saint John** in the United States Virgin Islands, **Tobago**, and **Trinidad**. The following companies are geared to this aspect of adventure travel.

Eco-Summer Expeditions
1516 Duranleau Street
Vancouver, BC V6H 3S4
Tel: (800) 688–8605 (U.S.)
    (800) 465–8884 (Canada)
    (604) 669–7741
(Bahamas)

Ibis Tours
7040 West Palmetto Park Road
Suite 2119
Boca Raton, FL 33433
Tel: (800) 525–9411
(Trips through the Exumas
    of the Bahamas)

Safari Centre International
3201 North Sepulveda Boulevard
Manhattan Beach, CA 90266
Tel: (800) 223–6046
　　(800) 233–6046 (Canada)
　　(310) 546–4411
(Tobago and Trinidad)

Music

The best time to hear authentic music is during the local festivals. Musical instruments include accordions, cowbells, cymbals, drums (goatskin to steel), flutes, gourds, horns (homemade to saxophones), pans, pots, shells, string instruments (from *marimbula* to güiros and guitars), whistles, and so on. A very partial listing of the popular music that runs through the veins of all Caribbeans would include band (military style with a deep Caribbean influence), *béguine* (Martinique), *bomba* (Spanish-speaking areas), calypso (Trinidad), *compas* (blend of merengue with other styles), dance hall (disco, rap, and reggae; new and popular with the young), dub (reggae with rap), folk (many native styles), goombay (Bahamas) or goombey (Bermuda), gospel, *gro-ka* or *gwo ka* (drum music on Guadeloupe), jazz, merengue (a variation of calypso, best in Santo Domingo in the Dominican Republic), pan (the steel drum music of Port-of-Spain in Trinidad), reggae (Jamaica), *salsa* (San Juan in Puerto Rico), scratch or rake n' scrape, *soca* (blend of soul and calypso, originated in Montserrat), spouge (Barbados' blend of calypso and reggae), *tumba* or *tambu* (drum music and dance similar to salsa on Curaçao), and zouk or zouc (Guadeloupe and Martinique). Musicians are constantly blending these forms to create new music, just as they have converted much of the earlier forms from their ancestors into more modern music.

Native Culture

The Caribbean is really a blend of African, British, Chinese, Danish, Dutch, East Indian, French, Spanish, and native Amerindian cultures (Arawak and Carib dominated). On Dominica there is a special reserve for Carib Indians, but there is doubt as to whether this group really is authentic. The culture of the Caribbean is reflected in art, dance, festivals, and music.

Natural History

Specifics on birding, turtle watching, whalewatching, and so on have been mentioned in other sections of this chapter. However, the following company prides itself on being oriented strictly to natural history.

Holbrook Travel
3540 Northwest 13th Street
Gainesville, FL 32609
Tel: (800) 451–7111
    (904) 377–7111
(Dominica)

Photography

The Caribbean islands offer a visual feast for photographers. I'm assuming that you have a 35-millimeter camera. If you have some other type, some of these tips won't apply to your outfit.

Cameras and Lenses

- If you're serious about photography, bring a 50-millimeter lens, a wide-angle, and a good telephoto lens—but don't go overboard; try to keep it as light and compact as possible. If you specialize in extreme close-ups of insects and flowers, bring an appropriate lens.
- If you're on an extended trip, consider buying good but relatively inexpensive equipment that you can view as disposable. The salt and humidity often destroy cameras in the Caribbean. Stores specializing in used camera equipment will advise you on which cameras are cheap (disposable) but good.
- A lightweight tripod can be invaluable if you're extremely serious about your photos.
- A broad camera strap makes taking pictures easier and carrying cameras more comfortable.
- Be familiar with the workings of your equipment before traveling. Run a few rolls through the camera to make sure that things are working properly. It's very difficult to get cameras repaired during travel.
- Change all batteries, and carry a spare for each body. Batteries are hard to find abroad and often prohibitively expensive if available.
- Equip each lens with a Polaroid filter. Leave the filter on at all times (not only to improve photos but to protect the lens). If a filter gets scratched or broken, it's far less expensive to replace than a lens, and this will happen.

- Bring photographic lens tissue or liquid lens cleaner to clean lenses.
- Don't forget your instruction book if you're not completely familiar with your camera or haven't used it frequently in recent months.
- Finally, unless your camera is always at hand, you're going to miss some of the best spontaneous shots. Have your camera handy (but hidden if possible).

Register Your Equipment

- Don't forget to register equipment to avoid problems coming back through customs (see p. 190).

Film

- Bring more than the "legal" amount of film. Simply take the film out of the cardboard containers.
- Put the film in a plastic bag, which you hand to an inspector when going through security checks at airports. Although the inspectors will tell you that the x-rays do no harm, don't take any chances.
- Yes, you can buy film abroad, but it is extremely expensive and sometimes hard to find.
- Figure one 36-exposure roll for each day of shooting at the minimum.
- Avoid any film with "professional" printed on the label. These require refrigeration.
- Heat hurts all film, so keep it as cool as possible—often quite difficult in hot areas. Never put film in glove compartments.
- Specify either slide or print film. Slide film allows you to view every photo before deciding which ones you want made into prints—a real savings. But, at the same time, what you see is what you get. With print film you can make adjustments in the color.
- Get films with different ASAs (ISOs in some countries). ASA, often referred to as speed, is a measurement of light sensitivity. Lower speed films (most commonly ASA 100) are excellent for outdoor use. Much higher speed films are necessary for indoor shots.

Security Inspections

- Don't have film in cameras when you go through security inspections at the airport. They may be opened. If you forget or can't help having film in the camera, ask the inspector not to open the back. Just run it through the machine.
- The x-ray machines at airports can do damage to unexposed or undeveloped film, particularly those with ASAs over 400. Moreover, the effect is cumulative, so don't let the film go through these machines if possible.

- Ask the inspector politely for a visual inspection at all check points. If you carry film in a separate plastic bag, this takes only seconds. In general, inspectors cooperate fully with this request and with a minimum of hassle.
- Don't put film in checked luggage, which can be subjected to high-level radiation. Even lead pouches are no guarantee that the film will not be harmed. Carry all film on board with you.
- The affect of x-rays on film is highly controversial. Personally, I believe those who say it can do damage.

Protecting Camera Gear

- Dust, sand, and salt can be a problem; bring a plastic bag for each lens and camera to protect them, even if they're already enclosed in a leather carrying case. The plastic bags should lock shut.
- Humidity is also a problem. In highly humid areas, get cameras out of plastic bags as soon as possible. The same applies to rain. Protect cameras from downpours, but get them out of bags once indoors.
- If you carry cameras in plain bags, potential thieves will be less likely to know what you've got—namely, something they want.
- Always zip up the bag, even if you're nearby. Leave nothing exposed to chance and sticky fingers.
- Hand carry all camera equipment onto a plane or bus. This way you won't lose it if you're luggage is lost or crushed.
- Wear a camera around your shoulder rather than around your neck in public places. A thief snatching at your camera can easily hurt your neck in his eagerness. Yes, it is easier to steal this way.
- Do not leave cameras in car trunks or glove compartments. They are vulnerable to theft, and the heat of the closed compartment can damage the camera.

Photography Etiquette

- In some areas, you must be sensitive about taking photos. If it's clear that someone doesn't want to be photographed, honor their feelings.
- You can often get good shots of people with a telephoto lens, and this can be done inconspicuously.
- If you're close to a person, however, don't sneak photos. If you want to take someone's picture, be forthright and friendly—it often works. "Can I take your photo?" "¿Puedo sacar una foto?" "Puis-je faire une photo?"
- Just lift the camera slowly, nod your head, and smile. If the person turns away or tosses his hand at you, don't take the photo. Or just

say "please?", "*¿por favor?*", or "*s'il vous plaît?*" as if it were a question as you lift the camera, to get a reaction.
- You may be asked for a small payment for some of the photos, which seems reasonable enough.
- Some professionals look for a good background and then just let people walk into the frame while they sit at a table or pretend to be doing something else.

Developing Film

- Do it at home. It's the safest place to take care of film that may represent very special memories or a lot of effort if you take photography seriously.

Tips on Taking Good Photos

Following are tips from professional photographers. These generalizations are not iron-clad rules, but they often result in truly memorable photos.

- Focus carefully so that the subject is clear, not at all fuzzy. If you cannot hold the camera steady, use any handy object to help you keep the camera still. If you have a tripod, use it.
- The key ingredient in good photography is light. In most instances, you want light shining on your subject. This means the sun should be behind you. Sometimes light may be shining through your subject, such as a flower, to intensify the colors.
- Professional photographers and filmmakers know that the light just after sunrise and before sunset is extremely rich. The bright light in the middle of the day often washes out color or creates harsh shadows. Overcast days are often excellent for getting good color saturation in the tropics.
- Look carefully at your subject. Cameras are objective. Whatever appears in the viewfinder will show up on film. Check all edges of the photo to make sure that nothing unwanted is left out.
- Keep photos simple. What do you want the photo to say?
- Keep photos simple by having a clear-cut background, nothing cluttered or confusing. Keep them simple by getting close to the object you're photographing, whether it's a person, flower, insect, butterfly, or fabric. In short, fill the entire frame with your subject.
- Vary angles of your shots. Shooting down on a market can lead to an excellent shot. Shooting up at people can be dramatic.
- Move your camera from vertical to horizontal a number of times when trying to decide what kind of shot to take. You'll develop an instinct over a period of time as to which position is really working.
- When you know that you have an interesting subject, take many

photos from different angles and at different speeds. One of them may turn out to be sensational.

- Composition requires a good eye and an ability to create interest. Avoid placing subjects directly in the middle of the frame. Horizons across the center of a photo are deadly. Look for powerful diagonal lines; rhythmic curves (especially sensual S-curves along rivers or shorelines); and unusual patterns in shape, texture, and color.
- It can be difficult getting good shots from a boat. If possible, get your horizon straight (almost comical to do at times).
- Use the appropriate film for the situation. A low-speed film is excellent for outdoor shots, but worthless in low-light conditions or for photographing things in rapid movement. For this reason, consider carrying two camera bodies—one loaded with low-speed film, the other with high-speed.
- Shoot lots of film. It's the quickest way to learn what works and what doesn't. Again, the camera is objective. It feels nothing. It simply records. It takes lots of shooting to see how what is subjectively so beautiful in person can be so objectively dull on film.

Underwater Photography

The Caribbean is an ideal place for underwater photography. Here are a few tips.

- Have a fully waterproof camera for all water-related sports and for underwater photography. Try it out before you leave. There are disposable cameras of this kind for limited photos.
- Underwater cameras with a built-in flash are readily available and a must for good coloration (you lose many colors in water).
- Proper filters are important.
- When shooting underwater, get as close to the fish or subject as possible. This results in crisp photos.
- Take photos in the middle of the day (just the opposite of advice for most land shots). Aim straight ahead or up toward the surface for best results.
- Many resorts in the Caribbean have underwater cameras for rent. You might want to try shooting a few rolls to get the hang of it.

Rafting

Rafting is popular on Jamaica. Prices are negotiable. Trips are most fun after the heavier rains. The most popular trips are on the Rio Grande. There are two people on each 30-foot bamboo raft poled by a guide. The trip lasts approximately 2½ hours. You dramatically improve your chance to see wildlife if you leave early in the morning and are extremely quiet.

Riding

Horseback riding is an enjoyable change of pace on many of the Caribbean islands. Ask locally about tours. It is often so hot and muggy in the tropics that riding is really the most enjoyable way of seeing off-the-beaten-path areas. You're "hiking" but not having to do all the work. Riding is most highly recommended on **Barbados**, the **Dominican Republic**, **Guadeloupe**, **Jamaica** (Chukka Cove Equestrian Center—very famous), **Martinique**, and **Puerto Rico**. If riding will be a central part of your vacation, contact the following organization:

FITS Equestrian
685 Lateen Road
Solvang, CA 93463
Tel: (800) 666–3487
    (805) 688–9494
(Jamaica at Chukka Cove)

Sailing (see Yachting)

The idea of renting a yacht and sailing throughout the Caribbean has been covered in detail (pp. 126–133). However, some companies specialize in larger groups wanting a sailing "adventure" in the islands. Here is one contact.

American Wilderness Experience
P.O. Box 1486
Boulder, CO 80306
Tel: (800) 444–0099
    (303) 444–2622
(Sailing in the British and United States Virgin Islands)

Scuba Diving

SCUBA (Self-Contained Underwater Breathing Apparatus) diving is excellent throughout the Caribbean and at its very best in Bonaire and the Cayman Islands. Numerous books have been written about the best dive spots in the Bahamas, on Bermuda, and throughout the Caribbean. The main points are to go to places that match your level of expertise, to go at the right time of year, and to match the type of diving to your budget (consider diving packages as a way of keeping costs reasonable). If you're traveling with someone less interested in diving, take that into account. Many dive resorts appeal to divers and non-divers alike. Please read the section on Snorkeling for further tips.

Some of the Best Diving Spots

The best diving spot near a specific island may be one known only to a few locals or one where there are relatively few divers to disturb the area. However, following are islands popular with divers with some of the better, if well-known, diving spots in parentheses: **Abacos** islands in the Bahamas (Blue Holes—inland and sea; Pelican Cay National Park off Abaco; Sandy Cay for one of largest Elkhorn Coral stands in world; Tarpon Dive off Man-O-War Cay; and Walker's Cay for sleeping sharks with a guide), **Andros** in the Bahamas—stay in Andros Town (Blue Holes; Brad's Mountain, Caves—extensive; Giant Staircase; The Barge wreck; The Black Forest; The Dungeons; and Turnbull's Gut), **Anguilla** (Deep South Reef, Dog Island, Paintcan Reef, Prickly Pear, and the wreck of the M.V. Sarah), **Antigua** (Ariadne Shoal—long boat ride), **Aruba** (Mangel Halto Reef, and the wreck of the SS Antilla), **Barbuda** (surrounded by acres of shallow reefs with 73 charted shipwrecks), **Barbados** (Dottins Reef), **Bermuda** (Constellation wreck, Lartington, and Montana wreck), **Berry Island** in the Bahamas (Fishbowl at Chubb Cay), **Bimini** in the Bahamas—"The Lost Atlantis" (Bimini Wall, Nodules, and Tuna Alley), **Bonaire** (Alice in Wonderland, Angel City, Boca Slagbaai, Calabas Reef, Carl's Hill, Ebo's Reef, Forest Reef, Hands Off Reef, Hilma Hooker wreck, Karpata, La Dania's Leap, 1000 Steps, Ol Blue, Pink Beach, Red Slave, Salt City, The Knife, The Lake, and Twixt), **British Virgin Islands** (Alice in Wonderland between Ginger and Cooper islands, Chikuzen 6 miles north of Beef Island, P.O.S. off the Dogs, RMS Rhone off Salt Island, and wrecks off Anegada), **Carriacou** (Kick 'em Jenny, Twin Sisters, and dives off the islands of Mabouya, Saline, and Sandy), **Cayman Brac** (Hobbit, Radar Reef), **Chub Cay** in the Bahamas (The Fish Bowl—grouper congregate here in October and November), **Curaçao** (Director's Bay, Sandy's Plateau, and Shipwreck Point), **Dominica** (one of the best, but requires written permission unless you're with a diver operator—good dives include Canefield Barge, Canefield Tug, Champagne, Coral Gardens, Danglebends Reef, La Bim or The Wall, Point Guinard Caves, Rodney's Rock, Scotts Head Dropoff, Scotts Head Pinnacle, Soufriere Pinnacle, The Condo, and Toucari Caves), **Dominican Republic** (Isla Catalina), **Eleuthera** in the Bahamas

(Current Cut and The Gardens), **Exumas** in the Bahamas (Blue Holes in Elizabeth Harbor, Coral and Sting Ray Reef), **Grand Bahama** (Edge of the Ledge, Lucaya National Park—caves, Theo's wreck, Treasure Reef, and UNESCO's Dolphin Experience or Shark Junction Dive—800–992–3483), **Grand Cayman** (Balboa wreck, Big Tunnels, Orange Canyon, and Trinity Caves), **Grand Turk** (Anchor, Gardens, and Tunnels—in one of the world's finest diving areas), **Grenada** (the wreck of the Bianca C is the largest in the Caribbean—see Carriacou), **Guadeloupe** (the reefs around North Pigeon Island are among the best in the world—only 5 minutes by boat from shore), **Little Cayman** (Bloody Bay Wall and Little Cayman Wall), **Long Island** in the Bahamas (Cape Santa Maria, Conception Island Wall, Grouper Village, and Stella Maris Shark Reef—the latter with guide only), **Montserrat** (dive off the nearby island of Redonda), **Nevis** (Gridiron, Monkey Reef, Redonda Reef, and The Caves), **New Providence** in the Bahamas (Cliffton Pier Dropoff, Goulding's Cay, and Rose Islands Reefs), **Providenciales** and **North Caicos** in the Turks and Caicos (Northwest Point, Pinnacles, West Wall, and Wheeland Cut), **Puerto Rico** (Basslet Reef, Monkey Reef, The Cracks near Humacao, and South Gardens near Desecho Island off Aguadilla), **Rum Cay** in the Bahamas (1861 HMS Conqueror wreck, Grand Canyon, Pinder's Pinnacle, and Summer Point Reef), **Saba** (Diamond Reef, Ladder Labyrinth, Man-of-War, Outer Limits, Shark Shoals, Tent Reef, Third Encounter, Torrens Point, and Twilight Zone), **Saint Croix** (King's, Long, and Northstar reefs), **Saint Kitt's** (Sandy Point), **Saint Lucia** (Anse Chastanet and Pinnacles—best January to April), **Saint Thomas** (Coki Beach—at night—and French Cap Cay), **Saint Vincent** (Bottle Reef, New Guinea Reef, The Gardens, and The Wall), **San Salvador** in the Bahamas (the whole island), **Sint Eustatius** or **Statia** (Anchor Reef, Caroline's Reef, Dropoff, Outer Crooks Reef, Supermarket, and Tommy's Temptation), **South Caicos** (Amos' Wall, Arches, Eagle's Nest, and Plane), **Tobago** (Divers' Dream; Divers' Thirst; Goat Island; Kelliston Deep—largest recorded brain coral in the world; Manta City—manta rays with wingspans of over 10 feet are commonly seen off Little Tobago; Saint Giles Island; and numerous other sites—some for highly experienced divers only), **Turks and Caicos** (see **Grand Turk**, **North Caicos**, **Providenciales**, **South Caicos**), and the **United States Virgin Islands** (see **Saint Croix** and **Saint Thomas**).

Diving Companions

If you need someone to dive with, the following organization has a list of potential buddies. You pay a yearly fee for the service.

Divers' Exchange International
37 West Cedar Street
Boston, MA 02114
Tel: (617) 723–7134

Handicapped Diving
If you're handicapped, contact the following organization for information.

Handicapped Scuba Association
1104 El Prado
San Clemente, CA 92672
Tel: (714) 498–6128

Diving Companies
Since diving is one of the main reasons people go to the Caribbean, most islands have dive facilities. Here's an extensive list of companies specializing in this activity (you can get many more from the tourist offices listed on pp. 18–26 or once you arrive on the island from local publications). Airlines also offer special diving packages. Comparison shop to save money.

Aggressor Fleet
P.O. Drawer K
Morgan City, LA 70381
Tel: (800) 348–2628
   (504) 385–2628
(Turks and Caicos)

Baskin In the Sun
P.O. Box 8309
Cruz Bay
St. John, USVI 00831
Tel: (800) 233–7938
   (809) 494–2858
(British Virgin Islands)

Blackbeard's Cruises
P.O. Box 66–1091
Miami Springs, FL 33266
Tel: (800) 327–9600
   (305) 888–1226
(Live-aboards for diving in the Bahamas)

Bottom Time Adventures
P.O. Box 11919
Fort Lauderdale, FL 33339
Tel: (800) 648–7691
    (305) 561–0111
(Live-aboards for dives in the Bahamas)

Caradonna Caribbean Tours
P.O. Box 3299
Longwood, FL 32779
Tel: (800) 328–2288
    (407) 774–9000
(Aruba; Bahamas—New Providence; Bequia; Bonaire; British Virgin Islands; the Caymans; Dominica; Curaçao; Nevis; Saba; Saint Kitt's; Saint Lucia; Saint Martin; Turks and Caicos—Grand Turk, Providenciales; and the United States Virgin Islands)

Caribbean Dive Tours
732 Johnson Ferry Road
Marietta, GA 30068
Tel: (800) 786–3483
    (770) 578–8028
(Live-aboards in the Bahamas, Bonaire, and Cayman Islands)

Go Diving
5610 Rowland Road
Suite 100
Minnetonka, MN 55343
Tel: (800) 328–5285
    (612) 931–9101
(Live-aboards from the Bahamas—New Providence; Bonaire; British Virgin Islands—Tortola; the Caymans; Curaçao; Dominica; Saba; Saint Lucia; and the Turks and Caicos.

Landfall Productions Dive and Adventure Travel
Suite 295B
39675 Cedar Boulevard
Newark, CA 39675
Tel: (800) 525–3833
    (510) 794–1599
(British Virgin Islands, Dominica, the Grenadines, Nevis, Saint Kitt's, Saint Lucia, and Saint Vincent)

Ocean Connection
211 East Parkwood
Suite 108
Friendswood, TX 77546
Tel: (800) 331–2458
   (713) 996–7800
(Aruba, Bonaire, the Caymans, Curaçao, and Turks and Caicos)

Ocean Voyages
1709 Bridgeway
Sausalito, CA 94965
Tel: (800) 299–4444
   (415) 332–4681
(Grenadines)

Paradise Expeditions
23 Route 23 S
Pequannock, NJ 07440
Tel: (800) 696–5880
   (201) 696–5880
(Dominica)

Peter Hughes Diving, Inc.
6851 Yumuri Street
Suite 10
Coral Gables, FL 33146
Tel: (800) 932–6237
   (305) 669–9391
(Curaçao and Turks and Caicos)

Poseidon Venture Tours
359 San Miguel Drive
Newport Beach, CA 92660
Tel: (800) 854–9334
   (714) 644–5344
(Bahamas, Bonaire, British Virgin Islands, and Caymans)

Regency Yacht Vacations
5200 Long Bay Road
St. Thomas, USVI 00802
Tel: (800) 524–7676
   (809) 776–5950
(Sailing and power vessels equipped for diving in the Virgin
   Islands)

Rothschild Dive Safaris
900 West End Avenue
Suite 1B
New York, NY 10025
Tel: (800) 359–0747
   (212) 662–4858
(Bahamas—Grand Bahama live-aboard; Bonaire; the Caymans;
   Curaçao; Dominica; Jamaica; Nevis; Puerto Rico; Saba; Saint
   Kitt's; Saint Lucia; Tobago; and Turks and Caicos)

Scuba Voyages
595 Fairbanks Street
Corona, CA 91719
Tel: (800) 544–7631
   (909) 371–1831
(Bonaire, Cayman Brac, Dominica, Little Cayman, Palm Island in
   the Grenadines, Saba, Saint Lucia, Tobago, Grand Turk in the
   Turks & Caicos, and Young Island off Saint Vincent)

Sea Fever Diving Cruises
P.O. Box 398276
Miami Beach, FL 33239
Tel: (800) 443–3837
   (305) 531–3483
(Live-aboard offering dives in the Bahamas)

See and Sea Travel Services, Inc.
50 Francisco Street
Suite 205
San Francisco, CA 94133
Tel: (800) 348–9778
   (415) 434–3400
(Live-aboards for the Caymans, Saba, Saint Kitt's, Sint Maarten,
   and the Turks and Caicos)

Tropical Adventures
111 Second Avenue North
Seattle, WA 98109
Tel: (800) 247–3483
   (206) 441–3483
(Land based on Bonaire and Curaçao; live-aboards from the Caymans and the Turks and Caicos)

Undersea Adventures
P.O. Box 21766
Fort Lauderdale, FL 33335
Tel: (800) 327–8150
    (954) 462–3400
(Bahamas—Bimini, Grand Bahama, Marsh Harbour, New Providence, Walkers—and Bonaire)

Virgin Islands Charter Yacht League
Flagship-Anchor Way
St. Thomas, USVI 00802
Tel: (800) 524–2061
    (809) 774–3944
(Yachts set up for scuba diving in the British and United States Virgin Islands)

Diving Emergencies

Although the need for airlifts and decompression is rare, it's helpful to know the location of the nearest chambers (assuming they're working). Also, there are organizations worth checking into (see p. 17 for other air evacuation companies).

DAN (Divers Alert Network)
P.O. Box 3823
3100 Tower Boulevard
Suite 1300
Duke University Medical Center
Durham, NC 27710
Tel: (800) 446–2671
    (919) 684–2948
    (919) 684–8111 (emergency number)
(Offers accident insurance plus emergency evacuation services.
  Knows doctors who specialize in underwater accidents and
  other illnesses mimicking these. Also keeps tabs on the operat-
  ing conditions of the 17 decompression chambers in the
  Caribbean—they're not always working properly)

Seclusion

While this is a chapter on Doing Things, doing absolutely nothing is the goal of a number of travelers to the Caribbean. What they want is peace, quiet, and isolation. Best bets for this are **Anegada** (British Virgin Islands), the **Out Islands** of the Bahamas, **Cayman Brac**, the

Grenadines, and the **Turks and Caicos**. More about individual islands is given in the chapter on Where to Go (pp. 32–71).

Shopping

Shopping is one of the most popular activities of travelers in any region. The Caribbean is known for its duty-free ports. It also offers some interesting buys in locally crafted items.

Know Before You Go

If you've been out of the country for a specified period of days, you're allowed to return with a specific amount of merchandise as defined by law without paying duty. The amount is higher for some islands than others. Request the pamphlet "Know Before You Go" from your travel agent or from the customs department (larger cities have local branches that will send you the pamphlet if you call them directly).

U.S. Customs Service
P.O. Box 7407
Washington, DC 20044
Tel: (202) 927–6724

- You can import many goods from developing countries free of duty. For information on this, contact the nearest customs office for a copy of "GSP and the Traveler." At this time there are over 4,000 items that can be brought into our country in quantity without duty.
- However, there are some things you can't bring in at all. Get the pamphlet "Traveler's Tips on Bringing Food, Plant, and Animal Products into the United States" from:

U.S. Department of Agriculture
Washington, DC 20250
Tel: (202) 720–2791

- Many credit cards have a guaranteed protection program against loss, theft, and breakage. Check into this before going abroad. This added insurance can be quite valuable for more expensive articles. Keep your receipt.
- *Warning:* If you live in an area with a state tax, you *technically* are supposed to pay a "use" tax on all imported items. This tax is essentially the same as a sales tax. Recently, a number of states have begun checking forms filed with the U.S. Customs Service to see whether they could begin collecting this use tax.
- This practice has not yet spread through all states that have a sales

tax, but it has begun in at least 10 states on a random testing basis. The people most likely to be affected by this policy are ones buying expensive items abroad (gems, jewelry, watches, and so on).

- Another tax rarely mentioned in guides is that on liquor. Each state has a different law in regard to how much liquor can be imported duty-free. If you intend to bring in a case or more of some exotic liquor (quality rum) or liqueur, be forewarned that states can impose taxes. Also possible is that no liquor at all will be allowed in—it may be confiscated. However, hardly any state bothers with travelers bringing in a single bottle from abroad.

Comparison Shop in the United States and Canada

- If you intend to buy goods manufactured in countries other than the Caribbean (many duty-free areas exist), study your prices before leaving home. It may be wiser to buy an item at home even if slightly more expensive in case you want to return it or have it repaired.
- Unless an imported item is much lower in price, don't buy it. You'll lose on the currency exchange (unless you pay in dollars), you'll have to lug it home, and you may even have to pay duty on it if you exceed your personal exemption. If you can't make a 40 to 50 percent saving, skip it.

Locally Crafted Items

Individual islands are not noted for a wide range of locally produced items, but when all of the islands are combined, they produce a fascinating array of things to buy: Agate jewelry (Jamaica), amber (beads and jewelry on the Dominican Republic—often forged, but authentic pieces among finest in world, especially those containing insects), Angostura bitters (Trinidad), ashtrays, bags (fabric and straw), bamboo (varied items), baskets (especially beautiful is the tri-color basketry of the Caribs on Dominica), batiks, beads (may be braided into hair on Jamaica), boats (wooden models), bowls (wood), black coral (do not buy—endangered and *illegal*), ceramics (everything from brightly colored fish to elegant vases), cigars (Dominican Republic, Guadeloupe), coasters, coffee (Dominican Republic, Jamaican Blue Mountain, and Puerto Rican brands—all should be ground, not whole beans, to get through customs), conch pearls and jewelry (Providenciales in the Turks and Caicos), costumes (used in local festivals), dolls, embroidery, fabrics (hand-screened), fans (*khus-khus*), fashions (Barbados), furniture (Dominican Republic and Jamaica), grass or "khus-khus" mats (Dominica), *guayaberas* (embroidered shirts on Puerto Rico), guitars (Puerto Rico), hammocks (originally created by the now extinct Arawak Indians), handbags (coconut shell), hats (straw hats common), jams and jellies, jewelry (creole, hematite, mother-of-pearl), jewelry boxes (wood), key rings (wood), lace (visit the Centre de Broderie on Guadeloupe, look for bobbin lace or *mundillo* on Puerto Rico, and "Spanish Work" on Saba including handkerchiefs, napkins, and tablecloths), Larimar (blue stone in Dominican Republic), leather goods, madras fabric (Guadeloupe and Martinique), masks, mats (sisal), mortars and pestles (wood—for grinding coffee on Jamaica), musical instruments (such as the *güiro* on Puerto Rico), musical tapes and CDs, needlework, paintings (primitive), pepper sauces (Barbados, Bermuda, Jamaica, and others), pottery, quilts (from Eleuthera in the Bahamas), rag dolls (favorites are the doudou dolls on Martinique), rag rugs, rum (some of the best anywhere), sculpture, shells, shirts, silkscreens, spices (Grenada and Jamaica), stamps (some of the most beautiful in the world), statues (wood), statues of saints or *santos* (some on Puerto Rico sell for thousands of dollars), steel drums (miniature and full-size ones on Trinidad), straw products of all kinds, tablecloths (Aguadilla or Moca on Puerto Rico), tapestries, turtle shell combs or jewelry (do not buy—*illegal*), wall hangings, Warri Boards (game on Antigua), wicker (Dominican Republic), wood carvings (prized are items from blue mahoe, mahogany, and teak). Blue mahoe or *Lignum vitae* is most common on Jamaica.

- *Never buy goatskins. These may contain deadly anthrax spores. Don't even touch them. They will be confiscated and destroyed should you bring them home.*
- *Don't buy any of the following items: birds (living or stuffed), butterflies, coral (especially black coral jewelry), feathers, furs, ivory, leather from Caymans or crocodiles, and turtle shell (in any form). The fines on these can be very high.*

If you buy jewelry, get a receipt. You may need receipts when leaving a country and definitely on passing through customs on your return.

Duty-free Shops

The term duty-free does not mean that an item may not be taxed on your return if you exceed the limits allowed for purchases abroad. It is just an inducement to tourists to buy locally. Some duty-free shops offer true bargains, especially in some ports. Others, mainly in airports, offer little for your money with a few exceptions, one being liquor. The latter often must be delivered to you once you've cleared customs (as a way of stopping its sale locally). Main duty-free shops are found in Aruba, the Bahamas (Freeport on Grand Bahama and Nassau on New Providence), Barbados, Curaçao (one of the best in Caribbean), Isla Margarita (off Venezuela), Saint Croix, Saint Martin/Sint Maarten (one of the best areas), and Saint Thomas (very famous).

- Anyone traveling by cruise ship should understand that shore orientations may be given, which include information on where to buy specific duty-free goods. You may be given a map showing you the locations of these shops. Most people recognize this for what it is—a form of paid advertising that generates huge amounts of revenue for cruise lines. The shops may or may not be good (cruise lines claim to check them out). Be wary. Cruise lines are interested in making money. Some may get kickbacks from the stores related to total expenditures of passengers. Others are paid a straight fee for the marketing onboard.

Markets

Regional goods are limited in most Caribbean areas, but some of the local markets are fascinating to walk through. The people selling their wares in these areas are poor. Some bargaining is appropriate, but frivolous bargaining is considered insulting. Food and fish markets are particularly picturesque—not only good places to buy things but also to take photos. One of the most photogenic markets is at Saint George's Market Square in Grenada.

Street Vendors

You can't walk anywhere on some islands without being hustled. It's just part of the culture.

- If you're not interested, just say no. A polite way of turning vendors off is to say that something is very pretty, but that you don't want it. *"Muy bonito, mas no lo quiero." "Très joli, mais je ne le veux pas."*
- Some vendors offer some pretty good deals on some fairly decent items, but many offer junk at not-so-good prices.

Snorkeling

Going to the Caribbean without snorkeling is like going to a zoo and not getting out of the gift shop. Most of the Caribbean islands offer very good to excellent snorkeling. Some are much better known for this than others. A few even have underwater markers and buoys to follow as a guided tour (as at Trunk Bay on St. John's in the United States Virgin Islands). Following are a few of the region's best snorkeling spots on an island-by-island basis (note that some of these are unfortunately deteriorating from overuse and abuse): **Abacos** islands in the Bahamas (North Point off Man-O-War Cay and Pelican Cay National Park off Abaco), **Anguilla** (Frenchman's Reef, Little Bay, Rendezvous Bay, Sandy Island—really the whole island and many of the islets offshore—Prickly Pear cays especially), **Andros** in the Bahamas (Love Hill, Trumpet Reef), **Anegada** (whole island great, Paramatta wreck), **Antigua** (Bird Island, Five Islands, Half Moon Bay, Horse Shoe Reef), **Aruba** (Arashi Beach, Barcadera Reef, De Palm Reef Island, Malmok, Palm Beach), **Barbados** (Folkstone Park), **Barbuda** (acres of shallow reefs, try Cocoa Point), **Bermuda** (Blue Holes), **Biminis** in the Bahamas (Rainbow and Sunshine reefs, Victory Cay), **Bonaire** (Boca Slagbaai, Leonora's Reef, Nukove Beach, Pink Beach, Playa Funchi, Salt Pier), **British Virgin Islands** (see **Anegada**, **Norman Islands**—note that almost all areas have good snorkeling), **Cayman Brac** (Windsock Reef), **Culebra** off Puerto Rico, (whole archipelago good, but especially fine around Culebrita), **Curaçao** (Curaçao Underwater Park—Jan Theil Reef, Sandy's Plateau, Tow Boat—all best in the morning when it's calm and the reefs around Klein Curaçao), **Dominica** (Canefield Barge, Champagne, Coral Gardens, Douglas Bay, Point Guinard Caves, Scotts Head Dropoff, Soufriere Pinnacle), **Dominican Republic** (Isla Catalina), **Eleuthera** in the Bahamas (Cienfuegos and Train Wrecks), **Exuma** in the Bahamas (Exuma Cay Land and Sea Trust—accessible only by boat, Stocking Island), **Grand Bahama** (Sweetings Cay, Taino Beach), **Grand Cayman** (Eden Rocks, Stingray City), **Grenada** (Molinère Reef, Petit Cabrits Point), **Guadeloupe** (Ilet du Gosier, Isles de la Petite-Terre, Saint François Reef, southwest shore of Grand-Terre, West Side Reef off North Pigeon Island), **Little Cayman** (Bloody Bay Point—strong snorkelers only), **Long Island** in the Bahamas (Poseidon's Pint, Southampton Reef), **Norman Island** in the British Virgin Islands (Caves—with underwater flashlight), **Providenciales** in the Turks and Caicos (Wheeland Cut), **Saba** (surrounded by reefs—Ladder Labyrinth, Torrens Point has snorkeling trail), **San Salvador** (the whole island), **Saint Croix** in the US Virgin Islands (Buck Island Reef), **Saint John** in the US Virgin Islands (Francis Bay, Reef Bay, Maho Bay, Trunk Bay—famous but just fair), **Saint Lucia** (Anse Chastanet, Pinnacles), **Saint Thomas** in the US Virgin Islands (Coki Beach, French Cap Cay), **Saint Vincent** (Bottle Reef, New Guinea Reef, The Gardens—best, The Wall), **Sint Eustatius** or **Statia** (Outer Crooks Reef), **Tobago** (Buccoo Reef from Pigeon Point or Store Bay beaches), **Turks and Caicos** (miles of unexplored reef), **United States Virgin Islands** (see **Saint Croix**, **Saint John**, **Saint Thomas**), **Vieques** (entire reef system throughout area), **Virgin Gorda** in the British Virgin Islands (Baths).

When to Go
Snorkeling is good somewhere in the Bahamas, Bermuda, or the Caribbean at any time of year. However, snorkeling is best in the

peak or dry season near any islands where there is a chance of runoff during the wet season. Low-lying coral islands, often referred to as arid, desert, or dry islands, are the best places to snorkel in the wet season (because they don't really experience a wet season and have little runoff even if it were to rain).

Turtle Watching

The chance to see a rare sea turtle lay her eggs on a deserted shore in the middle of the night is an unforgettable experience. Timing is critical, since turtles only nest at specific times of the year. There are six species of sea turtle in the Caribbean, and all are threatened with extinction: the leatherback (trunk turtle, tinglada, tortue luth), loggerhead (logrit, caguama), hawksbill (carey, tortue imbriquée), Kemp's ridley (Atlantic ridley), olive ridley (tortuga golfina, tortue olivâtre), and green turtle (greenback turtle, tortuga verde, tortue verte). Even under ideal conditions fewer than 1 in 1,000 hatchlings survive the two or more decades necessary to reach sexual maturity.

Throughout the Caribbean the hunting of sea turtles continues, despite the fact that it is illegal in many areas. Turtle eggs are relished and reputed to have aphrodisiacal qualities. Although sea turtle nesting has greatly diminished, you can still witness this memorable event in a few isolated areas. Always go with a competent guide, if one is available. If you happen on a turtle while enjoying a walk on a moonlit beach, observe the following rules: Never shine a flashlight on a sea turtle. The light may frighten her back to the sea or temporarily blind or disorient her, leading to her death. For the same reason, never take a flash photo. Never stand between the turtle and the sea once she has finished laying her eggs. Do not touch the eggs as the turtle lays them. Sunscreen and insect repellent can be toxic to sea turtle eggs. Never excavate eggs since this will kill the developing embryo. Report the nest to the local Fisheries Department.

Some sites where formal or informal guided tours are available: **Antigua**: Long Island (Jumby Bay) offers guests of this private resort an opportunity to observe hawksbill turtles nesting at Pasture Bay from June to November (best time: September). Adults weigh 150 pounds and are critically endangered because of the trade in tortoiseshell items. The resort is very expensive, but chances are good that you will see a turtle during peak season. Contact Jumby Bay Resort Reservations (800) 421–9016. **Dominican Republic**: Leatherback turtles (April to July) and green and hawksbill turtles (June to November) nest in Parque Nacional Jaragua. The most accessible beaches are Inglesa, Mosquea, and San

Luis. Park rangers sometimes grant requests for turtle watching. **Grenada**: Levera and Bathway beaches in Levera National Park on the northeast coast of Grenada support small populations of leatherback turtles (adults weigh from 500 to 1,100 pounds), as well as occasional green and hawksbill turtles. Likelihood of seeing a turtle is low. Contact Levera National Park Office (809) 442–1018. **Puerto Rico**: Puerto Rico and Culebra Island off the east coast both support nesting by leatherback turtles (April to July), as well as by green and hawksbill turtles (June to November). Formal turtle watching is sometimes available. Contact the Department of Natural Resources (809) 724–8774 or the U.S. Fish and Wildlife Service (809) 851-7297. Mona Island off the west coast is an arduous trip but worth it to see hawksbills. See Eco-Tourism in this chapter for a company offering trips to this distant island. **Saint Lucia**: Grand Anse on the east coast supports a small population of leatherbacks (April to July). Contact Saint Lucia's Naturalists' Society (809) 451–6957. **Tobago**: Great Courland Bay on the northwest coast offers a chance to see leatherbacks (April to July). Poaching is devastating the population. Contact the Rex Turtle Hotel (809) 639–2851. **Trinidad**: Trinidad offers you the best chance of seeing nesting turtles of any island in the Caribbean. Matura Bay Beach on the east coast boasts one of the largest leatherback nesting colonies in the Western Hemisphere. Nature Seekers, Inc., offers tours by highly trained guides every night during the season (April to July). Contact them at (809) 667–9075. Grande Riviere Beach on the north coast and other sites may also offer guided tours. Contact the Wildlife Section-Forestry Division (809) 662–5114. The following organization coordinates activities to help preserve sea turtles in 30 Caribbean nations. It needs donations to support dozens of projects throughout the region:

(WIDECAST) Wider Caribbean Sea Turtle Conservation Network
17218 Libertad Drive
San Diego, CA 92127
Tel: (619) 451–6894

Whale Watching

Humpback whales migrate past the Turks and Caicos between November and December to their breeding grounds in the Silver Bank (*Banco de la Plata*) area about 80 miles northeast of Puerto Plata in the Dominican Republic. Possibly as many as 2,000 to 3,000 humpbacks migrate here from December through March. You can arrange trips from the Turks and Caicos or from ports in the Dominican

Republic. You also have a good chance of spotting humpback whales in the Virgin Islands from January through March in the Anegada passage. Harassment of whales is illegal in many areas. If whales change direction, you are required to move off from the pod. The following companies offer diverse whale watching expeditions, some short, others long. Many also include other activities from birding to trekking.

Natural Habitat Adventures
(merged with Biological Journeys)
2945 Center Green Court South,
Suite H
Boulder, CO 80301
Tel: (800) 543–8917
   (303) 449–3711
Swimming with Atlantic spotted dolphins west of Grand Bahama
   in the White Sand Ridge area. Swimming with Humpback
   whales in the Silver Bank area between the Turks & Caicos and
   the Dominican Republic in February and March.

Oceanic Society Expeditions
Fort Mason Center, Building E
San Francisco, CA 94123
Tel: (800) 326–7491
   (415) 441–1106
Both dolphin and whale watching trips similar to the ones men-
   tioned above.

Windsurfing

Windsurfing in the Caribbean is extraordinary because of the prevailing winds. All populated areas offer windsurfing to some degree. Some of the finest islands for windsurfing are **Aruba** (steady winds and lots of good areas), **Bahamas** (many hotels on the main and Out Islands have good facilities), **Barbados** (ranked in top 6 places in world—varied difficulty and good winds in morning and afternoon at Club Mistral, Silver Sands, and the notorious Soup Bowl at Bathsheba), **Bermuda** (many areas but the south shore is dangerous), **Bonaire** (Lac Bay—very safe and shallow), **British Virgin Islands** (superb sailing between the islands from November to February), **Curaçao** (Marie Pompoen, Spanish Water Bay), **Dominican Republic** (Cabarete—phenomenal from January to August with best winds in the afternoon), **Grand Cayman** (very expensive but good off Marriott's Tortuga Club), **Guadeloupe** (Le Moule, Raisins Clairs, Saint François, Sainte Anne), **Isla Margarita** and its offshore islet of **Coche** off Venezuela (superb), **Puerto Rico** (Rincon, north shore superb), **Saint Croix** (Salt River highly recommended), and **Saint Thomas** (Bluebeard's Beach). Following are a few companies specializing in windsurfing.

Divi Winds
2200 Fletcher Avenue
Fort Lee, NJ 07024
Tel: (800) 822–6754
    (201) 346–9125
Aruba

Excursions Extraordinaires
923 East 25th
Eugene, OR 97405
Tel: (800) 678–2252
    (541) 484–0493
Isla Margarita (off
    Venezuela), Tobago

Vela Resorts
16 East 3rd Avenue,
Suite 6
San Mateo, CA 94401
Tel: (800) 223–5443
    (415) 373–1100
Aruba, the Dominican Republic
    (Cabarete), Isla Margarita with
    its offshore islet of Coche (off
    Venezuela).

Work

It is possible to work in Puerto Rico and the United States Virgin Islands as an American citizen. It is quite difficult to work on other islands unless you have a skill lacking in local residents. However, if you would like to work on a yacht as a paid professional, that is possible. The following two organizations specialize in staffing yachts with qualified people. The more experience you have, the better. However, some people are hired and trained by owners. If you're looking for a paid vacation, these companies are not suited to your needs. **These companies are looking for people who want to work.** Here are the contacts:

Crewfinders
404 Southeast 17th Street
Fort Lauderdale, FL 33316
Tel: (800) 438-2739
(305) 522-2739

Hassel Free Inc.
1550 Southeast 17th Street
Suite 5
Fort Lauderdale, FL 33316
Tel: (305) 763-1841

Index

Abacos, 37
Acklins, 37
Accommodations, 141–179
  apartments, 144–157
  condos, 144–157
  hotlines, 143–144
  houses, 144–157
  hotel associations, 144
  villas, 144–157
Adventure travel, 271
Air conditioning, 211
Air evacuation companies, 17
Airlines, maverick, 110–111
Air temperature, 73
Andros, 37–38
Anegada, 46
Anguilla, 35
Animals, fauna, 275
Antigua, 35–36
Apartments, 144–157
Aquariums, 271
Architecture, 271–272
Art, 271–272
Aruba, 36
ATMs, 9

Babies, traveling with, 86–87
Bahamas, 36–43
Barbados, 43–44
Barbuda, 44
Bargaining
  on car rental, 240
  on rooms, 208
Barter, 117
Beaches, the best, 272
Bed and breakfasts, 157
Bequia, 53

Bermuda, 44–45
Berry Islands, 38
Biking, 140, 239
Bilharziasis, 253
Biminis, 38–39
Birding, 272–274
Black market, 218
Boardinghouses, 158
Boats, 139
Bonaire, 45
British Virgin Islands (BVI),
  45–46
Bumping, airline, 191–192
Buses, 134, 202, 239
Butterflies, 274

Cabins, 160
Camping, 158–160, 225
Canouan, 53
Cargo ships, 236
Caribbean Coalition for Tourism,
  26
Carriacou, 48
Car travel, 134–139, 239–242
Cat, 39
Cayman Brac, 48
Cayman Islands, 48–49
Chagas' disease, 247
Charters, 109–110, 236
Children,
  at Club Med, 160–161
  on cruises, 105
  in hotels, 211
Ciguatera, fish poisoning,
  247–248
Clearing customs, 191–201
Clearinghouses, 114–115

Club Med, 160–161
Clubs (private), 161
Condos, 144–157
Cooper Island, 165
Cottage colonies, 161
Couples, traveling together,
    82–83
Courier services, 117–118
Credit cards, 10–11, 215–216
Crooked, 39
Cruise Line International Associa-
    tion, 102
Cruises, 96–106
Culebra, 49–50
Curaçao, 50

Dance, 274–275
Dengue fever, 248
Diarrhea, 248–251
Dictionaries, 266
Directions, asking for, 266–267
Discount travel, 111–114, 173–176
Dogs, 225
Dominica, 50–51
Dominican Republic, 51–52
Driving, safety, 226
Drowning, 226–227

Electricity, 211–212
Eleuthera, 39
Exchanging money, 216–219
Exumas, 40

Fauna, 275
Family travel, 83–86
Faxes, 267
Ferries, 126, 204, 236–237
Festivals, 276
Fishing hotels, 161, 277–279
Film, 288
Flora, plants and flowers,
    279–282
Food, cutting costs, 262–264
Freeport, 40

Frequent Flyer programs,
    118–119

Gambling, 282
Gardens, 282
Gîtes, 161
Golf, 282–283
Grand Bahama, 40
Grand Caicos, 67
Grand Cayman, 49
Grand Turk, 67
Great Inagua, 41
Grenada, 52
Grenadines, 52–55
Group travel, 87
Guadeloupe, 55
Guana Island, 165
Guest houses, 162

Harbour Island, 39
Health care, 246–247
Hiking, 283–284
Hissing, 266
Historic sites, 284–285
Hitchhiking, 242–243
Home exchange, 162–163
Homes (rooms in private), 163
Hotel associations, 144
Hotels, 163
House rental, 144–157
Humidity, 74–75
Hurricanes, 75–76, 230

Ilet Oscar, 165
Ilet Thierry, 165
Inagua, 41
Information
    Caribbean Coalition for
        Tourism, 26
    island sketches, 32–71
    National Tourist Offices, 18–26
    tour companies, 29
    travel agents, 26–28
    travel magazines, 28–29

travel newsletters, 29
travel reports, 29
Inns, 164
Inoculations, 14–15
Insurance
  accident, 4
  baggage, 4
  car rental, 4, 138
  default, 4
  evacuation, 4, 16
  health, 5, 14–15, 88
  home, 5
  trip cancellation, 5
Isla Margarita, 56–57
Island index, 33–35
Isles des Saintes, 56

Jamaica, 57
Jellyfish, 251
Jost Van Dyke, 47
Jungle lodges, 164

Kayaking, sea, 285–286

La Désirade, 57–58
La Republica Dominicana, 51–52
Leishmaniasis, 252–253
Les Saintes, 56
Little Cayman, 49
Little Inagua, 41
Little Saint James, 165
Long Island, 41–42
Long Island (private), 165

Magazines, cruise, 97
Mail, 270
Mailboats, 237–238
Malaria, 251
Manchineel trees, 252
Maps
  map companies, 30–31
  National Tourist Offices, 18–26
Margarita, 56–57
Marie Galante, 58

Marina Cay, 165
Martinique, 58–59
Mayaguana, 42
Mayreau, 54
Medical
  cruises, 105–106
  doctors, 13
  evacuation insurance, 16–17
  organizations, 15
  trip preparation, 13
Middle Caicos, 67
Money
  carrying it, 11–12
  cost cutting tips, 7–8
  trip costs, 7
Montserrat, 59
Mosquitoes, 252
Mosquito Island, 165
Motels, 164
Motion sickness, 252
Motorboats, 238
Motorcycling, 140, 243
Music, 286
Mustique, 54, 165

Nassau, 42
National Tourist Offices, 18–26
Native culture, 286
Natural history, 287
Necker Island, 165
Networking, 30, 206
Nevis, 59–60
New Providence, 42
Newsletters, 29, 97
Noise, 212–213
North Caicos, 67–68

Older travelers
  discount airfare coupons, 117
  organizations, 87–89
  singles, 82

Packing, 180–186
Palm Island, 165

Paradise Island, 42
Paradores, 164
Parking
   at airports, 188
   at hotels, 213
Parrot Cay, 165
Passports, 3
Peter Island, 165
Petit Martinique, 60
Petit Saint Vincent Island, 165
Pets, 89
Photography, 287–291
Pine Cay, 165
Planes
   getting to the islands, 107–122
   travel between islands,
      124–125, 232–236
   travel on the islands, 134
   private, 122
Plantations, 165
Private islands, 165
Protecting valuables, 185,
   221–224
Providenciales, 68
Provo, 68
Puerto Rico, 60

Rape, 227–229
Rebators, 116
Rabies, 252
Rafting, Jamaica, 291–292
Refrigerators, 213
Relais créoles, 166
Registering with customs, 190
Reservations
   plane, 232–234
   restaurant, 258–259
   room, 176–179, 205–206
Resorts, 166–170
   checklist, 166–170
Restaurants
   as places to stay, 170
Riding, 292
Robberies, 229

Rum, best buys, 256
Rum Cay, 42

Saba, 61–62
Safety, personal, 225–231
Sailing, with a group, 292
Saint Bart, 62
Saint Barth, 62
Saint Barthélémy, 62
Saint Christopher, 62
Saint Croix, 69
Saint John, 69–70
Saint Kitt's, 62
Saint Lucia, 62–63
Saint Martin, 63–64
Saint Thomas, 70
Saint Vincent, 64
Salt Cay, 68
Sandflies, 252–253
San Salvador, 43
Schistosomiasis, 253
Scuba diving, 292–299
Sea urchins, 253–254
Seclusion, 299–300
Servi-bars, 213
Service charges, tips, 219
Sharks, 229–230
Shopping, 300–303
Singles
   Club Meds, 80
   cruises, 80, 104
   matching, 80–81
   older, 82
   resorts, 80
   tours, 92
   women, 82
Sint Eustatius, 64
Sint Maarten, 64–65
Snakes, 230
Snorkeling, 303–305
Solo travel, 79–88
South Caicos, 68–69
Spanish Wells, 39
Spas, 171

Spices, 255
Statia, 64
Stingrays, 254
Sun, 74
Sunburn, 254

Taxes, government, 219, 261
Taxis, 202–204, 243–244
Tea, afternoon tradition, 261
Telephone
    general tips, 268–270
    in hotels, 213
Time, saving it, 77–78
Tips, service charges, 219–220,
        261–262
Tobago, 65
Tobago Cays, 54–55
Tortola, 47
Tour companies
    checklist, 94–96
    for information, 29
    local, 244–245
    major companies, 91
    packages, 90
    special interest, 92–96,
        271–308
    TourScan, 90–91
Tourist offices, 18–26, 143, 205
TourScan, 90–91, 142
Townhalls, 171
Travel agents, 26–28
    cruise, 100, 104
    cruises for ill people, 104
Travel clubs, 173–176
Travel guides, 143, 206–207
Travel magazines, 28–29
Traveler's checks, 9, 215
Travel reports, 29
Trinidad, 65–66
Turks & Caicos, 66–67

Turtle watching, 305–306
Typhus, 254

Union, 55
United States Virgin Islands,
        69–70

Vieques, 71
Villa rental, 144–157
Virgin Gorda, 47–48
Visas, 3
Volcanoes, 230

Walking
    safety, 231
    seeing an island, 245
Water
    drinking, 214
    temperature for swimming, 74
    washing, 214
Watlings Island, 43
Weather, 72–76
Whale watching, 306–307
Wind, 75
Windermere Island, 165
Winsurfing, 307–308
Wines, 260
Work, 308

Yachts
    getting to the islands, 122–123
    safety, 231
    travel within the islands,
        126–133
    yacht hopping, 133
Yellow fever, 14, 254
Younger travelers
    general, 89
    tours, 91–92
Young Island, 165